Introducing Social Theory

For Ellen,
my wife and true companion

INTRODUCING SOCIAL THEORY

PIP JONES

polity

Copyright © Pip Jones 2003

The right of Pip Jones to be identified as Author of this Work has
been asserted in accordance with the UK Copyright, Designs and Patents
Act 1988.

First published in 2003 by Polity Press in association with Blackwell
Publishing Ltd

Reprinted 2003, 2004, 2005, 2006, 2007, 2008 (twice), 2009

Polity Press
65 Bridge Street
Cambridge CB2 1UR, UK

Polity Press
350 Main Street
Malden, MA 02148, USA

A catalogue record for this book is available from the British Library.

Library of Congress Cataloging-in-Publication Data
Jones, Pip.
   Introducing social theory / Pip Jones.
       p.   cm.
   Rev. ed. of: Studying society. 1993.
   Includes bibliographical references and index.
   ISBN 978-0-7456-2698-7—ISBN 978-0-7456-2699-4 (pbk.)
   1. Social sciences—Philosophy.   I. Jones, Pip. Studying society.
II. Title.
H61 .J568 2003
301—dc21   2002013552

Typeset in 10.5 on 12 pt Times NR
by Graphicraft Limited, Hong Kong
Printed and bound in Great Britain by TJ International, Padstow, Cornwall

For further information on Polity, visit our website: http://www.polity.co.uk

CONTENTS

Author's note

Where a term or concept is highlighted in the text, you will find it defined in the Glossary at the end of the book, on pages 196–203.

1 AN INTRODUCTION TO SOCIOLOGICAL THEORIES

Introduction

Humans are social beings. Whether we like it or not, nearly everything we do in our lives takes place in the company of others. Few of our activities are truly solitary and scarce are the times when we are really alone. Thus the study of how we are able to interact with one another, and what happens when we do, would seem to be one of the most fundamental concerns of anyone interested in human life. Yet strangely enough, it was not until relatively recently – from about the beginning of the nineteenth century onwards – that a specialist interest in this intrinsically social aspect of human existence was treated with any seriousness. Before that time, and even since, other kinds of interests have dominated the analysis of human life. Two of the most resilient, non-social approaches to human behaviour have been **'naturalistic'** and **'individualistic'** explanations.

Rather than seeing social behaviour as the product of interaction, these theories have concentrated on the presumed qualities inherent in individuals. On the one hand, naturalistic explanations suppose that all human behaviour – social interaction included – is a product of the inherited dispositions we possess as animals. We are, like animals, biologically programmed by nature. On the other hand, individualistic explanations baulk at such grand generalizations about the inevitability of behaviour. From this point of view we are all 'individual' and 'different'. Explanations of human behaviour must therefore always rest ultimately on the particular and unique psychological qualities of individuals. Sociological theories are in direct contrast to these 'non-social' approaches. Looking a little closer at them, and discovering what is wrong or incomplete about them, makes it easier to understand why sociological theories exist.

Naturalistic theories

Naturalistic explanations of human activity are common enough. For example, in our society it is often argued that it is only natural for a man and a woman to fall in love, get married and have children. It is equally natural for this nuclear family to live as a unit on their own, with the husband going out to work to earn resources for his dependants, while his wife, at least for the early years of her children's lives, devotes herself to looking after them – to being a mother. As they grow up and acquire more independence, it is still only 'natural' for the children to live at home with their parents, who are responsible for them, at least until their late teens. By then it is only natural for them to want to 'leave the nest', to start to 'make their own way in the world' and, in particular, to look for marriage partners. Thus they, too, can start families of their own.

The corollary of these 'natural' practices is that it is somehow *un*-natural not to want to get married, or to marry for reasons other than love. It is equally unnatural for a couple not to want to have children, or for wives not to want to be mothers, or for mothers not to want to devote the whole of their lives to child-rearing. Though it is not right or natural for children to leave home much younger than eighteen, it is certainly not natural for them not to want to leave home at all in order to start a family of their own. However, these 'unnatural' desires and practices are common enough in our society. There are plenty of people who prefer to stay single, or 'marry with an eye on the main chance'. There are plenty of women who do not like the idea of motherhood, and there is certainly any number of women who do not want to spend their lives solely being wives and mothers. There are plenty of children who want to leave home long before they are eighteen while there are many who are quite happy to stay as members of their parents' households until long after that age.

Why is this? If human behaviour is, in fact, the product of a disposition inherent in the nature of the human being then why are such deviations from what is 'natural' so common? We can hardly put down the widespread existence of such 'unnatural' patterns of behaviour to some kind of large-scale, faulty genetic programming.

In any case, why are there so many variations from these notions of 'normal' family practices in other kinds of human societies? Both history and anthropology provide us with stark contrasts in family life. In his book on family life in Medieval Europe, *Centuries of Childhood* (1973), Philippe Ariès paints a picture of marriage, the family and child-rearing which sharply contradicts our notions of normality. Families were not then, as they are for us today, private and isolated units, cut off socially, and physically separated from the world at large. Families were deeply embedded in the community, with people living essentially public, rather than private, lives. They lived in households whose composition was constantly shifting: relatives, friends, children, visitors, passers-by and animals all slept under the same roof. Marriage was primarily a means of forging alliances rather than simply the outcome of 'love', while women certainly did not look upon mothering as their sole destiny. Indeed, child-rearing was a far less demanding and onerous task than it is in our world. Children were not cosseted and coddled to anywhere near the extent we consider 'right'. Many more people – both other relatives and the community at large – were involved in child-rearing, and childhood lasted a far shorter time than it does today. As Ariès (1973) puts it, 'as soon as he had been weaned, or soon after, the child became the natural companion of the adult'.

In contemporary non-industrial societies, too, there is a wide range of variations in family practices. Here again, marriage is essentially a means of establishing alliances between groups, rather than simply a relationship between individuals. Monogamy – one husband and one wife – is only one form of marriage. Polygyny, marriage between a husband and more than one wife, and polyandry, between a wife and more than one husband, are found in many societies. Domestic life is also far more public and communal than it is in industrial societies. Each family unit is just a part of a much wider, cooperating group of mainly blood relatives associated with a local territory, usually a village. As in Medieval Europe, therefore, child-rearing is not considered the principal responsibility of parents alone, but involves a far greater number of people, relatives and non-relatives.

Clearly, then, to hope to explain human life simply by reference to natural impulses common to all is to ignore the one crucial fact that sociology directs attention to: human behaviour varies according to the social settings in which people find themselves.

Individualistic theories

What of individualistic explanations? How useful is the argument that behaviour is the product of the psychological make-up of individuals? The employment of this kind of theory is extremely common. For example, success or failure in education is often assumed to be merely a reflection of intelligence: bright children succeed and dim children fail. Criminals are often taken to be people with certain kinds of personality: they are usually seen as morally deficient individuals, lacking any real sense of right or wrong. Unemployed people are equally often condemned as 'work-shy', 'lazy' or 'scroungers' – inadequates who would rather 'get something for nothing' than work for it. Suicide is seen as the act of an unstable person – an act undertaken when, as coroners put it, 'the balance of the mind was disturbed'. This kind of explanation is attractive for many people and has proved particularly resilient to sociological critique. But a closer look shows it to be seriously flawed.

If educational achievement is simply a reflection of intelligence then why do children from manual workers' homes do so badly compared with children from middle-class homes? It is clearly nonsensical to suggest that doing one kind of job rather than another is likely to determine the intelligence of your child. Achievement in education must in some way be influenced by the characteristics of a child's background.

Equally, the fact that the majority of people convicted of a crime come from certain social categories must cast serious doubt on the 'deficient personality' theory. The conviction rate is highest for young males, especially blacks, who come from manual, working-class or unemployed backgrounds. Can we seriously believe that criminal personalities are likely to be concentrated in such *social* categories? As in the case of educational achievement, it is clear that the conviction of criminals must somehow be influenced by social factors.

Again, is it likely that the million or so people presently unemployed are typically uninterested in working when the vast majority of them have been forced out of their jobs, either by 'downsizing' or by the failure of the companies they worked for – as a result of social forces quite outside their control?

Suicide would seem to have the strongest case for being explained as a purely psychological act. But if it is simply a question of 'an unsound mind', then why does the rate of suicide vary between societies? Why does it vary between different groups within the same society? Also, why do the rates within groups and societies remain remarkably constant over time? As in other examples, social factors must be exerting some kind of influence; explanations at the level of the personality are clearly not enough.

Variations such as these demonstrate the inadequacy of theories of human behaviour which exclusively emphasize innate natural drives, or the unique psychological make-up of individuals. If nature is at the root of behaviour, why does it vary according to social settings? If we are all different individuals acting according to the dictates of unique psychological influences, why do different people in the same social circumstances behave similarly and in ways others can understand? Clearly there is a social dimension to human existence, which requires sociological theorizing to explain it.

All sociological theories thus have in common an emphasis on the way human belief and **action** is the product of social influences. They differ as to what these influences are, and how they should be invest-igated and explained. This book is about these differences.

We shall now examine three distinct kinds of theory – *consensus*, *conflict* and *action* theories – each of which highlights specific social sources of human behaviour. Though none of the sociologists whose work we will spend the rest of the book examining falls neatly into any one of these three categories of theory, discussing them now will produce two benefits:

- it will serve as an accessible introduction to theoretical debates in sociology; and
- it will act as useful reference points against which to judge and compare the work of the subject's major theorists.

Society as a structure of rules

The influence of culture on behaviour

Imagine you live in a big city. How many people do you know well? Twenty? Fifty? A hundred? Now consider how many other people you encounter each day, about whom you know nothing. For ex-ample, how many complete strangers do people living in London or Manchester or Birmingham come into contact with each day? On the street, in shops, on buses and trains, in cinemas or night clubs – everyday life in a big city is a constant encounter with complete strangers. Yet even if city dwellers bothered to reflect on this fact, they would not normally leave their homes quaking with dread about how all these hundreds of strangers would behave towards them. Indeed, they hardly, if ever, think about it. Why? Why do we take our ability to cope with strangers so much for granted? It is because nearly all the people we encounter in our everyday lives do behave in ways we expect. We expect bus passengers, shoppers, taxi-drivers, passers-by, and so on, to behave in quite definite ways even though we know nothing about them personally. City dwellers in particular – though it is true of all of us to some extent – routinely enter settings where others are going about their business both expecting not to know them, and yet also expecting to know how they will behave. And, more than this, we are nearly always absolutely right in both respects. We are only surprised if we encounter someone who is *not* a stranger – 'Fancy meeting you here! Isn't it a small world!' – or if one of these strangers actually does behave strangely – 'Mummy, why is that man shouting and waving his arms about?' Why is this? Why do others do what we expect of them? Why is *dis*order or the *un*expected among strangers so rare?

Structural-consensus theory

One of the traditional ways in which sociologists explain the order and predictability of social life is by regarding human behaviour as *learned* behaviour. This approach is known – for reasons that will become apparent – as *structural-consensus* theory. The key process this theory emphasizes is called *socialization*. This term refers to the way in which human beings learn the kinds of behaviour expected of them in the social settings in which they find themselves. From this point of view, societies differ because the kinds of behaviour considered appropriate in them differ. People in other societies think and behave differently because they have learned different rules about how to behave and think. The same goes for different groups within the same society. The actions and ideas of one group differ from those of another because its members have been socialized into different rules.

Consensus sociologists use the term *culture* to describe the rules that govern thought and behaviour in a society. Culture exists prior to the people who learn it. At birth, humans are confronted by a social world already in existence. Joining this world involves learning 'how things are done' in it. Only by learning the cultural rules of a society can a human interact with other humans. Because they have been similarly socialized, different individuals will behave similarly.

Consensus theory thus argues that a society's cultural rules determine, or *structure*, the behaviour of its members, channelling their actions in certain ways rather than others. They do so in much the same way that the physical construction of a building structures the actions of the people inside it. Take the behaviour of students in a school. Once inside the school they will display quite regular patterns of behaviour. They will all walk along corridors, up and down stairs, in and out of classrooms, through doors, and so on. They will, by and large, not attempt to dig through floors, smash through walls, or climb out of windows. Their physical movements are constrained by the school building. Since this affects all the students similarly, their behaviour inside the school will be similar – and will exhibit quite definite patterns. In consensus theory, the same is true of social life. Individuals will behave similarly in the same social settings because they are equally constrained by cultural rules. Though these **social structures** are not visible in the way physical structures are, those who are socialized into their rules find them comparably determining.

The levels at which these cultural rules operate can vary. Some rules, like laws for instance, operate at the level of the whole society and structure the behaviour of everyone who lives in it. Others are much less general, structuring the behaviour of people in quite specific social settings. For example, children in a classroom are expected to behave in an orderly and attentive fashion. In the playground much more license is given them, while away from school their behaviour often bears little resemblance to that expected of them during school hours. Similarly, when police officers or nurses or members of the armed forces are 'on duty', certain cultural rules structure their behaviour very rigidly. Out of uniform and off duty these constraints do not apply, though other ones do instead – those governing their behaviour as fathers and mothers, or husbands and wives, for instance.

This shows how the theory of a social structure of cultural rules operates. The rules apply not to the individuals themselves, but to the positions in the social structure they occupy. Shoppers, police officers, traffic wardens, schoolteachers or pupils are constrained by the cultural expectations attached to these positions, but only when they occupy them. In other circumstances, in other locations in the social structure – as fathers or mothers, squash players, football supporters, church members, and so on – other rules come into play.

Sociologists call positions in a social structure *roles*. The rules that structure the behaviour of their occupants are called *norms*. There are some cultural rules that are not attached to any particular role or set of roles. Called *values*, these are in a sense summaries of approved ways of living, and act as a base from which particular norms spring. So, for example: 'education should be the key to success'; 'family relationships should be the most important thing to protect'; 'self-help should be the means to individual fulfilment'. All these are values, and they provide general principles from which norms directing behaviour in schools and colleges, in the home and at work are derived.

According to this sociological theory, socialization into norms and values produces agreement, or *consensus*, between people about appropriate behaviour and beliefs without which no human society can survive. This is why it is called structural-consensus theory. Through socialization, cultural rules structure behaviour, guarantee a consensus about expected behaviour, and thereby ensure social order.

Clearly, in a complex society there are sometimes going to be competing norms and values. For example, while some people think it is wrong for mothers to go out to work, many women see motherhood at best as a real imposition and at worst as an infringement of their liberty. Children often encourage each other to misbehave at school and disapprove of their peers who refuse to do so. Teachers usually see this very much the other way round! The Tory Party Conference is annually strident in its condemnation of any speaker who criticizes the police. Some young blacks would be equally furious with any of their number who had other than a strongly belligerent attitude towards them.

Consensus theorists explain such differences in behaviour and attitude in terms of the existence of alternative cultural influences, characteristic of different social settings. A good example of this emphasis is their approach to educational inequality.

Educational inequality: a consensus theory analysis

Educational research demonstrates, in the most conclusive fashion, that achievement in education is strongly linked to class membership, gender and ethnic origin. There is overwhelming evidence, for example, that working-class children of similar intelligence to children from middle-class backgrounds achieve far less academically than their middle-class counterparts.

To explain this, consensus theorists turn to stock concepts in their approach to social life – norms, values, socialization and culture. Starting from the basic assumption that behaviour and belief are caused by socialization into particular rules, their explanation of working-class underachievement in education seeks to identify:

- the cultural influences which propel middle-class children to academic success
- the cultural influences which drag working-class children down to mediocrity.

The argument usually goes something like this. The upbringing of middle-class children involves socialization into norms and values that are ideal for educational achievement. Because of their own educational experiences, middle-class parents are likely to be very knowledgeable about how education works and how to make the most of it. Further, they are likely to be very keen for their children to make a success of their own education. These children will thus grow up in a social setting where educational achievement is valued and where they will be constantly encouraged and assisted to fulfil their academic potential.

In contrast, the home background of working-class children often lacks such advantageous socialization. Working-class parents are likely to have had only limited, and possibly unhappy, experiences of education. Even if they are keen for their children to achieve educational success, they will almost certainly lack the know-how of the middle-class parent to make this happen. Indeed, sometimes they may actively disapprove of academic attainment; for instance, they may simply distrust what they do not know. As a result, their children may well be taught instead to value the more immediate and practical advantages of leaving school as soon as possible. For example, boys may be encouraged to 'learn a trade' – to eschew academic success for the security of an apprenticeship in 'a proper job'.

Consensus theory: conclusion

Here is a clear example of the application of consensus theory to the facts of social life. From this theoretical point of view, different patterns of behaviour are the product of different patterns of socialization. It might seem that this contradicts the commitment of these theorists to the idea that social order in a society is the outcome of an agreement or a consensus among its members about how to behave and what to think. But consensus theorists say that despite differences of culture between different groups, even despite opposing sub-cultures within the overall culture, in all societies an overall consensus prevails. This is because all societies have certain values about the importance of which there is no dispute. They are called either *central values* or *core values*, and socialization ensures everyone conforms to them.

In Victorian Britain two central values were a commitment to Christian morality, and loyalty to the Queen and the British Empire. Today, examples of central values in a Western capitalist society might be the importance of economic growth, the importance of democratic institutions, the importance of the rule of law, and the importance of the freedom of the individual within the law. (Indeed, anything trotted out as 'basic to our country's way of life' at any particular time is usually a central value in a society.)

For consensus theory then, central values are the backbone of social structures, built and sustained by the process of socialization. Social behaviour and social order are determined by external cultural forces. Social life is possible because of the existence of social structures of cultural rules.

Society as a structure of inequality

The influence of advantages and disadvantages on behaviour

Other sociologists argue a rather different theoretical case. They agree that society determines our behaviour by structuring or constraining it. But they emphasize different structural constraints. For them, the most important influence on social life is the distribution of advantage and its impact on behaviour. Where advantages are unequally distributed, the opportunities of the advantaged to choose how to behave are much greater than those of the disadvantaged.

Educational inequality: an alternative analysis

For example, while it is perfectly feasible for two boys of the same intelligence to be equally keen to fulfil their potential in education and to be equally encouraged by their parents, their culturally instilled enthusiasm cannot, by itself, tell us everything about their potential educational successes or failures. If one boy comes from a wealthy home, while the other is from a much poorer one, this will be far more significant for their education than their similar (learned) desire. Clearly, the unequal distribution of advantage – in this case material resources – will assist the privileged boy and hamper the disadvantaged one.

The advantaged boy's parents can buy a private education, while those of the poorer boy cannot. The advantaged boy can be assured of living in a substantial enough house, with sufficient space to study, whereas the disadvantaged boy may have to make do with a room with the television in it, or a bedroom shared with his brothers and sisters. The advantaged boy can rely on a proper diet and resulting good health, whereas the disadvantaged boy cannot. The advantaged boy can be guaranteed access to all the books and equipment he needs to study, whereas the disadvantaged boy cannot. Probably most importantly, the advantaged boy will be able to continue his education up to the limit of his potential unhindered. For those who are less advantaged it is often necessary to leave school and go out to work to add to the family income. This stronger impulse usually brings education to a premature end.

Structural-conflict theory

So, one primary objection some sociologists have to structural-consensus theory is that where societies are unequal, people are not only constrained by the norms and values they have learnt via socialization. Such theorists argue that it has to be recognized that people are also constrained by the advantages they possess – by their position in the structures of inequality within their society. This emphasis on the effects on behaviour of an unequal distribution of advantage in a society is usually associated with *structural-conflict* theory. Why are such theories called conflict theories?

The kinds of inequality structures in a society vary. Ethnic groups can be unequal, young and old can be unequal, men and women can be unequal, people doing different jobs can be unequal, people of different religious beliefs can be unequal, and so on. The kinds of advantages unequally possessed by such groups can vary, too. Different groups can possess unequal amounts of power, authority, prestige, or wealth, or a combination of these and other advantages.

Notwithstanding the different kinds of inequality conflict theories focus on, and the different kinds of advantages they see as unequally distributed, such theories nonetheless have in common the axiom that the origin and persistence of a structure of inequality lies in the domination of its disadvantaged groups by its advantaged ones. Conflict theories are so-called because for them, inherent in an unequal society is an inevitable *conflict of interests* between its 'haves' and its 'have-nots'. As Wes Sharrock (1977) puts it:

> The conflict view is . . . founded upon the assumption that . . . any society . . . may provide extraordinarily good lives for some but this is usually only possible because the great majority are oppressed and degraded . . . Differences of interest are therefore as important to society as agreements upon rules and values, and most societies are so organised that they not only provide greater benefits for some than for

others but in such a way that the accrual of benefits to a few causes positive discomfort to others. (pp. 515–16)

So conflict theory differs from consensus theory not only because it is interested in the way an unequal distribution of advantage in a society structures behaviour, but also because it is interested in the conflict, not the consensus, inherent in such a society. According to conflict theory, there is a conflict of interest between a society's advantaged and disadvantaged, which is inherent in their relationship.

However, there is another conflict theory objection to consensus theory too. Conflict theorists not only accuse consensus theorists of putting too much emphasis on norms and values as determinants of behaviour at the expense of other influences. They also argue that in any case, consensus theory misunderstands and therefore misinterprets the role of its key concern – socialization into culture.

Ideas as instruments of power

Consensus theory argues that people behave as they do because they have been socialized into cultural rules. The outcome is a consensus about how to think and behave, which manifests itself in patterns and regularities of behaviour. In contrast, conflict theorists argue that we should see the role of cultural rules and the process of socialization in a very different light. For them, the real structural determinants of behaviour are the rewards and advantages possessed unequally by different groups in a society. Other things being equal, those most disadvantaged would not put up with such a state of affairs. Normally, however, other things are *not* equal. Where a society is unequal, the only way it can survive is if those who are disadvantaged in it come to accept their deprivation. Sometimes this involves naked coercion. Plenty of unequal societies survive because their rulers maintain repressive regimes based on terror. However, the exercise of the force necessary to maintain unequal advantage need not take such an obvious or naked form. There are two other related ways in which structures of inequality can survive – and with a surer future than by the naked use of force. First, it can do so if those most disadvantaged by them can somehow be prevented from seeing themselves as underprivileged, or second, even if this is recognized, it can do so if they can be persuaded that this is fair enough – that the inequality is rightful, legitimate and just. According to the conflict view, the way this happens is through the control and manipulation of the norms and values – the cultural rules – into which people are socialized. In effect then, for conflict theorists, far from being the means to social order via consensus, socialization is much more likely to be an instrument of power – producing social order by means of force and domination.

Imagine the following scenario. It is early morning in a Latin American country. A group of agricultural labourers, both men and women, are waiting by a roadside for a bus to arrive to drive them to work. Suddenly two vans draw up and four hooded men jump out. At gunpoint they order the labourers into the backs of the vans, which then race away deep into the surrounding countryside. At nightfall they are abandoned and the labourers transferred into a large covered lorry. This is driven through the night, deep into the mountains. Before daybreak it reaches its destination – a huge underground mine, built deep into the heart of a mountain. Here the labourers are horrified to find a vast army of slaves toiling away, under constant surveillance by brutal guards. After being given a meagre meal, the labourers are forced to join this workforce.

As they live out their desperate lives within this mountain world, some of the slaves try to escape. When caught they are publicly punished as a deterrent to others. Two attempts to escape result in public execution. As the labourers get older, they rely on each other for companionship, and on their memories for comfort. They keep sane by recounting stories of their former lives. In the fullness of time, children are born to them. The parents are careful to tell these children all about their past. As the children grow up and have children of their own, they, too, are told tales of their grandparents' land of lost content. But for them these are handed-down, historical stories, not tales based on experience. As the years go by, though the facts of life within the mountain remain the same, the perception of life in it by the participants alters. By the time five or six generations of slaves have been born, their knowledge of the world of their ancestors' past lives has become considerably diminished. It is still talked about, sometimes. But by now it is a misted world of folklore and myth. All they know from experience is slavery. So far as any of them can remember, they have always been slaves. In their world, slavery is 'normal'. In effect, to be a slave means something very different to them from what it meant to their ancestors.

A similar process occurs with the oppressors. As the slaves' view of themselves has altered over time, so the necessity for naked force has become less and less. As, through socialization, their subordinates have begun to acquiesce in their own subordination, the guards no longer brandish guns and clubs. Because of this, they no longer see themselves as the original guards did. Both the dominant and the subordinate, knowing nothing else, have, through socialization, come to see the inequality in their world in a very different light from the original inhabitants.

Though this story is rather larger-than-life, it does allow us to see the role of socialization into cultural rules as conflict theorists see it. Their argument is that we must be careful not to dismiss the presence of conflict in societies just because a consensus seems to prevail. Naked force is only necessary so long as people see themselves as oppressed. If they can be persuaded that they are not oppressed, or if they fail to see that they are, then they can be willing architects in the design of their own subordination. The easiest way to exercise power, and gain advantage as a result, is for the dominated to be complicit in their own subordination.

Conflict theorists tell us that rather than simply describe cultural rules in a society, therefore, we must carefully examine their content. We must ask: 'Who *benefits* from the *particular* set of rules prevailing in this society, rather than some other set?' Cultural rules cannot be neutral or all-benevolent. Of course, consensus theorists are right to say that people are socialized into pre-existing norms and values. But for conflict theorists this tells us only half the story. We must also find out whether some groups benefit more than others from the existence of a particular set of rules and have a greater say in their construction and interpretation. If they do, then the process of socialization into these is an instrument of their advantage – it is an instrument of their power.

Ideas exercising power: the example of gender inequality legitimation

For example, even a cursory glance at the kinds of occupations held by women and the kinds of rewards they receive for doing them clearly indicates the advantages men have over women in our society. Of course, Britain once had a female prime minister, and today has some female civil servants, MPs, judges, and university vice-chancellors as well an increasing number of women in leading positions in business. But this cannot hide the fact that there is still markedly unequal occupational opportunity, and unequal economic reward, based on gender. The facts are that males dominate the best-rewarded and most prestigious occupations and (despite the Equal Opportunities Commission) usually receive greater rewards when they perform the same jobs as women.

Clearly, there is a considerable potential conflict of interests between men and women here. It is in men's interests for women not to compete in large numbers for the limited number of highly rewarded jobs. It is in men's interests for women to stay at home and provide domestic services for them. If women were to want something different, this would conflict with the desires, interests and ambitions of men.

So why is it that so many women do *not* object to this state of affairs? If women are as systematically deprived of occupational opportunities and rewards by men as this, why do so many of them acquiesce in their deprivation? For example, why are some of the fiercest critics of the feminist movement women? Why do so many women *choose* to be (unpaid) houseworkers for the benefit of their husbands and children? Why is the extent of so many girls' ambitions to 'start a family'? Why do they not wish to explore their potential in other activities instead, or as well?

Clearly, a substantial part of the answers to these questions is that women have been socialized into accepting this definition of themselves. For conflict theorists, this is a clear example of particular norms and values working in the interests of one section of society and against another. Through the ideas they have learned, women have been forced to accept a role that is subordinate to men.

There is one final question to be asked about this theoretical approach. How does the exercise of force by means of socialization into particular ideas happen? Conflict theorists say it can be intentional or unintentional. The rulers of many societies in the world today deliberately employ propaganda to persuade the ruled of the legitimacy of this arrangement. They also often control and censor mass media in their countries, to ensure lack of opposition to this controlled socialization.

The exercise of this kind of force can be less deliberate too. Take our example of the inequality between men and women in our society. To what extent does the image of women presented in advertising promote an acceptance of this inequality? Though the intention is to sell various products – from lingerie and perfume to household goods, to alcohol, cigarettes, cars and office equipment – the images of women used in advertising are so specific that there are other, less intentional effects, too. Two images dominate. One is of the woman as the domestic at home, using the 'best' products to clean, polish, launder and cook. The other is of the woman as a sexually desirable object, guaranteed to either (1) magically adorn the life of any male who is sensible enough to drink a certain sort of gin, drive a particular car or use a specific shaving lotion; or (2) be transformed into an irresistible seductress when she wears particular underwear or perfume, or is given a particular brand of chocolates.

Such advertising socializes both men *and* women, of course. The outcome is a stereotypical view of womanhood and of the place of women in society, embraced not only by those whom it disadvantages, but also by those who benefit from it. There *is* a consensus about such things. However, it is not the kind of consensus portrayed by the consensus theorist. It is an imposed consensus, preventing the conflict that would break out if people were allowed to see the world as it really is.

Conflict theory: conclusion

There are a number of sociological theories that can be called structural-conflict theories, in that they are based on two main premises:

- social structures consist of unequally advantaged groups; the interests of these groups are in conflict, since inequality results from the domination and exploitation of the disadvantaged groups by the advantaged ones
- social order in such societies is maintained by force – either by actual force, or by force exercised through socialization.

Consensus theory versus conflict theory

Structural-consensus theory and structural-conflict theory emphasize different kinds of influences on thought and behaviour. Though both theories see the origin of human social life in the structural influences or determinants of society external to the individual, they disagree about what this outside society consists of. Consensus theory is based on the primacy of the influence of culture – what we learn to want as a result of socialization. Conflict theory, in contrast, pays most attention to the conflict inherent in the relationship between unequally advantaged groups in society and argues that the content of culture should be seen as a means of perpetuating relationships of inequality.

Society as the creation of its members

The influence of interpretation on behaviour

A third kind of sociological theory leads in a rather different direction. It still attempts to explain why human beings in society behave in the orderly ways they do. But instead of looking for the answer in the influence of a social structure which people confront and are constrained by, this theory argues something else. From this point of view, the most important influence on an individual's behaviour is the behaviour of other individuals towards him or her. The focus is not on general cultural rules, or on the unequal distribution of advantage in whole societies. It is on the way individual social encounters work – on how the parties to them are able to understand and thereby interact with one another. This is not to say that structural theories do not try to explain this, too. In consensus theory, for example, people are role players, and act out parts learnt through socialization. But how do they decide which roles to play, in which social setting? Consensus theory does not try to explain why people choose one role rather than another. It is assumed that we somehow learn to make the right choices. This third theory, however, argues that the choice of role playing is much more complex than in this rather robotized view. It argues that the essence of social life lies in the quite extraordinary ability of humans to work out what is going on around them – their ability to attach meaning to reality – and then to choose to act in a particular way in the light of this interpretation. This is called **interpretive**, or **action theory**.

Action theory

Action theorists stress the need to concentrate on the *micro*-level of social life, the way particular individuals are able to interact with one another in individual social encounters, rather than on the *macro*-level, the way the whole structure of society influences the behaviour of individuals. They argue that we must not think of societies as structures existing independently of, and prior to, the interaction of individuals. For action theorists, societies are the end result of human interaction, not its cause. Only by looking at how individual humans are able to interact can we come to understand how social order is created. To see how this happens, let us reflect on the kinds of action of which humans are capable.

Some human action is like the action of phenomena in the inanimate world – purpose*less*, or lacking intention. We all do things involuntarily – like sneezing, blinking or yawning. We do not *choose* to feel fear, excitement, or pain, or choose to react in certain ways to those feelings. So far as we know, the actions of non-human animate phenomena are purely instinctive (automatic or reflex responses to external stimuli). It is true that animals, for example, often appear to act in a purposive way by using their brains. They seem to choose to eat or sleep or be friendly or aggressive, or to choose to evacuate their bladders over the new living-room carpet. Nevertheless, the usual zoological explanation is that even these often quite sophisticated patterns of animal action are involuntary. They are reactive and conditioned, rather than the product of voluntary creative decision-making.

In contrast, nearly all human action *is* voluntary. It is the product of a conscious decision to act, a result of thought. Nearly everything we do is the result of choosing to act in one way rather than another. Furthermore, this is purposive, or goal-oriented choice. We choose between courses of action because, as humans, we are able to aim at an end or a goal and take action to achieve this. Nearly all human action, therefore, is *intentional* **action**: we *mean* to do what we do in order to achieve our chosen purposes.

Where do these chosen purposes, or goals, come from? What action theory emphasizes is that we decide what to do in the light of our *interpretation* of the world around us. Being human means making sense of the settings or situations in which we find ourselves and choosing to act accordingly. To use the usual action theory phrase for this, we choose what to do in the light of our 'definition of the situation'. For example, suppose you wake up one summer morning to find the sun shining in a cloudless sky. You decide to sunbathe all day and to mow your lawn in the evening, when it will be cooler. At lunchtime, you see large clouds beginning to form in the distance. Because you decide there is a chance of a thunderstorm, you cut the grass immediately. You get very hot. It does not rain. In the evening, you go for a walk in the country. You come to a country pub and stop for a drink. As you sit outside you notice smoke rising on a hillside some distance away. As you watch the smoke gets thicker and darker. You decide the fire is unattended and out of control. You dash inside the pub and ring the fire brigade. Shortly afterwards you hear a fire engine racing to the fire. You climb a nearby hill to have a better look. When you get there you see that the fire is, in fact, deliberate; it is a bonfire in the garden of a house on the hillside which you had been unable to see from the pub. Shortly afterwards you hear the fire engine returning to its base. You go back to the pub to finish your drink. It has been cleared away in your absence. You have no more money. You decide it is not your day. You decide to go home.

Of course, nearly all of the settings we have to make sense of involve more than this because nearly everything we do in our lives takes place in the company of others. Most of the situations we have to define in order to choose how to act are *social*; they involve other humans doing things. You see a very large man shaking his fist and shouting at you, and conclude that he is not overjoyed that you have driven into the back of his car. As a result you decide not to suggest that he was responsible for the accident because of the way he parked. You see a traffic warden slipping a parking ticket under your wind-screen-wiper, and decide not to contribute to the Police Benevolent Fund after all. This is *social* action. It is action we choose to take in the light of what we interpret the behaviour of others to mean.

Meaningful social interaction

There is more to social action than interpretation leading to action, however. Most of the time when we interact with other humans, they *want* us to arrive at certain interpretations of their actions – they *want* us to think one thing of them rather than another. The man whose car has just been damaged is not behaving in the rather distinctive manner described above because he wishes the culprit to come round to his house for tea. The man scratching his nose in the auction room is not (usually) alleviating an itch. He is communicating his bid to the auctioneer, and he expects that the latter will interpret his actions as he wishes. Pedestrians in London streets do not wave to taxi-drivers because they are, or want to become, their friends. They do so because they want a lift.

Dress can often organize interpretation just as effectively as gestures, of course. Though the punk rocker, the skinhead, the bowler-hatted civil servant, the police officer and the traffic warden whom we encounter in the street make no *apparent* attempt to communicate with us, they are certainly doing so, nevertheless. They want us to think certain things about them when we see them, so they choose to communicate by the use of uniforms. They are making a symbolic use of dress, if you like; after all, like gestures, garments symbolize what their users want us to interpret about them.

The most effective symbols humans have at their disposal are words – linguistic symbols. Though dress, gesture, touch and even smell can often communicate our meanings and organize the interpretations of others adequately enough, clearly the most efficient – and most remarkable – way in which we can get others to understand us is through language. This is why action theorists are often interested in the way we use language to exchange meanings with each other. Language, verbal or written, is the uniquely human device which we are able to use to interact meaningfully with one another, and thereby to create society.

From this point of view, societies are made up of individuals engaging in a countless number of meaningful encounters. The result is social order. But this is no *determined* order. It is not the result of the imposition of cultural rules, as the consensus theorist sees it. Nor is it the result of the constraints of a world where advantages are unequally distributed, and where cultural rules legitimate these constraints, as the conflict theorist sees it. Instead, society is an order created, or accomplished, by the capacities of the members themselves. It is the outcome of innumerable occasions of interaction, each one accomplished by interpreting, meaning-attributing actors who can make sense of the social settings in which they find themselves and who choose courses of action accordingly.

The social construction of reality

There is another important difference between structural and interpretive conceptions of society. For structural theorists, the character of a society – its social structure – is not in doubt. It is a 'real' thing that exists outside of its members. For the interpretivist, however, it is much more difficult to describe a society that is the outcome of interpretation as somehow 'true' or 'real' in this structural sense.

For the interpretivist, being human involves interpreting what is going on around one – saying: 'This is what is happening here', and choosing an appropriate course of action in the light of this interpretation. However, such interpretations of 'what is going on here' can only ever be considered 'correct' or 'true' for the particular person doing the interpreting. What is 'really' going on depends on how the individual sees it. Reality is in the eye of the beholder. We act in ways we consider appropriate. What we consider appropriate depends upon what we think the behaviour of others means. It is therefore by no means inconceivable that other people, in exactly the same social situations as ourselves, would have taken the behaviour around them to mean something very different, and would therefore have taken very different courses of action from us.

For example, a car crashes into a wall on a wet winter's evening. The police officer called to the scene discovers a dead driver and a strong smell of drink in the car. A search reveals an empty whisky bottle underneath a seat. Like all humans encountering a social situation, the officer engages in a process of interpretation, defining the situation. Weighing up the evidence, he or she decides that the crash was an accident caused by the driver being drunk and losing control of the vehicle in difficult driving conditions. Another officer called to the scene might use this evidence to interpret things rather differently, however. He or she might consider the possibility that the driver deliberately drove the car into the wall as an act of suicide, having first given himself courage to do so by drinking the whisky. The second officer would then make inquiries that the first would not. The dead man's domestic and work affairs would be looked into and it might be discovered that he had become severely depressed about his future. The officer would decide that his suspicions of suicide had been sufficiently confirmed by this additional evidence, and that it should be given at the Coroner's court when the inquest was held.

How the death is finally interpreted depends upon the decision of the court, of course, when the evidence is reassessed by a new set of interpreters – particularly the Coroner. The Coroner's decision will define the death as either accidental or a suicide. But is this judgment the 'truth'? Who is to say what the 'reality' of the situation was? What 'really' happened here? In the case of this kind of example, of course, no one will ever know for certain.

Even in more conclusive circumstances, actions still always depend upon the interpretation of the beholder. Suppose you come across a middle-aged man grappling with a young girl in the bushes of a park. What you do depends on what you think is going on. You may decide the man is assaulting the girl, and take a course of action you see fit in the light of this interpretation (and depending how brave you feel at the time). Or you may decide it is horseplay between lovers, or a father admonishing his daughter – or any other interpretation that may spring to mind. What matters is not so much that you are right, that you see what is *really* happening, but that:

- you cannot help but come to some sort of interpretation or other (even if it is that you do *not* know what is happening); and
- what you decide to do will be the result of this interpretation.

Though subsequent events may 'prove' things one way or another, initial action undertaken by human beings in such social circumstances, though always involving a process of interpretation, can never be assumed to be definitely 'true' or 'real'. It can only ever be how we choose to see things. The world 'is' what we think it is. As W. I. Thomas (1966) puts it: 'If man defines situations as real, they are real in their consequences.'

Action theory: conclusion

In contrast to the structuralist view then, social 'reality' is not a factual, objective, unambiguous state of affairs. Reality can only ever be what the actors involved in interaction *think* is real, and what they *think* is real determines what they decide to do. Reality is therefore quite definitely the negotiated creation of individuals in interaction with one another. Furthermore, because the social worlds so created are dependent on the interpretations of particular individuals in particular social settings, they are much more precarious constructions than suggested by the notion of social structures determining behaviour.

Consensus, conflict and action theories thus identify different factors as significant in explaining the nature of social life, and of the relationship between the individual and society. We will look in detail at the work of some of the most significant sociologists of the nineteenth, twentieth and twenty-first centuries. As we shall see, for most of the time sociology has been in existence as a distinct discipline, the kinds of issues highlighted by consensus, conflict and action approaches have been central to sociological theorizing. Although only some of this theorizing falls neatly or exclusively within one of these traditions alone, they are nonetheless useful as reference points from which to understand differences and debates in sociological thought.

Classical sociological theorizing: analysing modernity

The work of three nineteenth-century sociologists in particular has reverberated through the twentieth and twenty-first centuries and it is for this reason that they are regarded as the classic figures in the discipline. They are a Frenchman, **Emile Durkheim** (1858–1917), and two Germans, **Karl Marx** (1818–1883) and **Max Weber** (1864–1920). Despite the great differences in the content and direction of their sociological theories, the work of Durkheim, Marx and Weber each represents an intellectual and political response to the same historical circumstances. The most powerful set of forces at work in nineteenth-century Europe was unleashed in the eighteenth century during the period historians call the **Enlightenment**; today these forces are summarized in sociology as **modernity**. Sociology came into being because of modernity, and the theories of many of its major figures in both the nineteenth and twentieth centuries can be seen as different kinds of responses to the birth of the modern world. This is particularly true of the classic writings of Durkheim, Marx and Weber.

As we shall see later (chapter 9), there are those today who believe that over the last few decades a new set of social changes has once again transformed the world. According to *postmodernists*, the circumstances in which we live now and the ways in which we think – particularly the ways in which we think about ourselves – are so completely different from those described by the theorists of modernity such as Durkheim, Marx and Weber that we should realize that the world of modernity has been superseded by a new world, of *postmodernity*. However, as chapter 9 will show, the many critics of postmodernism hotly dispute this depiction of contemporary life. Indeed, the debate between modernist theorists and postmodernists has been one of the principal features of recent social theorizing. But we must leave an examination of the ideas of postmodernism and the competing ones of its critics until the end of this book. At this early stage in our journey we need to examine the profound changes to human existence ushered in by the emergence of modern life that gave birth to the discipline of sociology.

Modernity

The idea of the 'modern' originated as an account of the kinds of institutions, ideas and behaviour that grew out of the decline of medieval society in Europe. Although the seeds of modernity had been sown hundreds of years before, it was not until the nineteenth century that modern life became securely established. The changes involved were so momentous that Karl Polanyi (1973) does not overstate the case when he uses the phrase *The Great Transformation* to describe them. Marx and Engels are even more graphic in their famous depiction of modernity:

> All fixed, fast-frozen relations, with their train of ancient and venerable prejudices and opinions, are swept away, all new-formed ones become antiquated before they can ossify. All that is solid melts into air, all that is holy is profaned, and men at last are forced to face . . . the real conditions of their lives and their relations with their fellow men. (Marx and Engels, *The Communist Manifesto*, 1848)

In very summary form, the changes wrought by modernity involved the emergence and establishment of:

- capitalism
- mass production based on the factory
- a hugely increased, and largely urbanized, population
- the nation-state as the modern form of government
- Western domination of the globe
- secular forms of knowledge, particularly science.

Capitalism

In pre-capitalist economies, though there is some manufacturing and some trade, people more usually produce goods for their own consumption. This is particularly true of pre-capitalist agriculture. Capitalism means something very different. Capitalists employ workers to produce their goods for them, in return for a wage. The point of producing these goods is to sell them in the marketplace for more than the costs involved in their production. That is, capitalist production is about the pursuit of profit. The more efficient the production, the more profitable it can be. In the systematic pursuit of profit, what matters most is the market value of a good, the availability of markets, and the efficiency with which an enterprise is organized. In particular, this involves the rational management of the labour force so that costs are kept down.

Capitalism thus involves the establishment of new ways of thinking and acting, largely absent in the pre-modern world. Workers have to sell their labour to employers as a commodity in a labour market. Their survival depends not on what they produce for themselves but on the wages they receive, with which they have to purchase the goods and services they need. As a result, their life-chances are crucially determined by the rewards they receive for the work they do. That is, a system of class inequality emerges, largely based on occupational rewards. In addition, identity becomes intimately linked to work and class membership; how you see yourself and how you are seen by others becomes defined by the work you do and the rewards this work brings. One of the social expressions of this aspect of modernity is the emergence of a labour movement: organizations, such as Trade Unions, become established to represent the collectively held interests of workers in similar occupational groupings. Gender inequality develops too. Not only do male workers tend to receive greater rewards than working women but, over time, and as the mechanization of production increases, women become progressively excluded from the workplace. This produces a separation of life and life-chances into, on the one hand, a male-dominated public sphere, of the world of work and wages, and on the other, a female-dominated private sphere, of the world of unwaged domestic labour. Women thus become economically dependent on their husbands and defined principally in terms of their role in managing the domestic world.

Agricultural production and trade became capitalized first and then, in the nineteenth century, capitalism became the dynamic behind the huge and rapid growth in industrial production.

Techniques of production

Alongside the emergence of capitalism, the so-called Industrial Revolution allowed new ways of working and producing goods to be instituted. Rapid technological advances led to large-scale manufacturing being located in a designated workplace – the factory – and the organization of production became the object of rational calculation. The factory system involved the workers being systematically organized and controlled, with the separation of the process of production into specialized tasks a distinctive feature of this regulation. Later on, and with further technological advances, modern mass production techniques became ever more sophisticated, culminating in what is known as Fordism – the rational and efficient organization of manufacturing. (The name is derived from the founder of the assembly line in motor manufacturing, Henry Ford.) Fordism involves not only the mass production of a standardized product (Ford is famously remembered for saying that his customers could have any colour Model T Ford that they liked so long as it was black), but rigidly bureaucratic organizational structures, the pursuit of high productivity and collective wage bargaining.

Population change

The Great Transformation included an unprecedented growth in population and its concentration in urban settings. Birth rates rose and death rates fell; according to Kumar (1978), the population of Europe grew from around 120 million in 1750 to around 468 million in 1913. The urbanization of the population was another major feature of modernity; there was mass migration from the countryside to the towns and cities that were springing up around the centres of industrial production. This provided the template for a typical feature of modern twentieth-century life – the urban conurbation.

The nation-state

Modernity saw a new form of polity – the nation-state – come into being. States have a centralized form of government whose absolute power extends over a national territory. Governmental decrees – laws – are passed which apply to all those living on this territory and the state's ultimate power resides in its monopoly over the use of force, for example, by means of its control of the armed forces. The emergence of state government spawns a civil authority too – a system of political administrators and officials whose task it is to enforce state-sponsored decisions across the national territory. By the twentieth century, global political power resided in the nation-states of the West and ideas of citizenship, nationalism, democracy, socialism, conservatism and liberalism dominated political thinking and discourse.

Global domination by the West

The establishment of the power of the nation-state triggered the political, economic and cultural domination of the globe by European states. The rapid economic development of the West in the nineteenth century depended crucially on easy access to raw materials from around the globe. The political and military power of these states enabled them to plunder the material and human resources of weaker global areas and began the process of the unequal development of the First and Third Worlds with which we live today. Later on, this Western domination was cemented politically and culturally by colonialism and economically by the control of global markets.

Cultural change: the rise of rationality and the secularization of knowledge

The Enlightenment provided the cultural shift necessary for the final triumph of modernity. An historical moment of the eighteenth century, the Enlightenment refers to the emergence of a new confidence in the power of human reason. Knowledge production before the Enlightenment typically involved experts translating religious texts or signs. In this way it became possible for people to know what their God or gods had in mind for them. In complete contrast, the Enlightenment promoted the essentially secular view that by using reason, by thinking rationally, humans could, for the first time in human history, produce certain knowledge and could therefore harness this knowledge in the pursuit of progress. The exemplar of rationality was scientific thinking and scientific activity. The intellectual engine of modernity was thus the belief that nothing could remain a mystery, nothing would remain undiscovered, if reason were made the guide. Moreover, this would allow humankind to not only know things for certain but to know how to make things better – to achieve progress. The pre-modern dependence on the virtues of tradition and continuity gave way to a commitment to the benefits of reason-inspired change, innovation and progress. This way of thinking is called **modernism**. It is the rise of modernism, a cultural change in belief about what constitutes knowledge and what knowledge is for, that directly promoted the rise of sociology and sociological theorizing.

Modernism and sociology

Modernist thinking involves the idea that the purpose of acquiring knowledge is, as Giddens (1987) puts it: 'To influence for the better the human condition.' Modernity implies the constant pursuit of improvement in human lives and of the pursuit of progress. Unlike traditional settings, where virtue lies in things remaining the same, in modern worlds change, development and improvement are the goals. As Cheal (1991) has pointed out, believing in the ideal and possibility of progress means: 'believing that things tomorrow can always be better than they are today, which in turn means being prepared to overturn the existing order of things in order to make way for progress. It means, in other words, being prepared to break with tradition' (p. 27).

How should this progress be achieved? Underpinning the belief in the possibility of progress is a belief in the power of reason – in the ability of humans to think about themselves, their condition and their society reflexively and rationally – and to improve it in the light of such rational thought. The idea that humans can not only think about, and explain, their lives – to produce *social theories* in fact – but can employ them to change society for the better, is a specifically modern notion. The idea that reason can provide an agenda and a set of prescriptions for living, rather than relying on divine intervention and instruction, only began to prevail after the Enlightenment. Summarizing the effects of the Enlightenment, Badham (1986) says:

> It was during this period that faith in divine revelation, and the authority of the Church as interpreter of God's will, were increasingly undermined by this new confidence in the ability of human reason to provide an

understanding of the world and a guide for human conduct. Similarly, the understanding of history as the chronicle of the fall of man from God's grace, with spiritual salvation only attainable in the next world, was largely replaced by a belief in human perfectibility and the increasing faith in man's power and ability to use his new-found knowledge to improve mankind's state. The importance of these two assumptions should not be underestimated. Without the faith in reason, social theory could not be regarded as playing any important role in society. Without the belief in the possibility of progress, whatever reason's ability to understand the nature of society, social theory would not be able to fulfil any positive role in improving upon man's fate. (1986, p. 11)

So sociology is not only a product of modernity – of a belief in the power of human reason to create knowledge which can be used to achieve progress. In addition, the world created by modernity is its principal subject matter: Giddens (1987, pp. vii–viii) has said that in sociology, the 'prime field of study is the social world brought about by the advent of modernity'.

As Giddens (1987, p. 26) also puts it, the very existence of sociology is 'bound up with the "project of modernity"'. The construction of social theories thus reflects a concern not only with *how* we live, but how we *should* live; social theories of modern society try not only to describe and explain our social world, but to diagnose its problems and propose solutions. According to Giddens (1987, p. 17), this places sociology in the 'tensed zone of transition between diagnosis and prognosis'.

The problem, of course, concerns the goal and direction of desirable change. The following chapters attempt to summarize the contributions of some influential nineteenth-, twentieth- and twenty-first-century sociological figures to this enterprise – the contribution of sociology to the **'project of modernity'**.

Further Reading

There are five different kinds of texts included in the Further Reading sections at the end of each chapter of this book. These are:

- the classic texts in social theory
- readers consisting of extracts of classic work by the major theorists
- texts analysing the work of one or more of the major theorists
- readers consisting of commissioned chapters by experts on specific theorists and/or particular areas of social theory
- introductory theory textbooks covering similar ground to this one.

What you use as further reading and how you use these books depends on the stage you have reached in your studies. A-level students will get most benefit from the theory textbooks as will undergraduates in other subjects taking sociology modules. First-year undergraduates reading sociology should try and go beyond a reliance on such texts and also use at least the famous extracts contained in the readers. Second- and third-year undergraduates should consult the original texts themselves as well as the books dedicated to particular theorists and the commentaries contained in the commissioned readers.

Textbooks

Some of these are a lot more difficult than others. Decide for yourself which ones you find most accessible and helpful. In no particular order, I suggest you look at:

Bauman, Zygmunt and May, Tim: *Thinking Sociologically*, 2nd edn, Blackwell, 2001.
Baert, Patrick: *Social Theory in the Twentieth Century*, Polity, 1998.
Bernstein, R. J.: *The Restructuring of Social and Political Theory*, Blackwell, 1976.
Bilton, Tony et al.: *Introductory Sociology*, 4th edn, chapters 17, 18, 19 Palgrave, 2002.
Craib, Ian: *Modern Social Theory*, 2nd edn, Harvester-Wheatsheaf, 1992.
Craib, Ian: *Classical Social Theory*, Oxford University Press, 1997.
Cuff, E. C., Francis, D. W., Sharrock, W. W.: *Perspectives in Sociology*, 4th edn, Routledge, 1998.
Dodd, Nigel: *Social Theory and Modernity*, Polity, 1999.
Fidelman, Ashe: *Contemporary Social and Political Theory: an introduction*, Open University Press, 1998.
Lee, David and Newby, Howard: *The Problem of Sociology*, Hutchinson, 1983.
May, Tim: *Situating Social Theory*, Open University Press, 1996.
Ritzer, George: *Sociological Theory*, 5th edn, McGraw-Hill, 2000.
Seidmore, Steven: *Contested Knowledge*: *social theory in the postmodern era*, Blackwell, 1998.
Skidmore, W.: *Theoretical Thinking in Sociology*, Cambridge University Press, 1975.

Readers including extracts from the classic works

Craig Calhoun et al.: *Classical Sociological Theory*, Blackwell's Readers in Sociology, Blackwell, 2002a.
Craig Calhoun et al.: *Contemporary Sociological Theory*, Blackwell's Readers in Sociology, Blackwell, 2002b.
James Farganis (ed.): *Readings in Social Theory: the classic tradition to post-modernism*, 3rd edn, McGraw-Hill, 2000.

Charles Lemert (ed.): *Social Theory: the Multicultural and Classic Readings*, Westview Press, 1993.

Commissioned readers on theories and theorists

Robert Bocock and Kenneth Thompson (eds): *Social and Cultural Forms of Modernity*, Polity, 1992.

Stuart Hall, David Held and Tony McGrew (eds): *Modernity and its Futures*, Polity, 1992.

George Ritzer (ed.): *The Blackwell Companion to Major Social Theorists*, Blackwell, 2002.

Bryan Turner (ed.): *The Blackwell Companion to Social Theory*, 2nd edn, Blackwell, 2000.

2 EMILE DURKHEIM

Emile Durkheim

AKG London

Emile Durkheim: born Lorraine, France, 1858, died Paris, 1917

Major works

The Division of Labour in Society (1893)
Rules of Sociological Method (1895)
Suicide (1897)
The Elementary Forms of Religious Life (1912)

Introduction

Durkheim's response to modernity has two main elements:

- he wanted to ensure that modern societies were harmonious and orderly
- he wanted to create a *science* of society to generate the knowledge necessary to show how this could be done.

Social structure

Durkheim had a quite orthodox consensus view of social structures. Their crucial feature, he said, is that they are made up of *norms* and *values* – cultural definitions of behaviour considered appropriate and worthy in different settings. Since it is through socialization that we learn these normative definitions, it is only this process which makes individuals members of society and therefore makes social life possible.

According to Durkheim, though we may think we choose to behave in one way rather than another, in reality the choice is made for us. It was Durkheim who first of all stressed the consensus view that even the possibilities of thought and experience are *inherited*, not invented. For example, people who attend a religious service may believe sincerely in their god. But the beliefs and practices of their religion were in existence before they were – they *learned* them. Like all other social activity, religious belief and practice is structured by society and by the positions of people in it. Durkheim himself makes this point, so fundamental to the consensus view of social life:

> When I perform my duties as a brother, a husband or a citizen and carry out the commitments I have entered into, I fulfil obligations which are defined in law and custom and which are external to myself and my actions. Even when they conform to my own sentiments and when I feel their reality within me, that reality does not cease to be objective, for it is not I who have prescribed these duties; I have received them through education . . . Similarly the believer has discovered from birth, ready fashioned, the beliefs and practices of his religious life; if they existed before he did, it follows that they exist outside him. (Durkheim, 1982, pp. 50–1)

For Durkheim, then, the achievement of social life among humans, and the existence of social order in society, which he calls **'social solidarity'**, is ensured by socialization – the process whereby different individuals learn collectively held standards or rules of behaviour. Durkheim's phrase for these rules was 'social facts'. Although these are only *visible* through the conformity of individuals to them, they are, nevertheless, in Durkheim's words, 'external to, and constraining upon' these individuals. Though not capable of being seen, such structures of cultural rules are as real to the individuals whose behaviour is determined by them as the world's physical structure by which they are also constrained. Society, in a famous phrase of Durkheim's, is a reality '*sui generis*' – it has its own existence.

Forms of solidarity

According to Durkheim, the central problem of social existence is the problem of order – how to achieve social solidarity in a society. Different types of society achieve solidarity in different ways. In premodern, traditional societies, where people live very similar kinds of lives, solidarity is achieved more or less automatically. This form of **mechanical solidarity** is the result of a simple **division of labour**. There are so few roles to play or different ways of living available that the need for the society's members to see the world in the same way – to share a collectively held set of rules about how to behave – is satisfied without much difficulty.

Things are much more problematic in modernity however. By definition, a modern society has a highly complex division of labour. There are so many different roles to be played and so many different ways of living possible that social solidarity is much more difficult to achieve. For Durkheim, this is the main danger in modernity. The forces separating and dividing people are so profound that social disintegration is a real threat. Furthermore, Durkheim believed that human beings are not naturally consensual. He believed that if left to our own devices, we are *anti*-social. The natural, as opposed to structurally constrained, state for a human is to be self-centred, greedy, insatiable and overly competitive. The problem of modernity is that it encourages such excessive, rampant individualism. So not only are our natural propensities dangerously individualistic, but the very institutions of modernity encourage such anti-social individualism, a condition Durkheim termed **anomie**. According to Durkheim, unless such impulses promoting anomie are checked by counter-balancing social structural forces promoting cohesion and integration, social solidarity and social order are seriously threatened.

He sees two sources of hope. In modernity, we play very different roles in the division of labour and therefore live very different lives from each other. However, both our survival and the survival of our society depend on the fact that these roles are interdependent. The only way we can survive to live our particular lives is if others are living theirs. In a modern economy, for example, the main reason any particular task needs to be performed is because all the other tasks depend on it. That is, the roles are interdependent. Durkheim sees this as a kind of metaphor for modern existence. To survive, we need each other; our existence and our futures depend on our interdependence. To use his phrase, modern societies need to achieve **organic solidarity**. But our instincts are self-centred and anomie threatens. How can we members of modern societies be made to realize our mutual dependency, and as a result act in ways that can promote it to thereby achieve organic solidarity?

Solving this problem is at the heart of Durkheim's theorizing. He wants to demonstrate the truth of his assertions that stable societies are interdependent societies and that the members of these societies need to be taught to think and behave in ways that guarantee this interdependency, both for their own good and for the good of their society. This leads Durkheim in three separate, but related, directions:

- first, he argues that only if sociology is a science can we acquire the evidence we need to understand social arrangements
- second, he shows how societies work as interdependent social systems by using functionalist theorizing
- third, he demonstrates the crucial role of religion in inhibiting anomie and guaranteeing social solidarity in human societies.

A science of society

It is his conception of his subject matter that leads Durkheim to advocate the use of science to explain social life. The scientific method he favoured is known as **positivism**.

The guiding principle for the positivist scientist is that if something exists in nature, it has been caused by something else in nature. That is, natural phenomena cause other natural phenomena. For example, when water reaches a certain temperature (cause) it freezes (effect). Furthermore, this always happens. There are no circumstances (depending on atmospheric pressure) when water will not become ice at a particular temperature. Such invariable cause and effect relationships are called *laws*. Science sets out to discover the laws of nature. These laws are 'given' for us. Whether we like it or not, water will freeze at a certain temperature. Whether we like it or not, the temperature is higher in the summer than in the winter. Whether we like it or not, leaves will fall from deciduous trees in the autumn. We live in a natural world that is organized in a particular way and we are stuck with this world, whatever our views about it. Science therefore only reveals *why* nature is as it is. We can describe this 'given' character of nature by saying it is an *objective* world. It exists, as a matter of fact, independently of any subjective feelings or judgements we may have about it.

For Durkheim, social structures are as objective and given as nature. For him, structural features are as given for the inhabitants of a society who encounter them at birth as is the natural world given for phenomena, animate and inanimate, that make *it* up. Daffodils do not choose to be yellow; frogs do not choose to croak and have bulging eyes; water does not choose to freeze. They do so, nevertheless. Humans do not choose to have two eyes, a nose and a mouth. Nor do they choose to have two arms and two legs. These are simply biological facts of life.

In the same way, for Durkheim, a society consists of a similar realm of *social* facts 'external to and constraining upon' the individual. We do not choose to believe the things we believe or to act in the way we act. We *learn* to think or do these things. Pre-existing cultural rules determine our ideas and behaviour through socialization. Thus, in the same way as the characteristics of natural phenomena are the products of laws of nature, so people's ideas and acts are the product of external social forces that make up social structures. Consequently, sociology must be scientific in its method of enquiry. In Durkheim's words 'sociology can and must be objective, since it deals with realities as definite and substantial as those of . . . the biologist' (Durkheim, 1970).

For positivist science this method involves *empirical observation*: only if you can muster evidence of causal relationships identifiable by the senses can you claim to have demonstrated their existence. Thus, Durkheim argues for sociology to rely on empirical evidence too. Since behaviour and belief are determined by external structural forces, when we quantify the incidence of action or of thought among people, what we have is empirical evidence of the extent to which the forces that have produced this behaviour and belief exist.

The attraction of this method of relying on empirical evidence to produce knowledge was that it seemed to offer the possibility of certainty – of demonstrable proof. For many of those engaged in a project dedicated to social reconstruction and societal progress – the sociology of the modern world – such a prospect was indeed enticing. Durkheim's French predecessor, Auguste Comte (1798–1857), was the first to proclaim the virtues of an empirically based social science. According to Bilton et al. for someone like Comte, born during the aftermath of the French Revolution, the implications of such a social science were enormous: 'for positive sociological knowledge could offer the means for peaceful reconstruction of social order by the elite of enlightened scientists and intellectuals – social change need not depend upon revolutionary violence and the manipulation of the mob' (1996, p. 586).

Durkheim inherited this tradition and built upon it. He saw as his mission the establishment of a science of society that could prescribe how societies could be organized, in the light of knowledge of the laws governing social behaviour, in an ordered fashion.

As we discussed above, according to Durkheim, order flows from consensus – from the existence of shared norms and values. For him, the key cause of social and individual ill-health stems from anomie – a lack of regulating norms. Anomie is the result of the potential scourge of modern competitive society – the promotion of unrestricted desires. Without norms constraining behaviour, 'humans develop insatiable appetites, limitless desires and general feelings of irritation and dissatisfaction' (Durkheim, 1974, p. 72). He argues that a strong, ordered society and individual liberation are only guaranteed where beliefs and behaviour are properly regulated by socialization: 'The individual submits to society and this submission is the condition of his liberation. For man freedom consists in the deliverance from blind, unthinking physical forces; this he achieves by opposing against them the great and intelligent force which is society, under whose protection he shelters' (ibid.).

But why is order, harmony, and consensus the right state of affairs? To answer this question, Durkheim turned to **functionalism**.

Functionalism

Durkheim was the first major sociological theorist to use functionalist ideas. Other significant functionalists have been leading British social anthropologists in the years between 1920 and 1960. Of particular importance has been the work of anthropology's first two major figures, **Bronislaw Malinowski** (1884–1942) and **A. R. Radcliffe-Brown** (1881–1955). In addition, the later writings of anthropologists like **E. E. Evans-Pritchard** (1902–73), **Meyer Fortes** (1906–83) and **Max Gluckman** (1911–75) all helped to establish functionalist theory in British social science.

In twentieth-century sociology, undoubtedly the major figure (from the 1930s to the late 1950s) was the American functionalist **Talcott Parsons** (1902–79), though other US functionalists like **R. K. Merton** (1910–) and **Kingsley Davis** (1908–97) were important too. Until the 1960s America dominated sociology, and social anthropology dominated British social science. So, from the years between the early 1920s and the late 1950s, though other theoretical perspectives had long been in existence, they had little impact. The theoretical stage was dominated by the functionalist version of structural-consensus theory.

Though it has since lost much of its influence in sociological theory, particularly outside the US, an understanding of contemporary theoretical alternatives in sociology must begin with an understanding of functionalism. The rise to prominence of conflict theories (mainly in the forms of Marxist theory and in some versions of feminist theory) and action theories (like Weberian theory, symbolic interactionism and ethnomethodology) as major sociological approaches can only be understood in the light of the criticisms that began to be made (and by the late 1950s, very loudly) of functionalism. Conflict theories and action theory did not come into being in opposition to functionalism. However, they rose to prominence when they did because for many sociologists they provided questions and answers about social life which functionalism could not. Let us see why.

The organic analogy

Durkheim used the work of an Englishman, Herbert Spencer, to argue that we can best understand the existence and character of social

structures by comparing them to the origins and workings of biological organisms. As the name suggests, an organism is a living entity
whose existence and health depend on all the organs that make it up
working properly together. In the human body, for instance, all the
organs are interdependent. The workings of the brain depend on the
workings of the lungs, which depend on the workings of the heart,
and so on. Furthermore, all (or nearly all, in the case of the human
body) of these organs are indispensable. Each exists because it satisfies
a particular need of the human body which no other organ can. For
example, the heart exists because of the need for an organ to pump
blood round the body, the liver exists because of the need for the
blood to be purified, the kidneys exist because of the need to dispose
of waste matter and so on. In other words, the reason why each of
the constituent parts of the body exists is because each performs
a particular *function* for the overall system. Furthermore, all these
necessary parts have to function together in an integrated way for the
system as a whole to work properly. The difference between referring
to integrated wholes as 'systems' rather than 'structures' can be understood as simply the difference between a static picture of the whole
– its structure – and what this looks like when it is actually working,
as a system. In sociology the terms are often used in association with
each other for just this reason. A society both has a structure and
works as a system.

Durkheim and later functionalists argue that a **social system** works
like an organic system. Societies are made up of structures of cultural rules – established beliefs and practices – to which their members are expected to conform. Sociologists describe any established
way of thinking or acting in a society into which its members are
socialized as being *institutionalized* in that society. For functionalists,
the institutions of a society – for example the kind of family form
it has, its political arrangements, its educational arrangements, its
religious arrangements, and so on – are analogous to the parts of
an organism. Societies consist of parts that are integrated and interdependent. As with organs, the reason why an institutionalized way
of thinking or acting exists in a society is that it plays an indispensable part – or, to use the functionalist phrase, *performs a necessary
function* – in maintaining the society in a stable and satisfactory state.
In the case of the human body, if any organ fails to perform properly,
ill-health, or even loss of life, is the result. For functionalists, such
a functional failure by an institution – if it malfunctions – also leads
to a comparable state for the whole social system. Functionalists
have various phrases to describe this; a 'loss of social solidarity',

a 'lack of integration', or a 'loss of equilibrium' are three favourite ones.

Crucially, therefore, this account of the origins and workings of societies means that the existence of a social institution, of a part of the social structure, is not the result of the members of a society deciding to act or think this way. After all, people do not *decide* to have bowels or a liver or a pair of kidneys. These organs exist because the body needs them to perform necessary functions. In the same way, in functionalist theory, the institutional arrangements of a society exist not because of any choice on the part of its members. They are there because they are performing a necessary function for the social structure as a whole. Durkheim and other functionalists therefore argue that we should always explain the existence of social arrangements by looking for the *function* being performed by them – for the needs of the social system as a whole that they are satisfying.

The use of this analogy makes clear the goals of the theory. The purpose is to specify the importance of seeing the good society as the integrated, stable society. Organisms do not remain healthy if the constituent organs fight, eat or kill each other. There is a unity of purpose in organisms – the pursuit, protection and retention of health. So it is with social systems.

Therefore, the role of sociology should be the use of science to reveal the laws governing social organization. These laws demonstrate that the function of institutions is to serve the needs of the social system. 'Institutions performing functions', or 'institutions serving the needs of the social system' is functionalist jargon for people living their lives in the right ways – from which society benefits. So, 'ensuring that institutions perform these functions', means people knowing, and agreeing, about how to behave; thus, socialization into the correct rules is the key. The end result is a world where everyone agrees about how life should be lived, institutions perform their functions, the needs of the social system are satisfied and the society is healthy.

The corollary of this is that if the society is *un*healthy – you can tell because it will be disordered, riven with conflict, division and disagreement – it is because socialization is deficient. In these circumstances political action is necessary in the light of the social scientific evidence to ensure the correct cultural prescriptions are re-established. The end result is a harmonious society – integrated, stable, cohesive and healthy – and happy, normatively guided individuals.

How does science reveal the correct ways of living – the laws governing social organization? It demonstrates, empirically, the benefits for the social system of correctly functioning institutions. We can look at Durkheim's account of the role of religion in human societies as a good example of this. This analysis also shows us why Durkheim considered religion to be a vital instrument of social solidarity and such an important bulwark against the lurking threat of anomie.

Religion and society

The following is a simple example of the application of functionalist theory taken from one of Durkheim's own works, called *The Elementary Forms of Religious Life* (1976).

In Australia, there is an aborigine people called the Arunta. They are divided up into two kinds of group. *Bands* are their domestic groups who live together day to day, eking out a meagre survival by hunting and gathering in the Bush. The Arunta also belong to much larger groups, called *clans*. Much like the Scottish clans of great importance long ago, each Arunta clan consists of people who believe themselves to be descended from a distant common ancestor – that is, they consider themselves to be related. Each clan has a *totem* – an object in natural life which Arunta clan members believe to be special to them. In fact, the totem is so special that, according to Durkheim, they imbue it with a religious significance. On rare but important occasions the whole of the clan (including members of many different bands, of course) gathers to worship the totem. In addition, during their day-to-day life as band members, whenever they come across their particular totem they treat it with reverence – as a kind of *sacred* object.

How should we explain this? Employing the assumptions of functionalist theory, Durkheim is not interested in any intentions of particular Arunta individuals to have totemism in their society. After all, it was present among them before they were born, and will continue to be there after they die. He wants instead to identify the *function* that totemism performs for the Arunta social system. The answer he gives is this.

Living such a precarious life (without things we take for granted like hospitals or welfare institutions), the Arunta people above all need each other to survive. The groups to which the Arunta belong are their lifeline; the obligations others feel to help them, when they need it, are their only hope. In these circumstances, argues Durkheim, what is needed is some means of ensuring that the group *remains* important in the eyes of Arunta individuals. Furthermore, the recognition of the obligations must extend beyond band members alone. If not, all that would happen (as it does so often between people who feel no obligation towards one another) would be that individual bands would compete, and fight for, the limited resources available in their world. They would soon wipe each other out.

In the Arunta social system the answer to this problem of need for integration of separate groups is *totemism*. The totem is, as Durkheim puts it, 'the flag of the clan'. It is a symbol of those people in Arunta society with whom band members do not live, but whom they look upon as relatives. They are special people who should be helped and supported whenever necessary. Because of the totem, the group's symbol, its members are reminded of the group's existence when they might otherwise forget it. On the ceremonial occasions when the whole group gathers to worship the totem, a collective reaffirmation of its importance to them takes place. As Durkheim puts it, by worshipping the totem, the Arunta are really worshipping the group.

The *function* of totemism, then, is to integrate the Arunta social system (to draw its parts together and sustain it as a whole). It is, in Durkheim's terms, an instrument of *social solidarity*. Clearly, totemism is here being explained not in terms of what it *is* – what the content of its doctrines or beliefs are – but what it *does*, that is, the function it performs for the social system. Durkheim and his twentieth-century followers extended this analysis to all religions. For them, religion must always exist, since all social systems need integrating. They argue that what is interesting is not what is *different* about the beliefs and rituals characteristic of, say, totemism, Buddhism, Hinduism, Judaism, Protestantism and Catholicism. For them, what is interesting is what is *similar* about what they each *do* – about the *integrative functions* all these religions perform for their social systems.

Twentieth-century functionalism

In more recent times, of course, functionalists have been faced with the rather tricky problem of explaining how religion, which they saw as essential for the continuance of society, could have become so unimportant in so many of them. Undeterred, some have argued that even though religion has apparently lost importance in many societies (a process known as *secularization*), the function of integration continues to be performed by present-day functional equivalents of religion. Some theorists have claimed that this happens even in anti-religious societies, such as some (now-defunct) communist countries of Eastern Europe. Commitment to communist ideas, and the holding of rituals, like the May Day parades in the former Soviet Union, were said to be equivalent to religion. They were said to meet the need for a shared set of values and collective rituals met by more orthodox religious beliefs and practices in other societies.

Even in highly secularized Western societies some functionalists have seen a new kind of religion performing ancient functions. **Robert Bellah** (1927–) argues for the existence of a 'civil religion' in the USA, in which American history and institutions are utilized to ensure the reaffirmation of essential American values and sentiments. As Roy Wallis puts it:

> Bellah finds evidence for the existence of civil religion in such events as Presidential Inaugurations. Inaugural addresses tend to be couched in a religious idiom, referring to God in general terms and to the travails of America as a modern Israel led out of Egypt. This stylised rhetoric is taken as indicating a real commitment on the part of participants to symbols and values which unify and integrate the community and provide sacred legitimation for its affairs. Other more frequent ceremonials such as Thanksgiving Day and Memorial Day are similarly held to integrate families into the civil religion, or to unify the community around its values. (Roy Wallis, 1983, p. 44)

What is very apparent here is an interest in the effects of a religion, rather than its constituent beliefs. First, many different kinds of religious belief-systems are lumped together, because of the similar integrative function they all perform. Second, very different kinds of belief-systems, without any reference to, for example, gods or spirits or an after-life, are nevertheless thought of as equivalent to religion. Again, this is because of the similar function they are seen as performing. This directs our attention to a principal characteristic of functionalist explanation. Clearly, the inhabitants of India, Ireland or Israel would argue that their religions are not similar at all, since their focus would be on the beliefs themselves, not their effects. For the functionalist, however, the explanation of a belief or a pattern of behaviour observable in a society held by the *members* of that society is not usually thought to be particularly relevant. For them, the often unintended consequences of people's actions and beliefs needs to be identified – those consequences which, though not necessarily apparent to the people concerned, nevertheless have a crucial functional effect for the social system. To distinguish between these two levels of analysis, functionalists generally refer to the '*manifest*' function of institutions (those of which people are aware) and their '*latent*' functions (those of which people are often *un*aware). These latent functions are even more important to identify in order to understand the functioning and persistence of social systems.

These, then, are the characteristic features of functionalist analysis:

- an interest in the effect of an activity or belief, rather than its constituent ingredients: what it *does*, rather than what it *is*
- a stress on the need to go beyond people's own explanations of their activities in order to reveal the true functional significance of institutionalized behaviour and belief.

We will be able to see the character and consequences of these core functionalist interests by looking at a famous example from twentieth-century anthropology.

The kula

Bronislaw Malinowski was the first anthropologist to undertake a long-term piece of field research. For four years (between 1915 and 1918), he lived among the Trobriand islanders, who inhabit a group of tiny coral islands off the coast of New Guinea. He published a number of books describing and explaining various aspects of Trobriand life, but the most famous is *Argonauts of the Western Pacific* (1922). This is an account of an elaborate gift-exchange institution, called the *kula*, which is carried on by the Trobrianders among themselves and with the members of other tribal societies who live on surrounding islands. Malinowski described the kula as follows:

> The kula is a form of exchange, of extensive, inter-tribal character; it is carried on by communities inhabiting a wide ring of islands which form a closed circuit . . . along this route, articles of the two kinds, and these two kinds only, are constantly travelling in opposite directions. In the directions of the hands of a clock, moves constantly one of these kinds – long necklaces of red shell, called soulava. In the opposite direction moves the other kind – bracelets of white shell called mwali. Each of these two articles as it travels in its own direction on the closed circuit, meets on its way articles of the other class and is constantly being exchanged for them.
>
> On every island and in every village, a more or less limited number of men take part in the kula – that is to say, receive the goods, hold them for a short time, and then pass them on. Therefore every man who is in the kula, periodically though not regularly, receives one of several mwali (arm-shells), or a soulava necklace (necklace of red shell disks), and then has to hand it on to one of his partners, from whom he

receives the opposite commodity in exchange. Thus no man ever keeps any of the articles for any length of time in his possession. (Malinowski, 1922, pp. 82–3)

How is such an institution to be explained? Malinowski argues that from the point of view of those involved in it, the kula is a significant way of gaining prestige. In industrial society, objects are used in order to gain prestige too, of course. Thorstein Veblen (1970) coined the famous phrase 'conspicuous consumption' to describe the way people in Western societies do not simply own things for the practical uses they have – their *utility* value. He points out how we also seek to own things for the value they have for us as *symbols* of who we would like others to think we are. Though there might be a certain utility advantage for the Rolls Royce owner in terms of the extra comfort the car affords him or her, at least as important is its value as a status symbol. It symbolizes or expresses the resources, and, by implication, the importance, of its owner. The same goes for the possession of mink coats, diamonds, enormous houses in particular residential areas, and so forth.

Kula valuables similarly enable Trobrianders and their neighbours to gain prestige. But they do so in a rather different way. In the kula there is no advantage or prestige attached to *keeping* a valuable. You receive the admiration of others for two reasons. First, because *you* were chosen by your partner to be the recipient of the valuable article, rather than any other of his partners. Second, because you can show yourself to be generous by giving it away again in turn. As Malinowski puts it:

Ownership . . . in [the] kula, is quite a special economic relation. A man who is in the kula never keeps any article for longer than, say, a year or two. Even this exposes him to the reproach of being niggardly . . . on the other hand, each man has an enormous number of articles passing through his hands during his lifetime, of which he enjoys a temporary possession, and which he keeps in trust for a time. The possession hardly ever makes him use the articles, and he remains under the obligation soon again to hand them on to one of his partners. But the temporary ownership allows him to draw a great deal of renown, to exhibit his article, to tell how he obtained it, and to plan to whom he is going to give it. (Malinowski, 1922, p. 94)

Here then, social honour is not attached to the acquisition in order to possess. The purpose of wanting to acquire is not to own, but to give away again. In Malinowski's words: 'a man who owns a thing is naturally expected to share it, to distribute it, to be its trustee and dispenser . . . the main symptom of being powerful is to be wealthy and of wealth is to be generous . . . the more important he is, the more will he desire to shine by his generosity (Malinowski, 1922, p. 97).

It would appear that here we have the answer to the kula. It is a system of 'conspicuous generosity', to parody Veblen. It is a way of allowing people to gain importance and to be seen to be important. Status-seeking is not the prerogative of the materialist West. The Trobrianders wish to be thought of as important and powerful too – they just use different ways to do it. From the point of view of individual Trobrianders this is almost certainly the whole story. For them, the kula is an institution geared to the pursuit of status. But is their story the only one about the kula that needs to be told? After all, they learnt to kula; it existed before they did. Since they did not invent it, can we rely only on their views of what it is about? The functionalist in Malinowski will not allow him to stop here. He also wants to know why the kula is necessary for the Trobriand social system. He wants to know what the kula *does* – what its function is.

The answers that Malinowski and later functionalist analysts of his material give run along these lines: because many kula exchanges take place between partners who live on islands many miles apart, its existence allows economic and political relationships to take place between people who would otherwise never meet. The result is a greater economic and political integration of the whole of Trobriand society, and of different societies with each other, than would otherwise have been possible.

The economic function of the kula

Though kula partners are not allowed to engage in ordinary trading with one another, non-partners are. Thus an expedition of a large number of members from one island to another will not simply result in kula exchanges. Between men who are not kula partners, bartering for non-kula goods is quite normal. According to Malinowski, this is an important *latent* function of the kula. It makes trading relations possible between people who would otherwise never come into contact with one another, for their mutual economic benefit. 'Side by side with the ritual exchange of arm-shells and necklaces, the natives carry on ordinary trade, bartering from one island to another a great number of utilities, often improcurable in the district to which they are imported and indispensable there' (Malinowski, 1922, p. 83).

Here, then, is an economic function of the kula of which members would either be unaware, or certainly consider of secondary importance to the kula exchanges. In contrast, for functionalists it is such *unintended* consequences of people's activities that are usually of the greatest importance to identify.

The political function of the kula

It is the fact that the kula makes possible such long-distance social interaction, embracing the whole of Trobriand society and linking the Trobrianders with more distant tribal societies, that functionalists have usually pounced on as its key. Two excerpts from *Argonauts of the Western Pacific* give a flavour of the kula's political function which is identified by Malinowski himself:

> An average man has a few partners near by . . . and with these partners he is generally on very friendly terms . . . the overseas partner is, on the other hand, a host, patron and ally in a land of danger and insecurity. (Malinowski, 1922, pp. 91–2)

> The kula is thus an extremely big and complex institution . . . It welds together a considerable number of tribes, and it embraces a vast complex of activities, inter-connected and playing into one another, so as to form one organic whole. (Malinowski, 1922, p. 83)

Malinowski's functionalism and the integrative consequences of the kula which he sees as so central to its significance are clearly apparent here. In a later study of Malinowski's data, J. Singh Uberoi (1962) argued that the integrative function of the kula is even more fundamental than Malinowski himself acknowledged. His thesis is this. Only kula objects among valuable things are owned by individuals, rather than by groups of kin. Only in the kula do people enter into relations as individuals rather than as representatives of their kin groups. Only in the kula is self-interest, rather than group-interest, the motivating force.

How does this reduction in the importance of kinship relations in the kula allow it to enable a great political integration of the whole community? Uberoi argues that because the kula enables people to be released from obligations to their kin groups, they are better able to perceive Trobriand society as a wider whole. Rather in the way that the totem tells the Arunta about the wider society on which they ultimately depend, the kula encourages the Trobrianders to think of their society as a whole, rather than as a collection of competing kin groups. This is how Uberoi puts it:

The kula extends the political society beyond the district by periodically depreciating the ties which bind an individual to the other members of his own local lineage or district, and re-emphasising his obligations towards his kula partner, who belongs to an otherwise opposed district . . . on a kula expedition . . . each individual . . . stands by and for himself, released from the normal restraints of group solidarity; but because he pursues his individual self-interest through wooing his kula partner, he stands not only for himself, but also for the whole chain of partners which goes to make up the kula ring . . . [the kula valuables symbolise to] the normally kin-bound individuals . . . the highest point of their individual self-interest [and also] the interest of the widest political association of which they all partake [the kula]. (Singh Uberoi, 1962, pp. 159–60)

This is a typical functionalist analysis. The accounts of activities by the people involved in them are forgotten. The interest is in what *good* an institutionalized activity does, or has done, for the society as a whole. The assumption is that an institution would not exist unless it was necessary. The observer's job is to see *why* it is necessary, what *function* it is performing. The Trobriander sails to distant islands to pursue his self-interest and to maximize his prestige. Unknown to him, but perfectly apparent to the perceptive functionalist, is the fact that he is really integrating his society, both economically and politically.

Social change

So far, so good. Here we have an explanation of the source of individual happiness and societal health. However, the problem of social change has to be addressed:

- not only do functionalists have to take account of the fact that change *does* occur in societies, but also
- the idea of modernity – the modern ideal – is that knowledge is supposed to provide humans with the chance to create a *good* society and that change can represent progress, a good thing.

The functionalist is faced with a problem here, though. The functionalist model of the individual is the structural-consensus one of a determined, constrained, regulated social actor, whose choices are created for him or her by socialization. To be modernist, and allow that social change and social reconstruction can be actively promoted, and achieved, by social actors – that people can create society – turns the relationship between the individual and society on its head. The functionalist way around this is to use the organic analogy again, and to say that social progress occurs as it does with organisms – as *evolutionary* change.

Change takes the form of *structural differentiation*. As Bilton et al. say:

> Just as the evolution of animals produces more sophisticated special-ised organs to perform particular functions for the whole creature [so differentiation means] society comes to develop a range of distinct institutions which deal more adequately with particular needs of the social whole.
>   . . . differentiation is a type of splitting or separation of a previously undivided unit. The new units created by this process differ from the earlier unit by being more specialised in the functions they perform. The two new units differ from each other since they are structured in such a way that each of them can perform unique functions that the other unit cannot. (Bilton et al., 1996, p. 588)

This emphasis on differentiation is apparent in the twentieth-century approach to social change of Talcott Parsons. Institutions change, says Parsons, if the needs of the system change. The rise of industrialization in modern societies has proved the major impetus to family change, for a new industrial economy requires a new form of family to perform new, specialist functions. A process of differentiation, thus ensuring evolution and progress, meets this need. In Parsons's own words:

> The kinship-organised household in predominantly [traditional, non-industrial] society is both the unit of residence and the primary unit of agricultural production. In [industrial] societies, however, most productive work is performed in specialised units, such as workshops, factories or offices manned by people who are also members of family households. Thus two sets of roles and collectives have become differ-entiated and their functions separated. (Parsons, 1966)

This splitting-off of the nuclear family household from production does not mean the family has lost significance however. After all, it is evolution – progress and improvement. The loss of the economic function to specialized workplaces means the new, non-productive household can concentrate on performing non-economic functions better than the dual-purpose, peasant household could. The removal of economic activity from the home means family members can pay more time and attention to each other: thus the emotional quality of the relationship between adult family members is enhanced, and more effort is put into the socialization of children. The social system benefits: 'these developments enhance the significance of the family as provider of a secure emotional base for its members' participation in society' (Parsons, 1971). At the same time, now that production takes place in locations specifically designed for this alone, the performance of this economic function is also superior. Once again, the social system benefits; through evolution, then, modern societies forge ahead.

So, just as social structures have the character they do – not because of the purposive intentions of individuals, but because of system needs – so social change occurs, not because people want to have it, but because of evolution. The analogy with the organism therefore explains both social structure and social change; functionalism can be a theory extolling the virtues of modernity, while still seeing the individual as a societal creation.

Criticisms of functionalism

Functionalism has exerted a tremendous influence on sociology. As we noted at the beginning of the chapter, for much of the first half of the last century it occupied a largely unchallenged theoretical position in the subject. Through the influence of anthropology in Britain, and of Talcott Parsons and his supporters in America, by the middle of the century sociology came to be more or less synonymous with functionalist sociology. Other theoretical approaches were kept well in the background. The sociological enterprise was seen as principally concerned with a search for the 'real' significance of social institutions – the contribution they make to the maintenance of the social systems in which they are found. Because its influence has substantially waned today, it is easy to be over-critical of the rather narrow vision of functionalism's adherents. Now it seems rather strange that during functionalism's ascendancy, so little attention should have been paid to relations of dominance and subordination, advantage and disadvantage in society. It also seems self-evident that humans must be recognized as more than just 'cultural dopes', obediently learning sets of cultural prescriptions for action so that their social systems can persist. Today it seems clear that sociology must take account of the interpretive abilities of people in order to properly understand their actions.

In our eagerness to demonstrate the errors and partialities in functionalism/structural-consensus theory, we must not forget to acknowledge the contribution this kind of theory has made to socio-logy. The unintended social consequences of people's beliefs and actions *are* important to recognize. Sociology *does* have an important revelatory task. It *is* necessary sometimes to go beyond people's own explanations for their actions in order to properly understand social behaviour. This is undoubtedly functionalism's contribution. Nevertheless, we would also be quite wrong to deny functionalism's weaknesses. Four main ones are usually identified. It is argued that functionalism:

- has an inherent tendency to 'reify' society
- is not able to explain social change adequately
- is based upon an oversocialized view of human beings
- does not take enough account of power and conflict in society.

Functionalism and the reification of society

Functionalists explain the existence of institutionalized patterns of behaviour and belief in terms of the good effects these have for the social system in which they are found. Institutions are not the product of decisions made by individuals, since they exist prior to these individuals. The problem of social order is not how human beings can create an ordered society. It is how social systems can create social beings, socialised into conforming to institutionalized rules of behaviour necessary for their existence. The insistence that societies acquire their functioning characteristics prior to the existence of their members leaves a rather awkward question, however. If *people* do not decide what is functional for their society, then who does decide? The functionalist seems to be left with the proposition that the social system itself decides what is good for it. Yet this is clearly absurd. Societies cannot think; only people can. This is known as the problem of **'reification'**. Functionalists seem to 'reify' society – to treat it as a thing – by endowing it with the ability to think and act intentionally that only humans have.

Functionalism and social change

Functionalism seems to promote a static and conservative picture of society. The functionalist position is that institutions continue to exist because they are functional – they are satisfying a need of the social system. The job of the sociologist is to reveal what the good effects of particular institutions are. This seems to come remarkably close to *automatically* justifying what the status quo in a particular society happens to be; it seems to imply that all persisting social arrangements in a society must be beneficial, otherwise they would not remain in existence. When the problem of social change *is* addressed, it is seen as evolutionary, benign and adaptive; a slow process, whereby the social system accommodates new circumstances. This leaves the theory unable to explain rapid, disruptive change – politically inspired innovation that dramatically overturns existing structures. The revolutionary overthrow of communist regimes in Eastern Europe in the late 1980s and 1990s could hardly be understood by using the functionalist notion of change as organic adaptation.

Functionalism and socialization

As we said in chapter 1, *action* theories have crucial objections to the functionalist/structural-consensus model. For them, the real criticism of functionalism is that it over-emphasizes socialization as an explanation of social behaviour. The interpretive emphasis of action theory is that people are not passive recipients of cultural recipes for social action. Among living things, humans alone are able to *choose* how to act. Far from being a simple reflection of cultural prescription, such choices are made in the light of how people see the world – particularly how they interpret the actions of others. Social action is thus *voluntary* action. It is action chosen in the light of the actor's interpretation of reality.

Functionalism, power and conflict

As we also saw in chapter 1, the criticism *structural-conflict* theory makes of the functionalist/consensus approach to social life has two elements. First, according to conflict theory, functionalism fails to take account of the influence on behaviour of society's structures of inequality. The argument here is that people are not only influenced by the norms and values of the culture into which they are socialized. Their social lives are also crucially influenced by the advantages they possess; there are practical, as well as normative, constraints on behaviour which bring the advantaged and the disadvantaged into conflict. Second, for conflict theorists, functionalism is based on a fundamentally flawed conception of the role of socialization into cultural rules. In any conflict theory, norms and values only have the character they do because their role is to obscure, as well as to legitimate, the facts of inequality in society. Far from socialization being the instrument of social order and cohesion, it is a mechanism of power and control.

Conclusion

It was not until the 1960s that these sorts of criticisms caused functionalism to lose its influence. Alternative theoretical approaches came to be considered attractive and, indeed, superior. It was at this time that changes in their experiences altered people's perceptions of modern society, and sociologists were no exception. This was the decade of social reappraisal. The complacency encouraged by the economic prosperity of the 1950s, when Prime Minister Harold Macmillan confidently proclaimed that his British constituents had 'never had it so good' was replaced in the 1960s by a genuine concern for social justice and a real awareness of inequality and deprivation. Poverty had been 'rediscovered', both in Britain and the USA.

The Civil Rights movement in America began to demand equality for blacks. The feminist movement began to demand equality for women. US imperialism – most notoriously in Vietnam – was denounced by many in the Western world. In such a context, where social change was being demanded and conflict between different groups in society was clearly apparent, functionalism began to be seen more and more as remote from the real world. As we have seen, this is a theory that sets out to explain the benefits of social institutions, to reveal the mechanisms by which social systems achieve cohesion and integration, and to show how they persist. Consequently, it seemed hardly relevant or adequate in a world where many had begun to see disadvantage and inequality, where conflict and a lack of social cohesion were clearly apparent, and where social change seemed necessary. In such circumstances it is not surprising that alongside the emergence of interpretive alternatives to functionalism, another kind of alternative theory, which *does* explain conflict, confront change, and attempt to predict the future, should have proved intellectually appealing to many. We will look at this theory in the next chapter.

Further Reading

Fenton, Steve: *Durkheim and Modern Sociology*, Cambridge University Press, 1984.
Giddens, Anthony: *Capitalism and Modern Social Theory: an analysis of the writings of Marx, Durkheim and Max Weber*, Cambridge University Press, 1971b.

Giddens, Anthony (ed.): *The Sociology of Suicide*, Frank Cass, 1971a.

Giddens, Anthony: *Emile Durkheim: selected writings*, Cambridge University Press, 1972a.

Lukes, Steven: *Emile Durkheim: his life and work*, Penguin, 1973.

Pearce, Frank: *The Radical Durkheim*, Unwin Hyman, 1989.

Taylor, Steve: *Durkheim and the Sociology of Suicide*, Macmillan, 1982.

Thompson, Kenneth: *Emile Durkheim*, Routledge, 1982.

3 MARX AND MARXISM

Karl Marx

Bildarchiv Preussischer Kulturbesitz, Berlin

Karl Marx: born Trier, Rhineland, 1818, died London, 1883

Major works

The Poverty of Philosophy (1847)
The Communist Manifesto (1848)
The Eighteenth Brumaire of Louis Bonaparte (1852)
Grundisse (Outline of a Critique of Political Economy) (1857)
Preface to a Contribution to the Critique of Political Economy (1859)
Theories of Surplus Value (1862–3)
Capital, vols 1–3 (1863–7)
Critique of the Gotha Programme (1875)

Introduction

Like functionalism, Marxism is a theory designed to promote the good society. Like functionalism, it is a *response* to modernity, and, like functionalism, it is a *part* of modernity – it is part of the modern belief that societies can be transformed for the better, that progress can be achieved in social organization through the application of human knowledge. Like functionalism, Marxism rests upon the belief that the potential for individual fulfilment and freedom is linked inextricably to the potential for progress in social organization – to the structure of society. There the similarity ends. According to Marx, the potential for individual fulfilment is linked to the economic or productive activity of a society; in particular, the opportunity to be free in modern society is only possible when the class-based productive system characteristic of capitalism is abolished.

Can this progress be achieved? The need is for people to come to realize the truth of Marxist theory – to realize that liberation depends upon the destruction of capitalism. Once they know that the key to freedom lies here, they will use it to unlock the door – they will take political action to abolish classes. How can they be made to see the truth and take action? This is the key problem, for what they think is the truth about the world is manipulated. In capitalism, as in all class societies, prevailing beliefs will deny the truth that class-based production prevents freedom by:

• legitimizing such systems of production and their consequences
• preventing people from recognizing evidence of lack of freedom.

However, according to Marx, capitalism has within it the seeds of its own destruction. The activity of producing goods in this system will, over time, inevitably produce consequences that will cause so much misery that false beliefs will be discarded. People will come to realize the truth of Marxist theory and the real facts of their social circumstances. Then, armed with the truth, they will act, change society and become free.

Marx and historical materialism

In Marxist theory the most important human activity is *economic activity* – the production of material goods. In a speech at Marx's graveside, Engels said that 'Mankind must first of all eat, drink, have shelter and clothing, before it can pursue politics, science, art, religion, etc.' (17 March 1883).

According to Marx, understanding the way a society organizes its production is the key to understanding the whole of its social structure. The Marxist view is that 'the production of the means of subsistence ... forms the foundation upon which the state institutions, the legal conceptions, art and even the ideas on religion, of the people concerned have been evolved' (Engels' speech at the graveside of Karl Marx, 17 March 1883).

For Marx, social structures are not randomly created. He argues that there is a quite definite pattern to the way societies in different parts of the world, and at different times in history, have organized the production of material goods. This theory of history and society is called **historical materialism**. For our purposes we can identify its following elements.

First, all societies that have existed or do exist today exhibit one of five different ways of organizing production. These different ways of producing goods Marx called **modes of production**. The five are (in chronological order) the *primitive communist, ancient, feudal, capitalist* and *communist* modes.

Second, apart from the first and last modes of production – the primitive communist and communist modes – each mode has one crucial characteristic in common. Each is a way of producing goods based on *classes*. Though the term 'class' has different uses elsewhere in sociology (and all sorts of uses in speech) the Marxist usage is a quite specific one. According to Marx, in all non-communist societies – in the ancient, feudal and capitalist modes – there are just two classes that matter. There is the class that owns the means of production – it is their property – and there is the class that does not own it.

In systems of production based on classes, goods are produced in a quite definite way. The majority of people, who do not own the means of production, do the productive work for the benefit of those – the minority – who do own it. In Marxist theory, this is the key feature of non-communist societies at any time in history. The production of material goods (the most important activity of humans, remember), *always* takes place by means of the *exploitation* of the labour of the majority, non-property-owning class by the minority class, which owns the means of production and does not work. That is, the relationship between classes is a *conflict* relationship.

There are no classes in either of the communist modes. In primitive communist societies people cannot produce a surplus. This is usually because of an inhospitable environment, or a lack of technological know-how, or a combination of the two. Because such peoples only produce enough to allow them to exist at subsistence level, everyone has to work. There is no surplus property, and there is therefore no possibility for classes to emerge to exploit it. In the communist mode there are no classes because private property has been abolished – people are not able to own the means of production. Because in any class-based mode of production goods are produced in this exploitative way, in Marxist writing the owners of the means of production are usually called the *dominant* class, while the non-owning, exploited class which performs the productive work is called the *subordinate* class.

According to Marx, the history of human society is the history of different kinds of productive systems based on class exploitation. He says we can divide up the history of any society into different *epochs* or ages, each of which is dominated by one particular mode of production, with its own characteristic class relationships. All societies will eventually pass through all these stages in history and all will eventually become communist. However, not all societies evolve at the same rate. This is why at any particular time in history different societies exhibit different modes of production – they are at different stages of historical development.

What distinguishes different modes of production from one another? All non-communist modes have in common the production of goods by means of the domination and exploitation of one class by another. What is different in each case is who the classes are. Each non-communist mode of production has a different, dominant, property-owning class and a different subordinate, exploited, non-property-owning class. Furthermore, each mode grows out of the death of the previous one.

The ancient mode of production

The oldest form of class production – hence its name – is the ancient mode of production. This mode grew out of the subsistence primitive communist mode primarily because of technological improvements. For example, in the Iron Age humans developed productive techniques that allowed specialist animal farming and settled agricultural production. This in turn enabled the production of a surplus, and allowed a more complex division of labour than was possible in a purely subsistence economy. In effect, a dominant class of *non-producers* could emerge.

The distinguishing feature of this mode of production is that people are owned as productive property by other, more powerful people. That is, it is production based on slavery. Here, then, there is a dominant class of *masters* and a subordinate class of *slaves*. Production takes place by means of the involuntary labour of people who are owned as property by others. Ancient Greece and Rome provide the classic examples of slavery as a mode of production. In the Greek and Roman empires about a third of the population was enslaved. Most had entered into slavery as prisoners-of-war, following battles undertaken as part of the imperialist (empire-building) policies of the Greek and Roman states. One of the main reasons why the ancient mode of production disintegrated was that the state power upon which it depended became eroded. As it became more and more difficult for the ancient states to control and coerce people living in distant parts of their empires, so did the possibility of sustaining slavery as a mode of production.

The feudal mode of production

In place of the ancient mode of production emerged a new mode of a much more local character, called feudalism. Feudal production was based upon the ability of warriors or nobles controlling small local territories by force of arms to coerce and exploit an agricultural labour force. In feudalism the dominant class controls the land, and comprises the *lords*. The subordinate class is made up of *serfs*. Production takes place by means of the labour of those who have to work the land in order to survive. Since these labourers do not own the land, but are merely tenants on it, they are obliged to give up much of the product of their labour as rent (in the form of a 'fee' called a *tithe*) to the landlords.

Feudalism dominated Europe from the Dark Ages until early modern times. Two factors in particular heralded its death and helped to usher in a new mode of production, based on a new form of class exploitation. First, strongly centralized political power was re-established in Europe not in the form of large, unwieldy empires, but in the form of absolutist monarchies. This allowed sufficient state control to be exercised within national territories in European countries for proper legal systems to be devised and enforced. This, in turn, provided an opportunity for economic activity to extend beyond local feudal boundaries, and for widespread trade to become possible, for example, through the gradual unification of tax and currency systems within major trading areas, and along major trading routes such as the Rhine.

Second, as a result of the changes brought about by the agricultural revolution, agricultural production became rationalized and more efficient. One of the most significant consequences of this was the Enclosures Acts. These Acts denied the bulk of the agricultural labour force the subsistence rights over the strips of land they had been entitled to under feudalism. Replaced by sheep, and by non-labour-intensive farming using machines, these labourers were made landless. As Marx (1976) described it in *Capital*, 'Sheep ate men.' Thrown off the land, and with no other means of subsistence than their labour power, workers were forced to sell their labour to employers for a wage. A *labour market* thus emerged for the first time.

The capitalist mode of production

Production now took on a new class character. The labour power of a class of landless labourers – the **proletariat**, as Marxists call them – could now be purchased for a wage by a class of property-owning employers, for whom the Marxist term is the **bourgeoisie**.

So capitalism developed in Britain before industrialization; agricultural goods were produced first of all in a capitalistic way. It was only later, when factories were built and industrial machines were developed, that industrial capitalism became established and an urban proletariat emerged. In capitalist society, the bourgeoisie are the dominant class because, like the masters in slave societies and the lords in feudal societies, they own the productive wealth – the means of production.

During the development of **capitalism**, the character of property in which capitalists have invested their wealth has, of course, altered. In the early stages of capitalism, as we have just noted, productive property primarily took the form of land, with the proletariat earning wages as agricultural labourers on it. Later, industrial production gave rise to capitalist investment in factories and machines, with the proletariat earning wages as industrial manual labourers. Still later, capitalism took on the form typical of contemporary industrial capitalism. Today, instead of actually owning and controlling industrial production themselves, the ownership of productive property usually takes the form of capital investment in stocks and shares. (Of course, capitalist landowners, and owners and controllers of their own enterprises – especially the smaller ones – still exist in plenty today.)

Despite these alterations to the nature of productive property in capitalist society, for Marxists the character of class relations between owners of property and non-owners of property is essentially the same as in earlier, class-based modes of production. Though the bourgeoisie do not make goods themselves, they nevertheless own the means of production. For this reason, they will always profit from the difference between the cost to them of the labour of the proletariat, and the value of the goods produced by the proletariat's labour power. The important fact is that workers will always be paid less than the value of the goods they produce. If this did not happen, the system could not work; without profit, reinvestment of this surplus into the productive power of capitalism would not take place, and enterprises would wither and die in the face of competition. This *surplus value* costs the capitalist nothing, and is a tangible symbol of the exploitation of wage-earners' labour power by employers. Though not as obvious as the exaction of tithes by feudal lords, or the ownership of people by slave-owners, the relationship between the capitalist and the wage-earner is of exactly the same kind. In Marx's (1976) words, 'The history of all hitherto existing society is the history of class struggle.'

The role of the superstructure

So far, our account of Marxist theory has concentrated on production – on economic relationships. What about the rest of social life? The defining characteristic of Marxist sociology is the view that economic activity is the architect that designs the character of other aspects of life. In order to convey this, Marx calls the way a society organizes production its **infrastructure/economic base**; economic activity, that is, is the basis of all else in that society. The rest of its social organization – its non-economic activities and its ideas, beliefs and philosophies – he calls its **superstructure**. The use of these terms is important. It stresses the way in which a society's superstructure is created by its base; one set of activities is built upon the other.

Institutions

First, at the level of social structure, non-economic institutions in any epoch are always organized in such a way as to benefit the mode of production. The task of the sociologist is to analyse this, as in the following accounts of the family and of education in capitalist society:

The family

Most Marxist analyses draw attention to the way in which families tend to encourage and reproduce hierarchical inegalitarian relationships, and to act as a safety-valve, dampening down discontent so that it is robbed of revolutionary content. In providing a place where children can be conceived, born and reared in relative safety, the family is providing tomorrow's labour force. At the same time, by offering a centre for relaxation, recreation, refreshment and rest, the family helps to ensure that members of today's labour force are returned to work each day with their capacity to work renewed and strengthened. This is what is meant when it is said that the family reproduces labour power on a generational as well as a daily basis.

Education

Bowles and Gintis argue that schooling operates within the 'long shadow of work': that is, the education system reflects the organisation of production in capitalist society. For example, the fragmentation of most work processes is mirrored in the breaking up of the curriculum into tiny 'packages' of knowledge, each subject divorced from all others; lack of control over work processes is reflected in the powerlessness of pupils with regard to what they will learn in school or how they will learn it; and the necessity of working for pay when jobs seem pointless and unfulfilling in themselves is paralleled by the emphasis in schools on learning in order to gain good grades, rather than learning for its own sake. Therefore, Bowles and Gintis claim there is a correspondence between the nature of work in capitalist societies, and the nature of schooling. (Bilton et al., 1981, pp. 292–3; 387)

This interest in analysing the ways in which the character of non-economic institutions benefits the system of production has a close parallel with functionalism. As with functionalism, the analysis of an institution takes the form of identifying its positive role in the system.

Indeed, the above accounts of the benefits for capitalism of family life and schooling could quite legitimately be said to be the identification of the 'function' that the institutions perform in meeting the needs of capitalism. Though both are 'systemic' theories, the crucial difference concerns the way they characterize the system, and whose needs are being met by it.

Ideologies

At the level of ideas, the relationship between the base and the super-structure is apparent in the way the prevailing beliefs in any epoch also support the organization of production. This is especially important in societies where the activity of producing goods involves the exploitation of the bulk of the population, rendering them grossly unequal and disadvantaged. While the compliance of the subordinate class in this arrangement can be secured by physical force, in the Marxist view the most effective way they can be persuaded to acquiesce in their own subordination is via what they think – their *ideas* and *beliefs*. What is distinctive about a Marxist approach to the world of ideas in a class society is its interest in the *ideological* nature of beliefs. As we said earlier, for Marxists, **ideologies** are systems of belief which:

- legitimate the class-based system of production by making it appear right and just, and/or
- obscure the reality of its consequences from the gaze of the people.

Here again there are parallels with functionalism. Just as conformity to shared ideas is the fundamental functionalist source of cohesion and order, so Marxists conceive of class societies persisting due to the commitment of individuals to the same ideological beliefs. Here, however, socialization determines what people think for the benefit of the property-owning class, and the maintenance of the system.

According to Marxists, the dominant ideas, beliefs and values in a class society (which are ideas about which there is most agreement) are not there by chance. They act as ideologies, propping up a structure which, without such ideological support, would collapse. Marxists argue that although from time to time dominant classes *do* have to resort to naked force to maintain their power and supremacy, the absence of such obvious coercion should not be taken to signify an absence of exploitation. On the contrary, they suggest, all a lack of naked oppression can ever indicate is a lack of opposition, and the lack of any need to use force. It does not mean that domination is not taking place. It is only that the dominated are unaware of their condition, because of the effectiveness of the ideologies into which they have been socialized.

How do such dominant ideas gain general acceptance? Like functionalists, Marxists argue that particular ideas prevail through various key agencies of socialization. In contemporary society, for example, both Marxists and functionalists would point to the important role played by institutions like the family, the education system and the mass media in promoting generally held beliefs and values. The essential difference between functionalists and Marxists concerns their interpretations of the role of the socialization process that such institutions ensure. For functionalists, it is the way we learn ideas that we need to know in order to think and behave in the ways required of us by the social system. For Marxists, it is the way we learn those ideas which serves to hide from our eyes, or justify, the real character of a class society. For both theories there is a prevailing culture which people learn through socialization. The difference between them concerns the job this culture does. For functionalists, it ensures social integration. For Marxists, it ensures social inequality and domination.

Ideologies in contemporary Britain

We can look at some prevailing ideas in contemporary capitalist Britain to see how a Marxist would explain their superstructural significance. From the Marxist viewpoint, the type of ideas in Britain which help to perpetuate capitalism in this society are ones that:

- divert people's attention away from the reality of class inequality
- reproduce demand for goods by encouraging consumerism
- encourage the wage-earning class to accept their subordinate role
- justify the inequality between the classes.

How is this done? How do such ideas come to prevail? A Marxist approach to the superstructure of contemporary Britain might be as follows.

Diversionary institutions

Capitalist production is exploitative, according to Marxists. A major reason for its survival is that institutions exist to divert the attention of the exploited away from the reality of their condition. One important vehicle for doing this is the entertainment industry. For example, much popular music, with its characteristic emphasis on the attractions of romantic love and/or sexual satisfaction as the pinnacle of human fulfilment hardly aims to shed light on the reality of class exploitation! Nor does much popular literature, not only by its emphasis on sex/love. Escapism of other kinds abounds: the never-ending production of gangster/detective novels, war novels, science fiction, and so on, bears testimony to this preoccupation. A substantial proportion of television and radio programmes has similar consequences. From situation comedies to quiz games, from soap operas to cops and robbers films, such entertainment promotes a trivialization of reality. Programmes like these create 'pretend' worlds, where the facts of life in a class society are ignored.

The family can also perform a similar task. A dominant belief in contemporary society is that individual emotional satisfaction can only be found in marriage and child-rearing. However pleasant or otherwise the successful accomplishment of such goals may be, we must realize that the pursuit of such an achievement renders a desire for fulfilment through other activities, like work, less likely. The result is that exploited, meaningless work is tolerated. Life becomes about the achievement of marital and parental satisfaction, in order to compensate. As a Ford car worker told Huw Beynon (1973) 'I just close my eyes, stick it out, and think of the wife and kids.'

Much of the news media perform an important diversionary role in capitalist society too. For example, in Britain, tabloid newspapers like the *Sun*, the *Star*, the *Daily Mirror*, the *Daily Mail* and the *Daily Express* traditionally concentrate on the trivial, the sensational and the titillating rather than on a serious reporting of events. This deliberate suppression and distortion of reality can only further encourage people living in a capitalist society to divert their gaze away from inequality, deprivation and exploitation. Indeed, since it is only through mass media that we gain most of our information about reality, a failure to provide such information is not only diversionary. It also means we are being provided with a picture of the world that is false.

Consumerism: the reproduction of demand

Capitalism depends on the reproduction of demand. Any social institution that promotes the purchase of goods perpetuates their production by capitalist means. Clearly, the main way in which we are encouraged to consume is by means of advertising. Whether on television and radio, or in the cinema, in newspapers and magazines or on billboards, advertisements glorify the possession of material goods (compare this with the values underpinning the kula) and thereby promote their acquisition. The family helps reproduce demand too. In Western societies, many people live in nuclear families – the smallest kind of family unit. Each family is economically independent, purchasing its own goods. This ensures that demand is maximized. In larger households, demand for consumer goods would decrease.

The acquiescence of wage-earners in their subordination

Capitalism depends on the bulk of the population being socialized into accepting a subordinate role. Once again, the family plays an important part. It is in the family that we first learn the meaning of authority and obedience. Learning to submit to the wishes of parents provides just the training necessary to cope with being a wage-earner and under the authority of an employer. Education obviously reinforces this training.

The justification of inequality

Capitalism depends on its inherent inequalities, if recognized, being accepted as just. It is in the classroom that we first encounter the inevitability of inequality. Here we learn that people do not only possess *different* abilities. They possess *better* or *worse* abilities. 'Clever' children succeed and are rewarded with good grades and exam results. 'Less able' children deserve poorer rewards. What better training for life in a society where different abilities are also judged as superior and inferior, and judged accordingly? Experiences in school can only encourage people to believe that inequality of reward is just. Such beliefs are expressed in such commonly held views as these: 'Of course doctors should be paid more than dustmen. They do a much more important job.' The unequal distribution of rewards among different occupations reflects their importance. Or again, 'Anyone could be a dustman. Only able/intelligent/skilled people can become doctors.' Achievement within an unequal world reflects merit. In a fundamental way, then, education, with its intrinsic emphasis on competition and selection, on success and failure, on merit and de-merit, teaches members of a capitalist society the justice of inequality. In particular, it teaches the 'less able' – the 'failures' – to expect, and accept, low rewards in their lives.

Marxists argue that such an analysis of the relationship between the infrastructure and the superstructure tells us a great deal about power in a class society. The dominant class rules, but not by necessarily being the actual office-holders who make decisions. It rules because its interests are considered superior by all those – property-owners and property-less alike – who have been subject to socialization into dominant ideas by superstructural agencies. In Marx's words: 'The ideas of the ruling class are, in every age, the ruling ideas' (1963, p. 39).

False consciousness and class consciousness

It is for these reasons that the concepts of **false consciousness** and **class consciousness** are of such importance in Marxist theory. Because the subordinate class subscribe to dominant ideologies, which obscure the real nature of class society from its gaze, its picture of the world and its place in it is wrong. Its consciousness of reality is false. Only when a class-based mode of production falters will members of a subordinate class start to discard their false images of the world, and come to see the reality of their exploited status. Then they come to see themselves as they really are – a class. In Marx's words, they develop class consciousness. Their *subjective* view of themselves and their condition comes to match its *objective* reality. It is the emergence of class consciousness in a subordinate class that is the key which unlocks the revolution which overthrows a mode of production and its dominant class. How does this happen? How does false consciousness become class consciousness?

As with the existence of false ideas, true consciousness cannot come into being independently of economic circumstances. According to Marx, the impetus for revolution does not arise randomly, or by chance. Ideas about how a society ought to be restructured can only develop under certain circumstances. In particular, when institutional arrangements (which have come into being to support a particular mode of production) no longer suit productive relationships, because of the alterations these have undergone through time, pressure for change builds up. The exploited class then embarks on a political struggle, designed to replace old social arrangements with ones more suited to new economic arrangements.

Social change

Feudalism to capitalism

In feudal society, the owners of land were the dominant class, owning the dominant means of production. The superstructure supported their dominance, and ideas that reflected their class interests were the ruling ideas. For example, feudal law bound serfs to the land, and political power was in the hands of landlords and nobles. Feudal religion legitimated these arrangements. As one Victorian hymn puts it, three hundred years later:

> The rich man at his castle,
> The poor man at his gate:
> God made them high or lowly,
> And ordered their estate.

For the Marxist, there is nothing surprising in the correspondence between the characteristics of production and the character of prevailing ideas. Clearly, if feudal legal, political or religious ideas had stressed something different, feudal production could not have survived. The correspondence between the material world and the world of ideas continued as economic change took place. As capitalism replaced feudalism, superstructural ideas necessarily changed in consequence, in order to support and justify the new economic arrangements, so that they could work. According to the Marxist, this is how this happened. As feudalism progressed, technological innovations began to transform the nature of production, from labour-intensive agriculture to mechanized agriculture, and ultimately to industrial production. As these agricultural and industrial revolutions unfolded, so the new capitalist class emerged as the owners of the foundation of the new and growing means of production – capital.

For a time, however, the superstructure lagged behind these changes, its character still reflecting and legitimating the old economic arrangements. For example, though capitalist production required a mobile labour force and land to be freely available for buying and selling, the old legal and political arrangements prevented this.

Eventually, the strain or contradiction between the interests of the new bourgeoisie and the power and practices of the old landowning class became too great and the landlord class was overthrown. Though this happened quite quickly and violently in other European societies, the change began earlier, and was more gradual, in Britain. By means of various political alterations which took place over a few centuries, the landlord class came to share political power, first with the capitalist landowners, and then with the new industrialists. Eventually the control of political decision-making passed irrevocably into capitalist hands, though a residue of influence has remained with the landlords up to today.

Capitalism to communism

Marx predicted that the same kind of process would be apparent in the revolutionary transformation of the capitalist mode of production into the communist one. Again, the ideas and actions of the people would be the motor of this change. However, these revolutionary ideas could only come about as a result of the emergence of class consciousness. This would only happen as capitalism developed as a mode of production. According to Marx, the evolution of capitalism can only occur by means of the continual exploitation of the working class. That is, though capitalism survives only by exploiting the wage-earning class to a greater and greater extent, an increase in such exploitation will inevitably transform false consciousness into class consciousness. As a result, the steps which are taken to ensure capitalism's 'progress' as a productive system will, at the same time, guarantee the sowing of the seeds of its own destruction. This is how it is supposed to happen.

As we said earlier, capitalism was established prior to the development of industry. But it was only with the Industrial Revolution, representing progress for capital, that the reality of capitalist society could start to be visible to its members. Industrial production created large urban settlements of workers, in similar positions for the first time. Living in the same overcrowded conditions of poverty and squalor, and working in the same factory workplaces, the urban proletariat could together begin to recognize their common exploited state. Furthermore, as capitalism develops as a mode of production, exploitation increases. As this happens, class consciousness begins to replace false consciousness.

Capitalist production depends on capital accumulation. Capitalists accumulate capital by increasing the return from the sale of their goods while at the same time lowering the cost of their production. One major way of lowering costs is to cut labour by constantly mechanizing – decreasing the labour force. This has two effects. First, smaller capitalists, lacking the capital to invest in new machinery, are unable to compete successfully. They go to the wall, and join the proletariat class. Second, unemployment increases among the proletariat. Since wage-earners are also consumers, an increase in the impoverishment of some of them reduces demand for goods. Faced with this loss in demand capitalists have to cut costs still further in order to retain profit levels and remain solvent. This is done by either decreasing their labour forces still further or by reducing wage levels. This can be done in two ways. Wages can be actually reduced. (The 1926 General Strike took place when miners' wages were reduced.) More topically, they can be 'increased' at a slower rate than the rate of inflation. As a result of either of these methods, demand decreases still further and this further affects supply. As this process continues, the gap in reward between the contracting bourgeoisie and the ever-growing proletariat increases. As the proletariat become increasingly impoverished in this way, the conditions emerge for the development of a fully fledged class consciousness among them. The proletariat is thus transformed from merely an *objective* class, a class in fact, to being a *subjective* class – a class in their thoughts – as well. It changes from being just a class *in* itself to being a class *for* itself. When this class consciousness reaches its fullest extent, the proletariat rise up and overthrow capitalism, taking over the means of production and the state apparatus, as the capitalists did before them.

According to Marx, this is the final revolution in a society. Unlike in earlier revolutions, there will be no new exploiting class. Rule by the proletariat means self-government by the workers. Class society is abolished, with all its evils, and a new realm of human freedom begins in communist society. Here, at last, is an abundant society where all benefit, and all are free to live and work in a flexible, creative way for themselves, rather than for others. People come to control their own destiny and 'make their own history'. Equality brings emancipation. According to Marx it will be 'possible for me to do one thing today and another tomorrow, to hunt in the morning, fish in the afternoon, rear cattle in the evening, criticise after dinner, just as I have a mind, without ever becoming hunter, fisherman, shepherd or critic' (Marx, 1963, p. 22).

So, only in communist society can human beings fulfil their potential for creativity and goodness. In all other forms of society, the production of material wealth by the dominance of one class over the rest denies this possibility. Despite the ways it is dressed up by those who have power, in the Marxist view people living in class societies inevitably experience **alienation** – they are always dehumanized and denied the chance of fulfilling their potential. For Marx, in a class society a human being is prevented from being truly human.

Controversies within Marxism

The base/superstructure approach to institutions, ideas, beliefs and social change is what makes Marxist sociology distinctive. According to Lee and Newby, 'This base/superstructure distinction lies at the heart of Marx's sociology . . . Marx himself refers to the base/super-structure distinction as the "guiding thread for my studies"' (1983, p. 115). Marx wanted to show how non-economic life is directly influenced by the activity of production; how only changes in the economic realm can enable people to see the world as it really is; and therefore how social change is ultimately only possible as a consequence of economic developments. Although revolution has to be undertaken by political action, the realization of its necessity can only come about as a result of the consequences of economic change. Ideas are therefore, in the end, contingent upon economic circumstances; crucially, changes in ideas, involving the shift from false consciousness to class consciousness and therefore the desire to change society, can only come about as a result of economic change. As Marx says, 'Men make their own history, but not under circumstances of their own choosing' (1954, p. 10).

Ever since these ideas appeared they have caused enormous controversy. One of the most common accusations has been that Marx's theory is a theory of **economic determinism** – that it argues that 'all social, political and intellectual development is caused by economic changes and even that all human action is economically motivated' (Lee and Newby, 1983, p. 116).

Since such a claim is patently untrue, twentieth-century Marxists have insisted that reading Marx this way is to 'vulgarize' Marxism (though they admit, as Marx did himself, that some of Marx's nineteenth-century followers did commit such an error; referring to such work, Marx complained, 'I am not a Marxist'). Marxists say that Marx certainly did not mean that at any particular time the whole of social life is economically determined, or that everyone is always guided by economic motives in their actions. According to Lee and Newby, for Marx such 'economic **reductionism**' was not historical material-ism, and 'neither was Marxism a dehumanizing theory which reduced all individuals to economic automata and denied them any free will' (Lee and Newby, 1983, p. 116).

Unfortunately, while Marxists agree about what Marx did *not* mean, they do not agree about what he *did* mean. Debates about the real meaning of the base/superstructure relationship dominated twentieth-century Marxist sociology. The problem is that to de-emphasize the economic as the determining influence on ideas is to water down what is distinctively Marxist about Marxism. On the other hand, to assert the economic as the driving influence over the rest of social life certainly makes you distinctively Marxist, but lays you open to charges of economic determinism.

The importance of the debate for Marxists cannot be over-emphasized. This is a modern theory *par excellence*: a set of prescriptions for political action. Here is the blueprint for the creation of the good society; here is the vehicle for human emancipation via societal progress. For the Marxist, the point is not just to understand the world, but to change it. So it is not just a matter of getting the theory right to explain capitalism; the theory *has* to be right, because it is a weapon of political transformation – the purpose of the theory is to destroy capitalism.

With this in mind, the fervour and intensity of the debate among twentieth-century Marxists is easily understood. For if Marxism is right, then surely it could be expected that at least some twentieth-century capitalist societies would succumb to the forces of progress specified by the theory? In effect, Marx is saying: 'Don't worry, this evil society will ultimately destroy itself. Be patient: perhaps slowly, but nonetheless inexorably, economic developments will, in the end, bring the proletariat to realise the truth. Eventually, they will act.'

But what is the evidence? As Lee and Newby put it, modern Marxism has had to come to terms with the occurrence of a non-event:

> In *no* advanced capitalist society has a successful proletarian revolution taken place . . . moreover . . . the most advanced capitalist nation in the world, the United States, appears ostensibly to be almost a living testament to the falsity of some of Marx's predictions. Not only have the majority of American workers persistently increased their standard of living, there is no significant attachment to socialism among American workers and certainly no widespread revolutionary movement aimed at overthrowing capitalism. In Europe during the 1930s, furthermore, many of the conditions which Marx's writings would lead one to believe would prompt the growth of working class consciousness were present – the widespread immiseration and unemployment of workers in the midst of a severe economic crisis in advanced capitalist societies. The outcome, however, was not the growth of revolutionary socialism within the working class but, equally often, the growth of Fascism . . . the proletariat has persistently failed to act in the ways which Marx both predicted and desired. (Lee and Newby, 1983, p. 134)

Living through such a consolidation of capitalism and confronted by a working class that was profoundly disinclined to emancipate itself cannot have been easy for twentieth-century Marxists. It is not therefore surprising that the efforts of most of them were dedicated to making sense of such disillusioning and dispiriting evidence and to modernize Marxism – to try and breathe new political life into the theory.

Two main schools of Marxism emerged:

- *Humanist Marxism*, whose leading figures were the Italian **Antonio Gramsci** (1891–1937), and the German members of the Frankfurt school, based in the Frankfurt Institute for Social Research (founded in 1928), whose work is otherwise known as *Critical Theory*
- *Structuralist Marxism*, associated primarily with Frenchman **Louis Althusser** (1918–90).

Humanist Marxism

Humanist Marxists shift the emphasis to the superstructure. For them, twentieth-century political events demonstrate that the ideological locks on the minds of the working class are so secure that the traditional Marxist method of waiting for economic crises to prise them open and precipitate class consciousness and political action should be rethought. The argument is that changes in the base by themselves are insufficient to promote changes in ideas, since under capitalism people's minds are too securely held in the distorting grip of ideologies. Theoretically, this means allocating greater importance to the role of the superstructure in explaining the survival of capitalism; politically, it means actively promoting the correct ideas – Marxist theory – to combat ideological indoctrination. However, the Frankfurt School and Gramsci differed over the chances of such superstructural change being effected. Whereas Gramsci was optimistic, the Critical Theorists ultimately lost all faith in the revolutionary potential of the working class.

Gramsci

Gramsci is famous for his notion of *hegemony*. He uses this concept to summarize the all-consuming way in which ideologies work to distort a person's view of the world. More than merely referring to the dominance of certain ideas from which capitalism benefits, hegemony conveys the inability of believers even to acknowledge that their beliefs are, in principle, capable of being different, so natural do they take them to be. Describing beliefs as hegemonic, therefore, means indicating that those who subscribe to them take them so much for granted that it requires deliberate and sustained effort to point out their existence, let alone change believers' minds.

Because of this theoretical view of the nature of belief under capitalism, Gramsci was led to insist on the political importance of directly challenging the hegemony of ruling ideas. Gramsci argued that of course Marx was right to say that social change depends on the proletariat seeing the world as it really is. However, he was wrong to assume that this would happen without deliberate action on behalf of the truth. Thus, custodians of the truth (Marxists, with their knowledge of the truth about capitalism) have to become persuaders, preachers and teachers. Before political action can be undertaken to overturn the system, the battle for the *minds* of the soldiers has to be won – bourgeois hegemony has to be deliberately taken on and defeated.

The idea that ideologies have to be exposed, that false consciousness has to be replaced by class consciousness before political action will be taken, is essential to Marxism. What is different with Gramsci is the account of how this will happen. He says it will not happen automatically through economic developments because of the strength of hegemonic beliefs; it has to be deliberately secured through education – by means of counter-socialization.

Critical Theory: the Frankfurt School

The three main Frankfurt School thinkers were **Herbert Marcuse** (1898–1979), **Theodor Adorno** (1903–69), and **Max Horkheimer** (1895–1973). Forced to flee Hitler's Germany (in 1933, to the USA), they watched the rise and fall of the Nazi state and then the post-war entrenchment of the capitalist way of life with increasing disillusion. They eventually came to view the emancipation of the working class as a hopeless prospect, principally because of their belief in the immutability of certain superstructural forces which they saw as inexorably suffusing, and dominating, modern life under capitalism. For many thinkers today, the conceptual tools that they used to explain the triumph of capitalism by means of these forces remain highly relevant for an understanding of contemporary life.

Just as Gramsci was concerned to emphasize the control of ideas as the principal source of the power of capital, so Critical Theory also focuses on instruments of mental domination as the key to capitalism's success. For Critical Theory, three features of the culture of capitalism in particular function as these instruments:

- the way of thinking called **instrumental reason**
- the role of mass, or popular, culture in stupefying the thought-processes of people and rendering them incapable of being critical of their world
- the prevalence of a type of personality that not only accepts domination, but actively desires it.

Instrumental reason

Instrumental reason echoes Weber's focus on rationalization as the key feature of modern life (see chapters 4 and 9). It is intended to convey the predominance of seeing things as instruments – as means to ends – rather than as having value in themselves. It is a focus on *how* things can achieve goals, rather than on whether the goals are worthwhile, or whether the instruments should be used for particular purposes.

The centrality of such reasoning in modern society is in many ways a consequence of capitalist activity, where a preoccupation with new and ever more efficient means of achieving productive ends becomes the be-all and end-all. In this, too, the key role of positivist science in modern life – characterized by a never-ending search for the causes of effects, for technical knowledge of how things produce other things – is crucial. Indeed, Marx's own dedication to science as the route to worthwhile knowledge itself eventually came under criticism from the Frankfurt theorists. In summary, for Critical Theorists, the essence of being human lies in the ability to reason about meaning and value and ultimate good. Subverting such potential by encouraging a preoccupation with instrumental reason is thus a crucial means whereby criticism of goals and values embodied in the existing order is likely to be prevented.

Mass culture

The rise of *mass culture* is another major instrument of mental domination identified by the Frankfurt writers. They insist that an examination of the role of cultural agencies such as popular music, the cinema and radio (writing today they would obviously have included television, videos and computer games) is essential for understanding the disinclination of modern humans to do anything but passively acquiesce in their subordination. Indeed, Critical Theorists are famous for their contemptuous dismissal of popular entertainment as dehumanizing, debasing and worthless. It has led to charges of intellectual snobbery and cultural élitism, but the Frankfurt writers were convinced that the superficiality of low-brow art, and its apparent mission to trivialize reality, is a root cause of the accommodation of the evils of modern society on the part of its members. Indeed, the term 'Critical Theory' to describe their ideas stems from this view. For them, only intellectuals or artists concerned about, and familiar with, serious and worthy cultural products can escape the shackles and impoverishment of mass entertainment and be capable of offering a critique of the modern world – to show how a substantially better world could be created. This position has also led to criticism of Frankfurt School thinking. Its implications seem to be not only that there are correct values, but that the ability to identify these – to know good and bad when they see it – is a virtue monopolized by the theorists themselves and their followers. Not only do they seem to be claiming that they alone are able to know what is good, but they also seem to be claiming that they alone know what is good for the rest of us – whatever we may think.

Personality manipulation

The final element in Critical Theory is an interest in the sort of *personality* characteristics created by the modern world. Marcuse in particular developed this theme. He uses Freud's ideas to argue that all societies need to promote the repression or *sublimation* of the desires of their members in order to prevent the collapse of social order in an orgy of individual self-gratification. As a result, any proper analysis of modern society must include an examination of how such repression is achieved in our sort of world. According to Marcuse, in the early stages of capitalism a high degree of repression is necessary to ensure that people concentrate on work and production. In later, mature, capitalism, however, there is less need for such an exclusive focus, so that the retention of such repression is surplus to the system's requirements. In such circumstances, continuing to insist on such surplus repression from people might well lead to discontent, so psychological pressure is exerted – via what Marcuse calls *repressive de-sublimation* – to allow us to realize and pursue our desires, but in ways that are useful to the system. Thus, the routine use of sexual images to sell commodities in capitalist societies – cars, cigarettes, alcohol, coffee, clothes, or whatever – is not only sales technique (associating the commodity with an enviable sexual state or circumstance) but also a way of satisfying desires whose *dis*satisfaction would be potentially dangerous. As with other forms of human potential, then, for Marcuse, the use of sex in this way takes an integral and profoundly fulfilling part of human existence and turns it into an instrument of domination or manipulation.

Today, the heir to Critical Theory analysis is **Jürgen Habermas**. We will examine some of his ideas in the final chapter, when we discuss **postmodernism** and its critics.

Althusser and structuralist Marxism

For structuralist Marxists like Althusser, humanist Marxism is wrong theory and therefore wrong practice. For Gramsci, human beings are potentially capable of seeing whom they have been forced to become by ideologies, and therefore in principle able to choose to rid themselves of these hegemonic chains and become who they really are. Like the supporters of other forms of structuralism (see chapter 8), Althusser rejects completely the idea that humans can be 'subjects' – creative agents – in this way, in charge of their lives and worlds. For him, human life is always entirely structured, and change can only ever come about at the level of a structure whose workings have nothing to do with human cognition, choice and purpose. Althusserian Marxism thus sees itself as the heir to the 'late' Marx – to writings produced towards the end of Marx's life, when he tried to build a scientific analysis of the structure of capitalism. As you might expect from the term 'late', such a view is opposed to the work of the 'young' or 'early' Marx, whose heirs are humanist Marxists like Gramsci and for whom the way we live is the product of the way we think. Whereas for humanist Marxists social change in capitalist society can only come about through alterations in human purpose and motivation, for Althusser it can only ever happen by change in the structural relations of capitalism.

Theoretically, Althusser is equally opposed to both crude, economistic Marxism and humanist Marxism. Concentrating on the base, on economic organization to the exclusion of the other structural features of the superstructure, is for him as faulty as concentrating on ideologies – the ideas believed by the working class. Althusser insists it is only scientific Marxism, resting on a proper understanding of the complexity of the structure of capitalism, which can lead to the destruction of such societies.

According to Althusser there are three levels in the structure of a class society: *economic, political* and *ideological.* He defines them broadly, so that they embrace most aspects of human life. The 'economic' concerns all aspects of material production, the 'political' all forms of organization, and the 'ideological' all kinds of ideas and beliefs. The political level and the ideological level are not the simple creation of the economic. Although the economic level is ultimately the determining level – 'determinant in the last instance' as he puts it – Althusser defines the political and ideological levels as having 'relative autonomy'. They are thus independent and important in their own right and the interplay between the three levels is complex and varied. Ian Craib uses a nice architectural analogy to explain this:

> We can look at the relationship between the floors of a multi-storey building: it would be nonsense to say that the first and second floors are caused by the ground floor, even though they rest upon it, have some sort of relationship to it. Each is separate from the floor above and below it, and what goes on on each floor is not determined by what goes on below it. The first floor might be a shop, the second floor offices and the third floor living quarters. Althusser's term for describing this relation where there is a causal connection but not complete dependence is 'relative autonomy'. The political and ideological levels are neither completely dependent on the economic nor completely independent. If we take this building as a single enterprise, the office work which goes on on the second floor obviously depends upon the sort of trading that goes on in the shop but there are various ways in which it might be organised, and the work relationships there may develop in ways not influenced by the economic activity going on below. Similarly if the owners live on the third floor their standard of living and way of life has its limits set by the nature of the business they run but there are choices within these limits and the development of a marriage and family life has its own dynamics. Althusser's next step away from crude Marxism is to argue that the causal processes are two-way: the political and ideological levels affect the economic. Returning to the example, decisions based on administrative criteria in the offices may have an effect on the trading in the shop – a 'streamlining of the management structure' for example, might lead to increased turnover. Similarly if the business is jointly owned and the marriage fails, the settlement between the partners might have an important effect on the nature of the business. (Craib, 1992, pp. 131–2)

As you might expect from this perception of the structure of class society, Althusser argues that the study of history reveals periods when one level dominates over the other two but that this is never a permanent state of affairs. Thus it could be argued that 'the structure in dominance', as he calls it, in nineteenth-century capitalism was the economic, with the industrial bourgeoisie dominating not only economic but eventually political life, too. The power of the ideological level, mainly represented by the church, could be said to have dominated feudal society, while today a strong case could be made for seeing the structure in dominance in present-day Britain to be the political, via the power of the state and its penetration into so many aspects of life.

Althusser is also well known for a conceptual separation of the two elements by which the state exercises its power. He refers to organizations like the police, the army, the law and so on as constituting a *repressive state apparatus*. Alongside this political apparatus is an ideological one – the *ideological state apparatus* – made up of educational, media, religious and cultural institutions. Althusser's conception of a layered, interconnected structure is apparent here too; just as different structures in dominance prevail at different times in history, so different elements of a particular level will dominate at different times. Thus in modern society, education has taken over from religion as the principal ideological instrument of oppression; the work of Bowles and Gintis (1976) on the correspondence between the needs of capitalism and the function of education referred to earlier on is Althusserian theory in practice.

Conclusion

Despite the efforts of such schools of neo-Marxist thought, capitalism still seems under no threat. Indeed, living in the twenty-first century we now have to add the (for Marxists) calamitous events in Eastern Europe in the 1990s. Not only did communist regimes collapse like cards, and not only did the Soviet Union self-destruct, but an ancient form of political ambition emerged to replace communism in Eastern Europe – nationalism. Furthermore, the new post-communist regimes are enthusiastically embracing capitalism, the free market and *laissez-faire* individualism.

None of this *necessarily* means that Marxist theory is a bad theory of capitalism, however. Just because it has been found wanting as a theory of political action does not mean it is therefore faulty as a theory of the political economy of capitalism. While events of the twentieth century may have brought into question Marx's version of the project of modernity, this does not mean that Marxist theory is failing to continue to provide us with the best set of analytical tools with which to make sense of modern capitalist societies. Here the questions are:

- Is the mode of production the defining characteristic of society?
- Is class always the central organizing principle?
- Are ideas ultimately influenced by economic organization?

It is against such conclusions that Marx's contemporary, Max Weber, presented his alternative analysis of modern capitalist society and it is to Weber's ideas that we now turn.

Further Reading

General introductions

Elster, Jon: *Making Sense of Marx*, Cambridge University Press, 1985.
Elster, Jon: *An Introduction to Karl Marx*, Cambridge University Press, 1986a.
McLellan, David: *Karl Marx: his life and thought*, Macmillan, 1973.
McLellan, David: *Marxism after Marx: an introduction*, 3rd edn, Macmillan, 1998.
Worsley, Peter: *Marx and Marxism*, Tavistock, 1982.

Collections of extracts

Bottomore, T. and Rubel, M.: *Karl Marx: selected writings*, Penguin, 1963.
Elster, Jon: *Karl Marx: a reader*, Cambridge University Press, 1986b.
McLellan, David: *The Thought of Karl Marx*, 2nd edn, Macmillan, 1980.
McLellan, David: *Marxism: essential writings*, Oxford University Press, 1988.
McLellan, David: *Selected Writings of Karl Marx*, 2nd edn, Oxford University Press, 2000.

Critical commentaries on Marxism

Anderson, Perry: *Considerations on Western Marxism*, New Left Books, 1976b.
Bottomore, Tom (ed.): *Interpretations of Marx*, Blackwell, 1988.
Callinicos, Alex: *Is There a Future for Marxism?* Macmillan, 1982.
Giddens, Anthony: *Capitalism and Modern Social Theory: an analysis of the writings of Marx, Durkheim and Max Weber*, Cambridge University Press, 1971b.
Held, David: *Introduction to Critical Theory*, Hutchinson, 1980.

Kolakowski, L.: *Main Currents of Marxism*, vols 1–3, Oxford University Press, 1978.

McLellan, David: *Karl Marx – the first 100 years*, Fontana, 1983.

Mann, Michael: *The Sources of Social Power*, vol. 2, Cambridge University Press, 1993.

Matthews, Betty (ed.): *Marx – 100 years on*, Lawrence and Wishart, 1983.

4 MAX WEBER

Max Weber

Bildarchiv Preussischer Kulturbesitz, Berlin

Max Weber: born Erfurt, Thuringia, 1864, died Munich, 1920

Major works

Methodological Essays (1902)
The Protestant Ethic and the Spirit of Capitalism (1902–4)
Economy and Society (1910–14)
Sociology of Religion (1916)

Introduction

As we have seen, functionalism and Marxism, while giving very different accounts of modern social life, are nonetheless similar types of theory. For both, the world is as it is because of the characteristics of the social structure; change occurs because of the dynamics of the system and these theories of the system show how it works and how change takes place.

Of course, people living in different societies have their own theories of their worlds, but these mental states usually do not correspond with structural reality, and usually have no influence on the way the social world is. This is why functionalists talk of 'latent' and 'manifest' functions and why Marxists talk of 'false consciousness'. The idea that people should see how the world really is is unimportant in functionalism. While it is ultimately crucial for Marxism (other than in Althusserian Marxism), it only comes about when economic developments via the workings of the system encourage it, or when it is deliberately promoted by education. For functionalism all of the time and for Marxism most of the time then, mental states have no consequence for the structure of society. Weber's sociology is opposed to this kind of theory.

For Weber, the world is as it is because of social action. People do things because they decide to do so in order to achieve ends they desire. Having selected their goals, and taken account of the circumstances they find themselves in, they *choose* to act. Social structures are the outcome of such action; ways of living are the product of motivated choice. Existing action-created social circumstances exercise constraint as structural forces, of course, but action is nonetheless still mental in origin – chosen in the light of the actor's perception of these structural constraints. Understanding social, action-produced reality involves explaining why people make the choices they do. Socio-logical theories are not theories of social *systems*, which have their own dynamics, but of the meanings behind actions – they are theories of the theories of actors.

Social action theory

Weber called the method by which this is done *verstehen*. Because sociologists are human too, we can put ourselves in the place of others, appreciate the structural circumstances in which they find themselves, take account of their goals and thereby understand their actions. This is what distinguishes a social science from a natural science. Daffodils do not choose to open their leaves; apples do not decide to fall from trees. Natural scientists therefore do not have to be like daffodils or apples to explain their behaviour.

Unlike most action sociology, however (see chapter 6), Weber's interest in actors' theories, in motivated, goal-oriented action, does not mean that he is only interested in the small-scale, in the meaning of specific interaction between individuals. Like Marx, Weber is inter-ested in the broad sweep of history and social change, and believes that the best way of understanding different societies is to appreciate the typical forms of action that characterize them. But unlike Marx and Durkheim, who saw their task as uncovering *universal* tendencies in human social life, Weber rejects such a project. Weber reconstructs the meaning behind historical events producing social structures and formations, but at the same time sees all such historical configurations of circumstances as unique.

Weber argues that you can compare the structure of societies by understanding the reasons for the respective historical actions and events which have influenced their character, and by understanding the actions of actors living in them now, but that it is not possible to generalize about all societies or all social structures. To assist this kind of comparison, Weber argues that sociology should use as wide a range of concepts as possible.

Types of action

Weber uses a classification of four types of action, differentiated in terms of the motives of actors:

Traditional action	'I do this because I always have.'
Affective action	'I can't help doing this.'
Value-oriented action, or the use of **value rationality**	'All I care about is this.'
Goal-oriented action, or the use of **instrumental rationality**	'This is the most efficient means to achieve *this*', but '*this* is the best way to do *that*.'

Types of inequality

Though, like Marx, Weber saw relations of inequality as central to social life, he rejects the Marxist notion that class inequality is always the most important. For him, comparative and historical analysis testifies that *status groups*, possessing certain amounts of prestige, and *parties*, possessing certain amounts of political influence, can be just as significant sources of advantage as *class* membership. Furthermore, Weber defined class not simply as the possession of productive property, as Marx did, but as the possession of all of the kinds of life-chances generated by 'market power' in a society. That is, he defines class in terms of the individual's capacity to solicit rewards for the sale of his or her skills in society's market-place.

Types of power

Similarly, Weber rejects the Marxist notion that power is always tied to class membership, although an interest in power and force suffuses his work. As he puts it: 'Domination . . . is one of the most important elements of social action . . . in most of the varieties of social action domination plays a considerable role . . . without exception every sphere of social action is profoundly influenced by structures of dominancy' (Weber, 1968, p. 141).

Parkin (1982) shows how Weber's typology of power identifies different appeals for legitimacy by the powerful:

Type of domination	*Grounds for claiming obedience*
Traditional	'Obey me because this is what our people have always done.'
Charismatic	'Obey me because I can transform your life.'
Legal-rational	'Obey me because I am your lawfully appointed superior.'

By developing his conceptual apparatus in this way, away from the sort of reliance on economic factors that characterizes Marx's work, Weber has often been portrayed as engaging in a major attempt to refute the economic determinism of Marxism. Since he sees ideas and motives as the driving force in social life, he certainly wants to refute economic determinism. His sociology is quite clearly wholly antagonistic to the view that all social behaviour can be understood as being economically caused. However, as we have seen, while some of Marx's contemporaries who followed him were crudely economistic, it is not a charge that can be fairly levelled at Marx himself, as Weber in fact recognized in his comments on Marx's work. But there is another reason why it is wrong to see Weber's writings as a deliberate attempt to *disprove* Marx. This is because of the way he views the human activity of theorizing.

Ideal types and sociological theorizing

According to Weber, the most obvious truth about thinking is that no human being can possibly grasp the whole of reality he or she confronts – the 'meaningless infinity of the world process' as he describes it. Humans can only make sense of an aspect of reality – a selection from the infinite aggregate of events. Your theory represents your selection – your choice of what you think is worth looking at and your choice of what you think explains these things. But this does not make your personal, selected, partial account objectively correct – objective truth is unavailable to a human theorist. As Weber puts it, 'all knowledge of cultural reality . . . is always knowledge from *particular points of view*'. There can be no such thing as an 'absolutely "objective" scientific analysis of culture or . . . of "social phenomena" independent of special and "one-sided" viewpoints . . .' (Weber, 1949, pp. 72, 81).

What we think exists depends upon what we think something's essence is. Thus, a functionalist might see a family as a system-integrating institution; a Marxist might see the same collection of people as a means of reproducing capitalism; while a feminist might see them as living lives which systematically oppress and subordinate the woman who is wife and mother. 'Seeing' therefore, is 'selecting'; 'seeing' is always theoretical. (It could be said that in some ways, these ideas of Weber anticipate the *relativism* underpinning *postmodern* thought today. See chapters 8 and 9.)

Since seeing from a particular point of view is an inevitable part of being human, says Weber, we should not try to ignore the fact, but make it explicit in our accounts of the world. We should describe and explain reality by highlighting and emphasizing our points of view to an extent which exaggerates the real world – by constructing **ideal types** of reality, as Weber calls them. To understand an aspect of social life, it is necessary to reduce it to what we think is its essence and then to highlight these features, so that others know exactly where we stand – what our point of view is. Our account of the world is 'ideal' not in a judgemental sense, but in a 'larger-than-life' sense. We paint our picture of the world – the aspects we consider significant or important to refer to – in bold strokes, so others can be left in no doubt.

Unlike Marx and Durkheim, then, Weber is not claiming to know the 'truth' about reality – only his version of it. Thus, in one of his most celebrated works (an account of the reasons for the emergence of modern capitalist society, and a portrayal of its principal features), Weber is not claiming that Marx is 'wrong' and he alone is 'right' in his theory. Weber regarded Marx's account as an ideal type and simply wanted to add his own account to Marx's, as an alternative, rather than claim to refute it.

However, it is easy to see why Weber's ideal-typical writings on modern society have been interpreted as an assault on Marxism, since he reverses the causal sequence Marx employs. Instead of seeing economic factors causing changes in ideas and beliefs, Weber explains the rise of modern capitalist society the other way round. Particular ideas and beliefs emerge first, and thereby allow the establishment of capitalist production. Furthermore, the defining feature of capitalism for Weber is not, as it is for Marx, a mode of production, but an attitude, or a 'spirit' – a way of looking at things.

Religion, capitalism and rationalization

Much of Weber's historical, comparative work is focused on the influence of religious beliefs on action. It is in this tradition that he sets out his account of the factors that encouraged the emergence of capitalism in those countries where it took root. This form of modern society, he argues, represents the institutionalization of *instrumental rationality* above all else. Whereas in other times and places other forms of action have prevailed, it is only in modern industrial capitalist societies that it has become routine for actors to act due to reasons of efficiency and calculability, rather than because of emotional or traditional reasons, or because of a single-minded dedication to an overriding goal. For Weber, modernity is best understood as the triumph of this way of thinking, this way of looking at the world, and this way of acting (though the last thing he wants to do is to join in the celebration). Modern capitalism is the end result of a **rationalization** process, rooted in the historical influence of specific intellectual traditions. The emergence of this way of living and acting is, for Weber, 'the central problem in a universal history of civilization'. His investigation into this history is guided by the question of why it was, in non-Western countries, that 'neither scientific nor artistic nor political nor economic development followed the path of rationalisation which is unique to the West'. In Weber's account, the role of religious leaders in promoting differing kinds of ideas and orientations in different societies is crucial: 'For example, the Buddhist monk withdrew from all worldly activity in order to achieve a spiritual elevation, while the Confucian Mandarin engaged in administration on the basis of highly traditionalistic and non-scientific literary knowledge. Only in the West did a cultural orientation emerge which favoured rationalisation' (Bilton et al., 1996, p. 602).

The part of Weber's argument that has become most famous concerns the role of Puritan Protestantism, and particularly Calvinism, in this process. In *The Protestant Ethic and the Spirit of Capitalism* (1977) Weber outlines the affinity he sees between the kind of lives Calvinists were encouraged to lead by their religion and the kind of behaviour and attitudes necessary for capitalism to work effectively. Weber explains how, unlike in most religions, Calvinists are encouraged to concentrate on worldly work as the most virtuous activity and, at the same time, are exhorted to live ascetic – frugal, thrifty and austere – lives. Weber argues that this emphasis on the importance of industriousness and hard work coupled with a demand for an ascetic lifestyle, is unique to Puritan religions, and that it was this combination of religious prescriptions that gave capitalism the chance to take root. Calvinists believe they cannot prove to themselves and others that they have been called by God to salvation, as a predestined member of his elect, unless they are successful and productive in their life's work. Their belief is that the Lord will only let the worthy prosper. Their lives therefore become a dedication to efficiency and rationality in order to maximize their productivity. But the symbols of their achievement, material riches accumulated through constant, ever-more-efficient labour, cannot be consumed in any profligate, ostentatious or self-indulgent fashion, since this would contradict the other Calvinist virtue of asceticism. Thus, although wealth accumulation is the symbol of virtuous and efficient hard work for Calvinists, the consumption of the fruits of this labour is denied the believer because of the need to live an ascetic life.

Here is the affinity with capitalism. Unlike other forms of economy, for capitalism to work, capital has to be accumulated; not to be consumed, but to be reinvested in the pursuit of ever-more-efficient, and profitable, techniques of production. The need is for the constant pursuit of rational means of production, by ploughing back the fruits of labour. The more wealth is made and the more successful the capitalist enterprise is, the more resources are available to improve the efficiency of production. Work is therefore an end in itself; profit to be reinvested is virtuous, and brings its own reward.

Weber's account is clear. Only Puritanism expects of its followers a way of thinking and a way of living that matches the peculiar demands made on capitalist producers. Without a population dedicated to worldly work for its own sake, prepared to eschew as sinful any sign of extravagance, capitalism could not have got off the ground. The creation of such a world thus represents the perfect example of the Weberian view of the role of beliefs and action in social change. According to Weber, capitalism is the child of a particular way of thinking and acting, not a mode of production spawned by economic forces. But for Weber, this is a child that should have been strangled at birth, because it has grown into a monster.

Here is a different commentary on modernity from those of Weber's two main nineteenth-century peers. Weber's story is one of the role of specific intellectual traditions in specific historical circumstances, rather than the unravelling of inexorable and universally applicable laws of societal development, as are those of Durkheim and Marx. It is also the story of the social destruction of the human spirit by modernity. Durkheim and Marx each constructed versions of a social theory that could specify the societal route to a future of progress and human emancipation. They both thought they had discovered the cure for social sickness and the recipe for societal, and thereby individual, health and happiness. For Durkheim, regulation through socialization is guaranteed to prevent anomie; for Marx, historical materialism is the prescribed medicine for the eradication of the modern disease of alienation.

But Weber is no doctor of social life; he has no cure for rationalization which is, for him, the scourge of modern society. For Weber, the pursuit of technical efficiency, whatever the (non-material) cost, is inevitable and irreversible in modern industrial capitalism, and while in bureaucratic administration it reaches its zenith, it also represents humanity's nadir. Weber tells us that the rise of this form of society means it is now wholly illusory to hope to build the sort of utopia that the birth of modernity promised for so many thinkers. A world dominated by instrumental rationality – a world where efficiency, calculability and predictability are the dominant goals – means a world bereft of meaning, or of mystery, or of a concern with spiritual fulfilment. Weber tells us instead to resign ourselves to the 'iron cage of bureaucracy' and the 'polar night of icy darkness' which modernity has created. For Weber, the triumph of capitalism as a form of life signals the end of the line for progress. The train bearing the hopes for humanity's spiritual welfare has run into the buffers of terminal instrumental rationality.

Durkheim, Marx and Weber: conclusions

Much sociological theorizing in the twentieth century can be seen to have its roots in the work of Durkheim, Marx and Weber. As we said earlier, until the 1960s (and particularly in the USA, through the dominance of functionalist analysis in the manner of Parsons and his followers), the influence of Durkheim outweighed that of his German counterparts. However, from the 1960s onwards this influence waned, particularly in Britain, and the work of modern followers of Marx and Weber (neo-Marxists and neo-Weberians) became much more significant.

But although much British neo-Marxist sociology since then has remained important – through the work of such as **Stuart Hall** (1932–) and **Alex Callinicos** (1950–) – it is fair to say that neo-Weberian analysis has had a greater influence on the character of contemporary British sociology. During the 1960s and 1970s, prominent neo-Weberians such as **David Lockwood** (1929–), **John Goldthorpe** (1935–), **John Rex** (1925–) and **Ralf Dahrendorf** (1928–) all argued, following Weber, that though sociological analysis has to take proper account of relations of inequality, power and conflict, it should not be assumed that such phenomena can be reduced to economic factors. Furthermore, again in the Weberian tradition, such writers insisted that sociology also acknowledges the central importance of systems of ideas as instruments of continuity and change in social life. These twin Weberian interests, in structural relations and in the role of ideas, have remained important in British sociology and can be seen to have reached their greatest significance in the *structuration* theory of **Anthony Giddens** (see chapter 9). Giddens has since developed his work in numerous ways beyond Weberian concerns, and, in recent years, French philosophy and social theorizing have had a considerable influence on British sociology (see chapters 7, 8 and 9). Nevertheless, it is fair to say that over the last forty years or so, of the classical theorists, it is the approach of Weber and his followers that has had most influence over sociological theorizing in Britain. In the field of *feminist* theorizing, however, it is the ideas of Marx that have had most impact, and it is to feminist theories that we now turn.

Further Reading

Giddens, Anthony: *Capitalism and Modern Social Theory: an analysis of the writings of Marx, Durkheim and Max Weber*, Cambridge University Press, 1971b.
Giddens, Anthony: *Politics and Sociology in the Work of Max Weber*, Macmillan, 1972b.
Parkin, Frank: *Max Weber*, Tavistock, 1982.
Turner, Bryan: *For Weber: essays on the sociology of fate*, Routledge and Kegan Paul, 1981.
Whimster, Sam and Lash, Scott (eds): *Max Weber, Rationality and Modernity*, Allen and Unwin, 1987.

5 FEMINIST THEORIES

Introduction

For most of the time that sociological theorists debated the nature of modern society, a source of disadvantage experienced by half the world's population went unattended. The assumption was that the world as experienced by men was the same as that experienced by women. It was not until the political clamour of the 1960s and the renewed vigour of a women's movement which originated at the turn of the century to secure the vote, that feminist theorizing became established as an indispensable part of sociology. During this so-called 'second wave' of feminism, sociological theories began to be constructed to explain the specific experiences of women and to point to, in good modernist fashion, the societal route to female emancipation and fulfilment. Just as the classic nineteenth-century theories were attempts to specify the possibility of progress via human theorizing, so feminist theorists became engaged in a similar project. The purpose of feminism has been to show how the acquisition of an understanding of the social conditions in which women live their lives opens up the opportunity to reconstruct their world and thereby offer them the prospect of freedom.

Liberal feminism

Liberal feminism sees gender prejudice as a matter of individual ignorance. As a result, it can be eradicated by the enforcement of anti-discrimination laws against the individuals concerned and by the promotion of non-sexist attitudes. In effect, for liberal feminism, this is a war that can be won by re-education. The important sociological work of writers like **Ann Oakley** (1944–), in which the discrimination and disadvantage experienced by women is revealed through systematic empirical investigation, is often used in support of this kind of project. Other feminist theorists take a more structural view of women's oppression however, locating it not in individual ignorance, but in institutionalized ways of living and thinking.

Marxist-feminism

The first truly theoretical response to the need for a sociology of women was the claim that Marxism offered the best theoretical tool with which to excavate the foundations of their oppression. According to Marxist-feminists, women's subordination serves the needs of capitalism. It is in the economic relationships and ideas characteristic of the capitalist mode of production that we should look for the structures of disadvantage that unequally constrain women's lives in contrast to men's. The solution to the problem of women's oppression thus lies in the destruction of capitalism.

Marxist-feminist approaches are of two main kinds – one more economistic than the other. The version of Marxist-feminism which focuses on the economic position of women in capitalist societies argues that women's subordination is best explained by understanding the economic disadvantages they experience as a result of the requirements of capitalism. The following arguments have been advanced by contributors to the debate from this sort of perspective.

Under capitalism, women live in families, as wives and mothers. In these families, women constitute a source of unpaid domestic labour, whose work is as vital for capitalism as that of the commodity producer in industry. Both by providing the domestic services necessary to sustain the male worker who is her husband, and by reproducing a new generation of workers through childcare, the woman as wife and mother is providing a crucial service for capitalism – free. It is therefore obviously far more profitable for capitalism to have women as unpaid domestic labourers than to have to pay male labourers the much higher wage they would need to purchase these domestic services in the market-place.

Also as a result of the normalcy of the nuclear family under capitalism, when women do enter the labour market, because they are seen as economically dependent on their husbands, they can be given low-paid, low-status and part-time work. Their work is seen as secondary and supplementary to that of their husbands, and so the rewards can be supplementary, too – married women's wages also need not be as high as those of single persons. In effect, married women are semi-proletarianized workers, economically more disadvantaged than the working class.

Again, because of their economic dependence on their husbands, women as wives form a useful 'reserve army of labour', to be used in the labour market when required, but for whom permanent work is not a necessity. In effect, women are marginal workers, not just able to be more poorly rewarded than males, but who can be brought in and out of the labour market as the need arises. The classic example of this was during the Second World War, when the absence of male workers meant that previously held prejudices against women had to be suspended so that crucial munitions work could be undertaken. Suddenly, women were needed in heavy industry, and all peacetime justifications for excluding them from such work were conveniently forgotten. Once the war was over, however, such ideologies and legitimations were trumpeted abroad once more.

It is precisely these kinds of ideologies, justifying the world of women in capitalism, that more humanistically inclined Marxist-feminists stress, rather than economic factors. Writers like **Michèle Barrett** (1949–) use the kind of approach advanced by Gramsci, arguing that the role of ideologies in extolling the virtues of family life, and of wifeliness and motherhood in domesticating women, are crucial in reproducing the features of the world from which they are disadvantaged. Thus Barratt emphasizes that the destruction of capitalist economic relations is a necessary, but not a sufficient, condition for the liberation of women. Also necessary is the transformation of ideas about sexuality, gender and parenthood, so that men and women are not ideologically coerced into living in one kind of marriage and in one kind of family.

Obvious problems present themselves with both Marxist-feminist accounts. If capitalism promotes women's subordination, why are women equally subordinated in non-capitalist societies? Though it is easy to see how the performance of unpaid domestic tasks clearly benefits capital, Marxist-feminism does not explain why it should be women who inevitably perform this labour. Why not men? Why not the old? Radical feminism attempts to explain the universality of women's oppression, and it does so by employing the concept of **patriarchy**. Patriarchy means the power of men over women; for radical feminists it is not an economic system that oppresses women – it is *men* who oppress women.

Radical feminism

For radical feminists, patriarchy is the key to understanding social structures and patriarchal relations are universal and elemental. Why should this be? Clearly, if there is one cause of patriarchy it must be found everywhere – as a ubiquitous part of the human condition. One of the first radical feminists, **Kate Millett** (1934–), (1977) argued that patriarchy is brought about by male control of ideas and culture. While this drew proper attention to institutionalized forms of belief oppressing women in ideologies at work, in education and in the family, Millet's explanation of these is rather tautological; in effect she tends to explain patriarchy by the exercise of patriarchy, which is hardly satisfactory (Millet, 1977). In other radical feminist work, three sorts of universals have been suggested: biological motherhood, marriage-based families and heterosexuality.

In another early radical feminist theory, that of **Shulamith Firestone** (1945–) the argument is that patriarchy is based on the biological fact that only females bear children. This approach claims that only when it becomes technologically possible to conceive and nurture children outside the womb will women be capable of being liberated. Then, gender differences will become irrelevant and the biological justification for trapping women in the role of mother in the family will disappear (Firestone, 1971).

Other radical feminists argue that the universal phenomenon at the root of patriarchy is not biological motherhood, but the social institution of the family based on marriage of one kind or another. For this version of radical feminism, marriage is what capitalism is for Marxist-feminists, according to Bouchier (1983), the 'real institutional source of exploitation'. Here we see a characteristic of radical feminist theorizing that became established quite early on in its development – the notion that the 'personal is the political'. The exercise of power by men over women is found not just in the public structural and ideological features of work, education, the media, and so on. Just as important is patriarchy on the personal level, in the private world of intimate relations between men and women. As Mary Maynard puts it: 'Politics occur in families and between individuals when one person attempts to control or dominate another. It is in the personal and private sphere that women are particularly vulnerable to the power of men' (1989, p. 66). Thus Sylvia Walby says, from this point of view: 'The question of who does the housework, or who interrupts whom in conversation, is seen as part of the system of male domination' (1990, p. 3).

This emphasis on the politics of the private sphere has led some radical feminists to focus not so much on general interactions in families and marriages, as on the assumption of the normalcy of heterosexuality on which these universal institutions are based. Here the questions are:

- Why should 'normal sex' be seen as 'heterosexual sex'?
- Why should 'normal' heterosexual sex always involve the penetration of the woman's body by the man?
- Why should the pursuit of vaginal orgasms (which benefit men) be seen as superior and necessary to sexual satisfaction rather than the pursuit of clitoral orgasm (for which men are not needed)?

The exposure of the vaginal orgasm as a physiological myth by Masters and Johnson (1966) added a new legitimacy to some radical feminist claims that the social construction of certain forms of sexuality as 'normal' and 'superior' to others is the universal device upon which patriarchy is founded. (Adrienne Rich (1980) calls this **'compulsory heterosexuality'**.) From this point of view, the symbolism involved in 'normal' heterosexual (penetrative) sex is poignant; the act of penetration represents the colonization of the woman's body and is, literally, a collusion with the enemy. Here sexual intercourse is the quintessential device by which men exercise dominance over women, for the argument is that once the body is controlled, the rest of a woman's life follows. As David Bouchier describes it:

> Once the myth of the vaginal orgasm was out of the way, it became possible to conceive of a complete sexual revolution which would enable women to escape the sexual domination of men. If women did not need men, and could make an unrestricted choice of heterosexual, bisexual, lesbian or celibate life-styles, the resulting liberation of sexual behaviour would break the hold of the monogamous family, the source of patriarchal power. (Bouchier, 1983, p. 79)

In practice, this goal of the transformation of women's sexuality as the route to the destruction of patriarchy has led many radical feminists to argue that only lesbian sexuality allows women the freedom to express their emotional selves – a solution known as 'separatism'.

The emphasis on heterosexuality as the basis of patriarchy has led radical feminist theorists to explore the links between sexual hegemony and violence against women. The work of **Adrienne Rich** (1929–) and **Andrea Dworkin** (1946–) among others, is notable here. In societies like Great Britain, a significant element in the social construction of heterosexuality is the public presentation of women as compliant and accommodating, available playthings for men to make use of in the pursuit of their sexual gratification. Hardly any thought is needed to see that such images abound in advertising, the media and along the top shelves of countless newsagents. The radical feminist point here is that if women are presented in this sexually available way, with the explicit invitation to be used by men, sexual harassment, assault or rape should not be seen as surprising. These are merely more violent expressions of 'normal' sexual relations between men and women. To see such acts as evidence of depravity or sickness is to miss the point about the definition of what sex should be about from which they spring (Rich, 1980; Dworkin, 1981).

For many radical feminists the woman's world is suffused with the prospect of real or potential violence by men, violence endorsed by the symbolic violence of heterosexual sex, and promoted by advertising and pornography. If some men structure some aspects of their lives because of the threat of physical assault – avoiding certain places at night, or refusing to drink in 'rough' pubs – then radical feminism points at the much more routine problems faced by women. According to Elizabeth Stanko:

> Women know about the unpredictability of men's physical and sexual intimidation. We plan our lives around it: finding the right street to walk down when coming home, cooking the eggs the way the husband likes them, and avoiding office parties are examples of strategies designed to avoid male sexual and physical intimidation and violence. (Stanko, 1985, p. 70)

Dual-systems theories

Dual-systems theories involve a fusion of Marxist-feminist and radical feminist ideas, recognizing the impact of both capitalism and patriarchy as instruments of women's oppression. Most contributions so far tend to use a version of patriarchy rooted in marriage and the family, rather than in sexuality and violence.

Christine Delphy (1941–), who calls her theory *materialist feminism*, employs Marxist methods and concepts, but eschews a straight-forward Marxist approach. According to Delphy (1984) there are two class-based modes of production in capitalist society, the industrial and the domestic. The industrial mode of production involves the exploitation of the proletariat by the bourgeoisie, while the domestic mode features the patriarchal exploitation of women by men. The usual view of the family, as a unit in which the class membership of the members is determined by the economic status of the husband, is thus supplemented by a view of the family as an arena in which representatives of two other classes co-exist and in which class exploita-tion also occurs of a kind that parallels the industrial mode. Thus, while working men are exploited in the industrial mode, they become the exploiters in the domestic mode; single women are exploited in the industrial mode, but most women's exploitation is experienced in the domestic mode because most women get married and become domestic workers.

Delphy's main effort is to explain the patriarchal exploitation of women. She is far less concerned with the impact of capitalism. Other dual-systems theorists have the balance of interests much more equal. **Zillah Eisenstein** (1948–) sees capitalism and patriarchy as being so intimately connected that they actually form one system, which she calls *capitalist patriarchy* (1979). Their interconnection is so profound that changes in one part of the system cause changes in the other. Thus, for example, an increase in women working in the labour market because of the needs of capital would necessarily cause pressure for political change, because of the impact of this on women's role as domestic labourers.

In *The Unhappy Marriage of Marxism and Feminism* (1981), **Heidi Hartmann** (?–) also insists on the need to see women as oppressed by both men and capitalism, but sees these features as constituting separate, though connected, systems of oppression. Thus, women are exploited by men both in the labour market, where men have the better rewarded jobs, and in the household – women do more domestic labour than men, even if they are also wage-earners. Patriarchy came into being prior to capitalism through marriage and family relations, and with the development of capitalist **relations of production** men have, as it were, 'done a deal' with capitalism to secure the kind of advantages over women in this new sphere of waged work which they had previously enjoyed in the domestic sphere. Thus the Labour move-ment in Great Britain has mainly promoted the interests of men, not women. Both parties benefit from women's exploitation at home and in work. Capitalism benefits from women's economic dependence on men because this ensures their availability for insecure, low-paid employment, and men benefit because they get the better jobs and have domestic services provided for them.

Juliet Mitchell (1940–) also sees capitalism and patriarchy constituting two separate but related sources of oppression for women, but believes patriarchy is rooted in the unconscious rather than in the household. Mitchell's approach is rather controversial in feminist circles because she sees the universality of patriarchy not as a consequence of ubiquitous domestic or sexual relations in human life, but as part of the process of the formation of the female psyche. She uses Freudian ideas to claim that women develop a sense of self that allows their domination by men, but that this process takes place at an unconscious level, rather than by overt ideological manipulation. This can make its alteration a matter for psychoanalysis rather than political action (Mitchell, 1975).

Anti-essentialism

One of the commonest objections to all these Marxist-feminist and radical feminist approaches is that they are based on the assumption that all women experience the world in the same way. The view seems to be that women can be classed together and theorized about en masse, as if there is an essence to *all* women's lives. Black feminists in particular object to this, arguing that it commits the same kind of error as gender-blind, male-oriented sociological theorizing. This is also the point of departure for post-structuralist feminists.

Black feminism

Black feminists point out that while gender may be the main source of oppression experienced by white, middle-class women, black women are typically oppressed by their race and class as well. This means that white feminist theorizing often misses the mark so far as black women's lives are concerned. What is a source of oppression for white women may be a source of liberation for blacks; whereas the family can be the principal instrument of subordination for white women, it can be a haven from a racist outside world for blacks. White women are often the racist oppressors, which hardly equates with the concept of 'sisterhood' – women's solidarity. When white women talk of the need to expand opportunities for women to work in the labour market in order to liberate themselves from the stranglehold of domesticity, they do not usually mean the kind of work many black women are *forced* to do, since most black women are working class. Again, when white women clamour for the 'right to choose' – the right to have abortions – this hardly makes sense to some Third World black women, who live in societies characterized by enforced terminations and sterilizations and the use of drugs like Depo-Provera. For them, it is the right to *keep* their fertility that is at stake. Finally, the preoccupation with sexuality among some white feminists is profoundly irrelevant for many women in the Third World, where poverty and starvation and a lack of education are ubiquitous; there is not much point concentrating your energies on orgasms if you have no food, shelter or medicine.

Post-structuralist feminism

We will look at the ideas of post-structuralism in detail in chapter 9. For our purposes here, it is sufficient to explain that post-structuralism is particularly interested in the role of language in social life, and how the meanings of the words we learn are important influences on how we see the world and make judgements about it. In the case of post-structural feminism, this interest has led its proponents to explore the implications of the use of the category 'women' in feminist analysis. In practice this means questioning whether feminism is correct to claim it speaks on behalf of all the human beings who are called women. If using the term masks, and therefore leaves unexplored, important differences between different kinds of women then feminism is falling short of its professed intent, to attend to the needs of *all* women.

Judith Butler (1956–) is a post-structuralist feminist who has argued this sort of case. According to Butler (1990), problems arise if we assume that being called a woman indicates a life being led in a common set of circumstances and with a common set of experiences. Furthermore, there are also problems if it is assumed that 'women' all have a similar sense of themselves – that all women share a common identity. Butler is critical of feminism for making both these assumptions. She points out that while it is useful at times to highlight the common interests of women over a specific issue, for example, over the question of equal pay, assumptions of a shared core identity between women usually backfires on feminism. Once feminism claims to be speaking for all women, a process of resistance and division almost always sets in among the very women feminism is supposed

Judith Butler

to be unifying. For example, feminist attempts to isolate a common experience of maternity among women served merely to draw out the differences between them on this issue. It is not difficult to see why, as Butler points out: 'Surely all women are not mothers; some cannot be, some are too young or too old to be, some choose not to be, and for some who are mothers, that is not necessarily the rallying point of their politicisation in feminism' (Butler & Scott (eds), 1992, p. 15).

Butler suggests that rather than trying to make the category of women the fixed point at the centre of feminism, feminist theory should encourage a flexible, open-ended exploration of what it means to be a woman. In this light, different experiences and attitudes among women are valued as sources of richness and diversity that help to empower, rather than undermine, feminism.

Further Reading

Abbott, Pamela and Wallace, Claire: *An Introduction to Sociology: feminist perspectives*, Routledge, 1990.

Barrett, Michèle: *Women's Oppression Today: problems in Marxist feminist analysis*, Verso, 1988.

Bouchier, David: *The Feminist Challenge*, Macmillan, 1983.

Brownmiller, Susan: *Against Our Will*, Penguin, 1976.

Butler, Judith: *Gender Trouble*, Routledge, 1990.

Butler, Judith and Wallace Scott, Joan (eds): *Feminists Theorise the Political*, Routledge, 1992.

Davis, Angela Y.: *Women, Race, and Class*, Random House, 1981.

Delphy, Christine: *Close to Home: a materialist analysis of women's oppression*, Hutchinson, 1984.

Dworkin, Andrea: *Pornography: men possessing women*, Women's Press, 1981.

Firestone, Shulamith: *The Dialectic of Sex*, Cape, 1971.

Freedman, Jane: *Feminism*, Open University Press, 2001.

Friedan, Betty: *The Feminine Mystique*, Dell, 1974.

Hartmann, Heidi: 'The Unhappy Marriage of Marxism and Feminism: Towards a More Progressive Union', in Lydia Sargant (ed.), *Women and Revolution*, Pluto, 1981.

Hill Collins, Patricia: *Black Feminist Thought: knowledge, consciousness, and the politics of empowerment*, Unwin Hyman, 1990.

hooks, bell: *Ain't I a Woman? Black women and feminism*, South End Press, 1981.

hooks, bell: *Yearning: Race, Gender, and Cultural Politics*, South End Press, 1990.

Jackson, Stevi (ed.): *Women's Studies: a reader*, Harvester, 1993.

Jaggar, Alison, M.: *Feminist Politics and Human Nature*, Harvester, 1983.

James, Joy and Sharpley-Whiting, T. Denean (eds): *The Black Feminist Reader*, Blackwell, 2000.

Kelly, Liz: *Surviving Sexual Violence*, Polity, 1988.

Lovell, Terry (ed.): *British Feminist Thought: a reader*, Blackwell, 1990.

Marshall, Barbara, L.: *Engendering Modernity*, Polity, 1994.

Millett, Kate: *Sexual Politics*, Virago, 1977.

Mitchell, Juliet: *Psychoanalysis and Feminism*, Penguin, 1975.

Mitchell, Juliet and Oakley, Ann: *What is Feminism?* Blackwell, 1986.

Nicholson, Linda, J. (ed.): *Feminism/Postmodernism*, Routledge, 1990.

Oakley, Anne: *Sex, Gender and Society*, Maurice Temple Smith, 1972.

Oakley, Ann and Mitchell, Juliet: *Who's Afraid of Feminism? Seeing through the backlash*, Penguin, 1997.

Putnam Tong, Rosemarie: *Feminist Thought: A More Comprehensive Introduction*, Westview Press, 1998.

Richards, Janet Radcliffe: *The Skeptical Feminist*, Routledge, 1980.

Rogers, Mary, F. (ed.): *Contemporary Feminist Theory: a text/reader*, McGraw-Hill, 1998.

Stanko, Elizabeth: *Intimate Intrusions: women's experience of male violence*, Routledge, 1985.

Thompson, Denise: *Radical Feminism Today*, Sage, 2001.

Walby, Sylvia: *Theorizing Patriarchy*, Blackwell, 1990.

6 INTERPRETIVE SOCIOLOGY: ACTION THEORIES

Introduction

In our earlier discussion of action theory in chapter 1, we emphasized how the behaviour of human beings must be seen as the product of how they interpret the world around them. It is not that behaviour is *learned* or *determined*, as structural theories suggest. Rather, it is *chosen* as appropriate behaviour in the light of how people define the situations they encounter – what they take social settings to *mean*.

But a question we did not consider earlier is this: how far does this process of interpretation, which, according to action theorists, is always the origin of behaviour, affect other people involved in these meaningful encounters? This is clearly important. As we said in chapter 1, most of the situations in which we find ourselves are inevitably *social* situations – they involve other people doing things. Nearly every time we interpret meaning in order to decide how to act we are interpreting the actions of other human beings.

Symbolic interactionism

Symbolic interactionism (SI) is the name given to one of the best-known action theories. It is with symbolic interactionism that the phrases, 'definition of the situation', 'reality is in the eye of the beholder' and, 'if men define situations as real, they are real in their consequences' are most usually associated. Though rather cumbersome, the name given to this perspective does clearly indicate the kinds of human activity which its proponents consider essential to concentrate on in order to understand social life. According to SI theorists, social life literally is the 'interaction of humans via the use of symbols'. That is, they are interested in:

- the way in which humans employ symbols of what they mean in order to communicate with one another (an orthodox interpretive interest)
- the effects that the interpretations of these symbols have on the behaviour of parties during a social interaction.

SI stresses that *inter*action is a two-way interpretive process. We must not only understand that someone's action is a product of how he or she interpreted the behaviour of someone else, but that this interpretation will have an impact on the actor whose behaviour has been interpreted in certain ways too. One of the major contributions of symbolic interactionism to action theory has been to elaborate and explain the different kinds of effects that the interpretations of others can have on the social identities of the individuals who are the objects of these interpretations.

The construction of self-image

The most common effect is that we use the interpretations of others – what they take our behaviour to mean – as evidence of who we think we are. That is, our self-image – our sense of identity – is a product of the way others think of us. In effect, it is a case of 'I am what I think you think I am.' For SI this is largely what socialization means. It is not, as structural theorists argue, a process whereby given, external, cultural rules are generally internalized by people. It is an outcome of the interpretive process – the allocation of meaning between people – that for action theorists is at the root of all social interaction. Our personalities are constructed by means of this interpreting process as follows.

During the course of our lives, we encounter a number of people, all of whom take our behaviour towards them to symbolize something about our selves. They interpret our behaviour in the light of the evidence they are provided with. They then act towards us in the light of this interpretation, indicating via the symbolic means available to them what kind of person they have decided we are. The image we have of ourselves is crucially influenced by the reactions of individuals we come into contact with. We cannot ignore what kind of person others are telling us we are; the image of our 'self' is seriously affected, if not created, by the image others have of us.

Take, for example, the relationship between a primary school teacher and his/her class. Being human, the teacher cannot help but make judgements about the children in the class, particularly about their ability. Equally, according to SI, since the children are human too, their view of themselves and their abilities will be influenced by the judgement of the teacher. So the little boy who sits attentively at the front of the class, behaves well and is keen and conscientious, is likely to be thought of as 'intelligent' or 'able'. In contrast, the girl sitting at the back of the class, who appears inattentive and lazy, is less favourably interpreted.

SI argues that often what matters is not whether the interpretations are correct, but the impact they can have on their recipients. In this case, even though the children are in fact of the same ability, the teacher has decided they are not, and as a result treats them differently. The little boy is encouraged to work, whereas the little girl is merely admonished for misbehaviour and kept under control. These different reactions of the teacher influence the way the children see themselves. Sustained by the support and encouragement of the teacher, the little boy works hard and fulfils his potential. Persuaded by the teacher that she has little academic ability, the girl concentrates on misbehaving. The teacher's judgements are thus confirmed; the prophecy about the children's abilities comes true. The justice of the interpretations matters less than the consequences of their application, particularly in the way the recipients are encouraged to see themselves.

The fortuity of the outcome of this process of interaction between interpreter and interpreted is plain to see. Our 'self' – the person we become – depends upon the particular people we happen to encounter in our journey through life. Other parents, friends, acquaintances, and workmates could make us into very different people. In our example, a different teacher might have encouraged both children equally, with much more positive consequences for the little girl's self-image.

Social acting: the presentation of self in everyday life

But the influence of the interpretations of others is only one half of the process of interaction emphasized by SI. Far from human personality being simply the passive construction of others, SI stresses the active role which humans play in the creation of their social selves. According to SI, since we soon come to learn that others will interpret our behaviour, our own interpretive abilities allow us to manipulate these interpretations to suit our vision of ourselves. We use our capacity to be self-reflexive in order to present the person we wish others to think we are. We play roles in a creative way to elicit from others the responses we desire. In effect, we manage, or orchestrate, the responses of others by presenting the image of our self that we wish them to hold. We become actors on the stage of life, writing our own lines.

The SI theorist most commonly associated with this emphasis on creative role-playing is **Erving Goffman** (1922–82). In *The Presentation of Self in Everyday Life* (1969), Goffman outlines his conception of social life as a stage upon which humans play themselves, and explains the social props that are pressed into service to present these selves to others. According to Goffman, very few human attributes, possessions or activities are not used in this theatrical way. The clothes we wear, the house we live in, the way we furnish it, the way we walk and talk, the work we do, and the way in which we spend our leisure time – in fact, everything that is public about ourselves can be, and is, used to tell others what kind of person we are. We thus 'manage' the information we provide for others. We control our dress, appearance and habits to encourage others to see us as the people we want them to see us as being.

For Goffman and his fellow interactionists then, socialization is usually about the triumph of the creative capacities of the individual over the reactions of others. Not all action theorists agree, however. *Labelling theory* is a perspective that has grown out of symbolic interactionism. Labelling theory is less interested in the ways in which people are able to influence others' interpretations of themselves than in the kinds of interaction where no such opportunities exist. Labelling theorists are mainly interested in the fact that sometimes people are victims, often helpless, of the interpretations, or *labels*, of others to such an extent that their social identities can be imposed upon them, even against their will. Why should this happen? Why should we find ourselves in social situations where we cannot manipulate the interpretations of others?

Labelling theory

Labels which contradict the self-image

Sometimes we are in no position to protest against misinterpretation, because we are dead. For example, as already briefly discussed in chapter 1, a verdict of suicide depends on the interpretations of a range of people – kin, friends, police officers and, in particular, coroners. Though bodies often indicate the truth, everything eventually depends on others' interpretations.

Sometimes we *can* protest against a wrong label, but this cuts no ice with our interpreters. For example, it is the public labelling of a person as a shoplifter in court, and later on in the local press, that will be the evidence others will go on, not our protestations of innocence. In any case, sometimes these protestations are merely seen as confirmation of the appropriateness of the label. For example, if you are diagnosed as being mentally ill even though you consider yourself perfectly sane, it is likely that you will make a considerable fuss about the prospect of being sent to a mental hospital. Normal though this reaction may be from your point of view, the danger is that your angry or excitable behaviour will be seen by others as confirmation that you are unbalanced. 'After all, no *normal* person would get into that state.' Finally, even if we rise above the interpretations of others and attempt to ignore what we consider a wrong label and act normally, it is perfectly possible that this can simply serve to confirm its justice to others as well. For example, when you are diagnosed as mentally ill, if you *don't* make a fuss and act as normally as possible in order to prove your sanity, this too may simply be interpreted as confirmation of your diagnosed condition. 'After all, no *normal* person would just *sit* there like that.'

Goffman's classic interactionist account of hoarding behaviour among mental patients in *Asylums* (1968) is a very good example of the confirmatory character of 'normal' behaviour once the 'abnormal' label has been applied. Hoarding is a very common feature of the behaviour of patients in mental hospitals. All sorts of apparently useless and trivial objects – like pieces of string, cigarette butts and toilet paper – are constantly in the possession of many of the inmates, who steadfastly refuse to let them out of their sight for a moment. The usual interpretation of this behaviour serves to confirm the label attached to the patient. It is argued that it is obviously abnormal to have such worthless items permanently about one's person and such hoarding can only be a reflection of considerable and deep-seated anxieties and emotional instability.

Goffman disputes this analysis, arguing that it only seems appropriate from the standpoint of life outside the mental hospital, where such 'useless' items are always available. Inside the institution, however, where, for the inmate, they are much more difficult to come by, it makes very good sense to look after them very carefully. Furthermore, since mental hospital patients tend to lack both privacy and storage facilities, an obvious place to keep them secure is about one's person.

Labelling theory argues that sometimes the process of labelling can be so overwhelming that even the victims of misinterpretation cannot resist its impact. Faced with a persistently applied label, the self-image of the labelled person can crumble. He or she comes to see himself or herself anew, embracing the alternative image others have applied. As in the earlier effects of labelling, the correctness, or 'truth', of the label has little to do with the power of its impact. Right or wrong in *fact*, its application and the reactions of others to its existence make it true. Once again, the prophecy is fulfilled, but in this case it becomes the reality for both the beholder and the beheld.

The alteration of self-image

The identification of this process has been a feature of the application of labelling theory to deviance – the area where it has probably been most influential. One of its most significant contributions to the study of deviant behaviour has been to show that the identification of deviance is a product of the interpretation of a particular individual in a particular social setting (as is all labelling). It has also shown that the reactions of others to a labelled deviant are sometimes so severe that they can produce a dramatic alteration in an already established self-image.

Edwin Lemert (1912–96) has provided a famous account of the social construction of paranoia (1967) that demonstrates both these aspects of labelling very clearly. Paranoia is a mental condition in which the sufferer imagines he or she is being persecuted by a conspiracy. However, as Lemert points out, if paranoia is suspected in somebody then such a conspiracy actually does come into being. The 'ill' person is observed secretly. Since mentally disturbed people do not know what is good for them and can act irrationally, attempts to organize treatment will also be clandestine. For example, visits to doctors and psychiatric hospitals will be organized behind the patient's back. Any suspicion on the part of the suspected paranoid that this sort of thing is going on will, naturally enough, lead him or her to complain about it. Normal though such resentment may be from the labelled person's standpoint, in the eyes of its applicators this will merely serve to confirm the justice of the label. Clearly, here *is* someone who believes he or she is being conspired against by others. The fact that this is actually what *is* happening won't deter the labellers from having their judgement confirmed.

Such confirmation may lead to a stay in a mental hospital for treatment. It is at this stage in the construction of paranoia that persons so labelled experience the most sustained pressure on their self-images. Lemert argues that however certain they are of their sanity prior to institutionalization, organizational confirmation of the 'insane' label, particularly by means of deliberate attempts to change behaviour, might well seriously damage the inmates' previously held self-images. The suspicion may grow that perhaps everyone else was right all along and that they *were* too ill to appreciate their condition. After all, why else would they be in hospital? For the labellers of such people, particularly the psychiatric staff, this stage of self-image alteration – an acknowledgement of the need for treatment – is the first major step en route to a cure. The fact that it might simply be the *last* stage in the *social* construction of a mental condition, which began not with any real illness, but with an initial labelling by others is, of course, not considered. The impact which organizational labelling is designed to have on the construction of social personality and, particularly, on the creation of a new self-image, has been powerfully articulated by Goffman.

Goffman and institutionalization

According to Goffman the official treatment of many kinds of deviant behaviour in organizations set up for the purpose, is, as in the case of mental illness, a quite self-conscious attempt to alter the deviant's self-image, so that he or she may become more amenable to 'cure'. In a celebrated account of what he calls *'total institutions'* (1968) Goffman advances the view that establishments like prisons, concentration camps and mental hospitals, where labelled deviants are completely incarcerated over considerable periods, are essentially agencies of resocialization. His argument is not confined to the treatment of deviants, since he claims that the same principles underpin the rigorous training undergone by, for example, soldiers and the members of some religious orders. However, the involuntary nature of the deviants' membership of such institutions makes any successful alteration to their self-images particularly noteworthy.

Goffman (1968) defines total institutions as: 'places of residence and work where a large number of like-situated individuals cut off from the wider society for an appreciable period of time, together lead an enforced, formally administered round of life'. He argues that in such establishments, the organization of life is deliberately designed to strip the inmate of his or her self-image and replace it with one more acceptable to the ethos of the institution. He calls this process **'institutionalization'**. For example, he says, admission procedures are often designed to remove all visible symbols of the inmate's former self and replace them with indications of the new person he or she is to be trained to be. Thus, names are often replaced by numbers (as in prisons, concentration camps and military establishments), or by new names (as in religious orders). The inmate's physical appearance is sometimes altered as visibly as possible; clothing is often removed on entry and replaced with institutional uniforms, and hair is cut in a severe fashion. Since the acquisition of possessions may be frowned upon and made difficult, all or most personal property is often confiscated on entry. Personal space may be denied, even for the most private of activities. In these ways, and in others, says Goffman, inmates are stripped of the props by which they retained a sense of their former selves and were able to communicate this to others.

Furthermore, attempts to alter the self-image of the inmate can be reinforced by its debasement, in ritual and other ways – a process Goffman calls the **'mortification of the self'**. For example, new inmates may have to undergo humiliation upon entry, such as strip-searching (in prison) or ritual ablution (in mental hospital). During their incarceration inmates are often obliged to behave in the most obsequious and obedient manner towards the institution's staff, sometimes in the face of provocation. Such degradations, often in public, are designed, argues Goffman, to kill off the former self of the inmate, to render it soiled and thereafter unusable, and to encourage its replacement by a new identity, more suitable to meet the demands of the institution.

Though labelling theorists would normally expect such processes to prove irresistible to their recipients, Goffman is true to his interactionist principles. Believing that social identities are not just imposed on people but are created and recreated as a two-way interpretive process, Goffman stresses not only the impact of institutionalization but the capacity of inmates to resist or adjust to the processes to which they are subjected to a greater or lesser degree. He talks of those who do become 'colonized', or institutionalized, preferring life in the institution to life outside, or of those who become 'converted', acquiescing to the staff's view of the model inmate and acting out the role to the limit. He also talks of inmates who protect their selves by withdrawing from interaction with others, or who do so by actively rebelling against the institution, as well as of those (the majority, in Goffman's view) who 'play it cool' – who stay out of trouble and maintain their self-image by playing whatever reactive role circumstances demand.

If some labelling involves victimization of the kind we have been discussing, then labelling theory argues that we have to ask a further, final question – where do these victims come from? For example, why do some people come to be labelled as mentally ill and not others? Why do certain children come to be labelled as uneducable, and not others?

For labelling theorists the answer lies not in any reality of different mental conditions or levels of intelligence. Rather, it lies in the origin of the perception of these attributes by others. The focus is on the reasons for these kinds of labels being attached to certain kinds of people, rather than on any characteristics the victims of these labels may or may not possess. The interesting question is therefore not 'How did these people get like this?' but 'Why did *these* people come to be labelled like this, and not others?

The usual labelling theory answer to these questions is that the application of such labels is ultimately about the exercise of power. According to labelling theory the most damaging labels in social life – those of *deviant* – usually become attached to the most helpless and least powerful members of society, those least capable of fighting back and resisting the process. This analysis of deviant labelling as a reflection of the exercise of power is described by Howard Becker, one of its leading exponents, as a process where the 'underdogs' in a society become victims of its 'overdogs' (1967).

This is a feature of labelling approaches to deviant behaviour in general; deviants are generally seen as victims, not as wrongdoers. It is particularly evident in the typical labelling analysis of crime. Crime is seen exclusively as a product of labelling, and of the all-pervading impact that the allocation of such a label can have. Labelling theory sees the relationship between labellers and labelled in this area of social life as essentially one of power. Quite contrary to the conventional view, then, victims are the underdogs who are made into criminals, whereas wrongdoers are the more powerful overdogs who impel the powerless down a never-ending spiral of criminal deviance.

Labelling theory and crime

Labelling theorists argue that there are two fundamental questions which have to be asked about crime:

- Why do some human activities come to be made illegal and not others?
- Why do some people become criminals and not others?

According to labelling theory, the answers to both these questions reflect the distribution of power in society. Not only are the powerful able to designate those acts which are illegal in a society, they are also able to influence who gets labelled as a criminal. Labelling theory argues that although we might like to think that laws are somehow God-given or quite definitely in everyone's best interest, things are not quite as cosy as this. They stress that we have to recognize that the construction of legal rules is a political act. The decision that *this* action should be allowed, whereas another should not, is made by those humans who have the power to decide. Furthermore, 'the powerful' in this regard does not simply mean the actual law-makers, but also individuals or groups who are able to influence the law-makers – those people in a society whom Becker calls its 'moral entrepreneurs'.

Because of the relationship between power and the construction of legal rules, it is not surprising, say labelling theorists, that the acts that are not illegal in a society tend to be the acts in which the powerful engage. So, although it is perfectly possible to imagine a society in which it is illegal to inherit wealth, or profit from rent, or exploit black labour in South African mines, or avoid paying taxes, yet legal to smoke marijuana, make homosexual advances in public, and engage in 'adult' activity at a much younger age than eighteen, this is not how things are. Laws reflect the distribution of power in that the less powerful are more likely to engage in those activities which the laws prohibit.

You might consider this a rather far-fetched view. After all, what about laws prohibiting tax evasion, the placement of contracts by public officials in return for reward, company fraud, or the monopolization of production? Labelling theory grants that of course there are some laws which particularly affect the activities of, say, the wealthy, but it argues that these tend to be the laws that are the least strenuously enforced. And even if they are vigorously enforced they tend to be the laws least likely to furnish a successful prosecution, because of the resources available to the powerful to defend themselves. In effect then, the SI position is that the role of power in the construction of crime is not just restricted to the definition of illegal acts, but influences the investigation of crime too. And nowhere is this latter influence more apparent than in the selection of the individual criminal to prosecute – in the labelling of a particular person's actions as illegal.

Law-breaking

Why should some people be labelled as criminals and not others? The obvious answer to this is that only some people choose to commit crime. From this point of view, the job of any explanation of criminality – sociological, psychological or biological – is to discover what it is about these kinds of people that led them down the criminal path. For labelling theory, however, things are not as straightforward as this, primarily because such an analysis ignores the huge discrepancy between the number of crimes committed and the number of criminals convicted.

Research demonstrates without doubt that the incidence of criminal activity bears little relation to the number of crimes known to the police (the CKP index), and even less to the number of crimes for which the police get a conviction (the 'clear-up' rate). The degree to which the official statistics underplay the real level of crime depends on the particular category of crime. Almost all cars that are stolen are reported, since it is the only way owners can receive compensation from insurance companies. Probably for the same reason (because more private property is now insured than before), the number of burglaries reported has increased. But other property crimes have much lower reporting rates. For example, very few acts of vandalism are reported, and it is estimated that probably only 1 per cent of all shoplifting offences are reported. Why should this be? Many crimes, such as vandalism, are not reported because of their petty nature. Yet even many violent crimes go unreported – only about 20 per cent of all woundings, sexual attacks and robberies are reported, for example. The main reason for this low rate seems to be the young age of many of the victims and their lack of faith either in the way the police will handle the complaint, or in the capacity of the police to solve the crime. Studies have also shown that even when crimes are reported to the police they are not always recorded. The reasons for this include overwork, doubts about the validity of the allegations and the temptation to improve the clear-up rates by not including insoluble crimes.

As well as such victim surveys, self-report studies also illustrate the wide gap between the commission of crime and the CKP index and the even wider gap between commission and clear-up. Such studies ask people to volunteer their past illegal actions under a guarantee of absolute confidentiality. They reveal that anything between 50 per cent and 90 per cent of people admit some kind of illegal behaviour that could result in a court appearance if detected. Even more significant, they also indicate that criminal activity is distributed across all sections of society. They show that crimes are just as likely to be committed by the middle class as the working class, and they certainly demonstrate the error of assuming that crime is more likely to be concentrated in the lower strata of the class structure. Yet this is precisely what the official conviction statistics – of crimes cleared up by the police – *do* indicate. The overwhelming impression from these figures is that crime is mainly committed by young, urban working-class males. Why should this be? If, as self-report studies indicate, crime is committed by no particular kind of person, why do only certain kinds of people get caught?

The labelling theory answer, of course, is that only certain kinds of people are likely to be *labelled* as criminal. Being human, police can only take action against acts and people they *perceive* as breaking the law. That is why certain kinds of people become criminals. It is not because they are the only people who have committed crimes. Indeed it is not even because they necessarily *have* committed any crime at all. It is simply because they have been interpreted as having done so. But why is there such a distinctive pattern to these interpretations? Labelling theorists argue that the perceptions of the police inevitably emanate from the stereotypes of criminals with which they and other agents of law enforcement operate. Why stereotypes should prevail in law enforcement is clear enough. If, as self-report studies show, criminal activity is distributed equally throughout any population, then whatever stereotype of the 'typical criminal' you choose to operate, your judgement is going to be vindicated. So, the next important question is: why have some stereotypes come to prevail in the pursuit of crime and not others?

According to labelling theory, we need look no further for our answer than at the distribution of power in society. In the same way that the powerful are able to influence the designation of certain acts as illegal rather than others, they are also able to encourage certain perceptions of the criminal – advantageous to themselves – to prevail. So although the official conviction statistics tell us very little about the actual distribution of crime in society, they do tell us much about the kinds of people policemen and other law enforcers are most likely to label as criminal. In turn, this tells us about the kinds of influences on stereotypes employed in law enforcement that the powerful have been able to bring to bear. The picture painted by the conviction statistics makes this clear. The chances of matching up to the stereotypes typically employed in law enforcement decrease as a person moves up the social hierarchy. According to Bilton et al. criminal labels await the least advantaged members of society because they are powerless:

> We should not be surprised to find blacks and working-class people over-represented in the official statistics of crime, since they and their

behaviour are more likely to fit law-enforcement agencies' perceptions of 'criminals' and 'crime', and they are less likely to be able to mobilise the material and social resources necessary to convince others that 'they're not like that'. (Bilton et al., 1981, p. 595)

Of course, once the powerless receive their labels, the self-fulfilling prophecy just referred to will come into effect. The successful application of the stereotype will mean that its validity is confirmed for its users and it can be employed with even more conviction in the future. The process of criminal labelling thus increases the chances of the least powerful becoming criminals and decreases the chances of the most powerful. In this way, inequalities of power in society are cemented by the process of law enforcement. Furthermore, once the stereotype is applied and the label attached, the existence of the label promotes the usual self-fulfilling prophecy so far as any particular individual actor is concerned. Others react to the label in such a way that makes future 'normal' activity very difficult. Because of a conviction, other people may ostracize the labelled person or treat him or her with suspicion. Occupational opportunities may also become unavailable, and so on. The stigma of being branded a criminal overwhelms all other attributes; something someone is supposed to have *done* becomes what he or she *is*. Because of the reactions of others to the stigma of the label, the labelled person – whether guilty or innocent in fact – is, according to labelling theory, often impelled into pursuing the 'career' of a criminal, simply because all other normal options are closed down. Obviously, this process of being forced into a deviant career by the reactions of others – known as *deviance amplification* – is not as immediately problematic for the self as, say, the misinterpretation of mental illness. After all, one usually knows whether one was guilty of an offence or not. Nevertheless, it can still mean that the labelled person's self-image is in danger of alteration, especially if the opportunities for a 'normal' existence are sufficiently restricted. Lacking any choice, labelled persons come to see themselves as the people they have been forced to become.

Structure versus action: the analysis of crime

In an area such as crime, therefore, structural and action assumptions meet head on. Pursuing the external determinants of any social activity located in the social structure, the structural theorist looks for the reasons why, as the conviction statistics show, certain kinds of people come to commit criminal acts and some not. Armed with conviction statistics, which feature the urban working-class male above all other categories of person, those giving structural explanations of crime attempt to identify the reasons why a person in this sort of structural location is impelled to commit crime more often than other kinds of person. One of the most popular explanations of this phenomenon is known as *sub-cultural theory*. Here crime is explained as the product of cultural or normative influences. The young working-class male, more often than any other kind of person, finds himself in a cultural setting where criminal activity is normal, and where conformity to such norms via socialization gives rise to law-breaking. The sociological task is therefore to identify those cultural features that promote crime in this kind of social world, and not in others. As in the case of all structural explanations then, the emphasis is on identifying the origins of the *external* social forces whose existence is manifested in the behaviour of individuals.

In contrast, labelling theory's approach to crime features the opposed action theory assumptions about social behaviour. Armed with their evidence – that crime is much more widespread among all social groups than the conviction rates show – labelling theorists are interested not in why young working-class males commit crimes more often than other people, but why they are more likely to be *labelled* as criminals than others. The interesting questions here, therefore, concern the reasons for their behaviour being interpreted as criminal, while that of other people is not. The labelling perspective focuses on the social construction of the reality of crime by the members of a society themselves, rather than on the determining influence on behaviour of a structural reality outside these members.

Yet, as the study of crime also shows, the structural and SI emphases are not as mutually exclusive as they might at first appear. The reason is that SI does not completely embrace an action theory approach to social life. We can see this in two aspects of its explanation of crime. First, the idea of 'stereotypes' in the application of criminal labels refers to generally held views among those whose job it is to enforce the law. Since such generally held views will, for example, be encountered and embraced and therefore perpetuated by new recruits, this is clearly much closer to the structural view of socialization into pre-existing normative definitions than pure action theory allows.

Second, the idea that powerful groups influence both the construction of laws, and the stereotypes of the criminal, is quite close to an orthodox structural perspective. For such a process to take place, particular groups must have the power to exercise influence while others must lack the resources to resist. This vision of social life as being crucially influenced by the unequal distribution of advantage between groups is, of course, a conventional structural-conflict standpoint.

The reason for this apparent contradiction is that sociological theories, especially when put into practice to explain a particular area of social life, are usually neither completely structural, nor completely interpretive. SI is a fairly moderate version of action theory which, while emphasizing the primacy of interpretation in the social construction of reality, does not deny the existence of a fund of commonly held definitions – a common culture, if you like – from which people choose their interpretations. Furthermore, the fact that it insists upon a recognition of the existence of some kind of structure of power and advantage within which the labelling of deviants takes place, also shows that it cannot be seen as adopting a fully fledged, anti-structural position.

In this sense, SI occupies the middle ground between pure structural theory and pure action theory. In fact, as you will discover, most sociological theories are somewhere between these extremes, neither concentrating exclusively on external determinants or on interpretation, but emphasizing one rather than the other. Most definitely at the interpretive extreme, however, is ethnomethodology.

Ethnomethodology

Ethnomethodology pushes the action theory case – that social reality is the creation of actors – to the limit. It rests upon three assumptions:

- social life is inherently precarious; anything could happen in social interaction; however:
- actors never realize this, because
- they unwittingly possess the practical abilities necessary to make the world appear an ordered place.

The primary ethnomethodological interest is rather different from that of other action theorists. Instead of being concerned mainly with the *outcome* of interpretation – the creation of self-image, or the consequences of labelling, for example – it focuses on *how* interpretation is arrived at. Ethnomethodology literally means 'people's methods'. The aim is to reveal the methods used by the participants ('members') in any particular social setting to communicate to each other what they think is going on – what the situation means to them – and the efforts they each make to have this interpretation corroborated by the others. Ethnomethodology is not interested in 'the' social world, but in specific pieces of interaction between its members. The stress is on how order in a social setting is the (unknowing) accomplishment of its participants.

This interest in describing the practical abilities of members derives from a theory of reality called *phenomenology*. Phenomenology emphasizes that things and events have no meaning in themselves. They only mean whatever human beings take them to mean. It stresses that for the members of such a meaningfully created world to live together, meanings must be shared. Members must agree about what things are and social order depends upon shared meanings. Members *do* share meanings. This is because of the way they interpret reality. They do so by using 'commonsense knowledge'. This is embodied in language. Through language we acquire an enormous amount of knowledge about the world, knowledge we can take for granted and which others who speak our language possess too. We have actually experienced only a tiny number of the things that we know about. The rest of the knowledge, shared with other members, is sense that is common to us all. In the words of the founder of phenomenology in sociology, **Alfred Schutz** (1932–98):

> I take it for granted that my action (say putting a stamped and duly addressed envelope in a mailbox) will induce anonymous fellow-men (postmen) to perform typical actions (handling the mail) . . . with the result that the state of affairs projected by me (delivery of the letter to the addressee within reasonable time) will be achieved. (Schutz, 1962, pp. 25–6)

Because members can take for granted this shared knowledge about reality, they can also take for granted the reality it describes. They can assume that the world is a given, objective place. It must be. After all, we all know what it is, and what happens in it.

This concept of shared, commonsense knowledge may sound rather like the consensus theorist's notion of culture. But culture refers to a body of rules which are *obeyed* by actors, thereby producing social order. For the ethnomethodologist commonsense knowledge is *used* by members to create order in a particular situation that would otherwise lack it. Ethnomethodologists define their task as showing how members do this.

Armed with commonsense knowledge and with a confident belief in the factual, ordered character of the world, members can go ahead and make sense of any situation in which they participate. Ethnomethodology stresses that each social situation is unique. The words people utter, the actions they take, are **indexical** – that is, they only make sense on the particular occasion in which they are used. But they also stress that members, unwittingly engaged in identifying order and an objective reality, see things differently. They identify the similarities of an event with other events. They select from all the things happening around them evidence which supports the view that things which exist or which happen are *typical* of the world. For them, a social situation is 'a lecture', 'a dance' or 'a meeting', and a pattern is imposed on it by the application of commonsense knowledge. By commonsense knowledge too, gaps in the accounts of happenings by others are filled in in similar ways by different listeners to reassure themselves that things are as they seem.

In a famous analysis of a two-year-old child's story, ethnomethodologist Harvey Sacks (see Silverman, 1998) gives an example of the way the use of commonsense knowledge can be depended upon to generate the same interpretations. According to Sacks, there is a predictable response upon hearing the two phrases uttered consecutively by the child:

The baby cried.
The mummy picked it up.

We can be assured that, on first hearing the two year old's story, any listener will hear the mummy as the mummy of the baby; will assume a relationship between the two events (that the mummy picked up the baby because it was crying); and that these interpretations will be arrived at without having to know anything about the mummy or the baby or of the two year old who told the story.

As R. J. Anderson says about this example:

The import of this . . . is enormous, for if it is the case that competent users of the English language are able to find the same things from the same fragment of talk, then the methods that are used to do so must be of the highest order of generality. They must be part of the foundations of our common culture. (Anderson, 1979, p. 64)

It is these methods that ethnomethodolgy is interested in. Without realizing it, members use them as they work to create the meaning that they believe occasions or events have. Having done this unwitting work, and having arrived at an interpretation, they then engage in yet more unwitting work to have this confirmed by the corroboration of other participants. The founder of ethnomethodology, **Harold Garfinkel** (1917–) delighted in showing how members identify sense in occasions, even when corroboration from others is actually lacking. This is how Paul Filmer describes a very well-known Garfinkel experiment designed to demonstrate the lengths members will go to create meaning, to discover sense in an occasion, in spite of deliberate efforts to frustrate them:

> Ten undergraduates were asked to participate in research being carried out by a university's department of psychiatry to explore alternative means of psychotherapy. Each was asked to discuss the background to a serious problem on which he wanted advice, and then to address to an experimenter – who had been falsely presented to him as a trainee student counsellor – a number of questions about it which would be amenable to monosyllabic 'Yes' or 'No' answers. The subject and the experimenter/counsellor were physically separated, and communicated by two-way radio. After the answer to each of his questions had been given, the subject was asked to tape-record his comments upon it, out of radio-hearing of the experimenter/counsellor. The subjects were told that it was usual to ask ten questions, and they were, of course, led to believe that they would be given bona fide answers to them. The experimenter/counsellors, however, were given a list of monosyllabic answers, evenly divided between 'yes' and 'no', but whose order had been pre-decided from a table of random numbers. Thus, in this experiment, certain crucial variables of everyday interaction situations had been neutralized: the shared language of subject and experimenter had been reduced to the verbal spoken dimension (intonation, in all probability, would also have been relatively unimportant as an agent of meaning, owing to the distortion of spoken sounds by radio); there was no chance of gestures or physical expressions intervening in the communication process because of the physical separation of subject and experimenter. Also, the possibility of the experimenter/counsellor's answers making sense to the subjects depended entirely on their interpretations of them; indeed, the possibility of answers even being those anticipated by the subjects was reduced to a matter of chance. Garfinkel published two unedited transcripts of the exchanges and of the subjects' comments upon them [see Garfinkel, 1984], plus a detailed explication of his interpretive findings from them. The burden of these is where the random answers to the carefully thought out and phrased questions of the subjects appeared nonsensical, irrational or in some other way inappropriate or unexpected, then the subject reinterpreted them by reformulating what he assumed to be the context of meaning he held in common with the experimenter/counsellor (and which he had attempted to communicate to the experimenter/counsellor by the phrasing and

content of his questions), in order that the latter's responses made sense after all. Even where a succession of plainly contradictory answers engendered the suspicion in the subject that he was being tricked, he appeared reluctant to proceed upon the assumption that this was so. (Filmer et al., 1972, pp. 223–4)

Conclusions

Ethnomethodology is clearly a very different kind of sociology from the others we have been looking at so far in this book. For structural theorists the most significant features of human social life are forces external to the individual actor. To understand social behaviour we have to understand the structural determinants of people's lives. We do this by going beyond our actors' *own* theories of their existence and instead construct expert, objective *observer* theories that explain social structures.

In contrast, for interactionists/labelling theorists, the actor comes to the fore. Whether a person is in control of the interpretations of others, or is a more passive recipient of their labels, the focus is on the capacity for meaningful interaction. To understand social action we must understand the processes of interpretation that give rise to it. We do this by taking advantage of the fact that, just like our subject-matter, we too are human beings. This means we can put ourselves in the place of the other humans in which we are interested, and, by using our ability to empathize – by using *verstehen* – work out how the world must seem to them.

For ethnomethodologists, however, the interest is different. They criticize other sociological approaches for taking for granted what they believe is actually the essence of social life – members' sense-making methods. They also criticize them for their assumption that the use of these methods to produce one human's account of an aspect of reality – a particular social theory, for example – can ever be considered a true, or correct depiction. According to ethnomethodology, calling an account produced by the use of members' methods a 'sociological theory' does not privilege it over non-sociological accounts. Any piece of sociological analysis is just another human account of the world – no better, and no worse, than anybody else's. Just because one particular human analyst is called a sociologist and has produced an account called a theory that is agreed with by some other humans who are also called sociologists means nothing so far as its approximation to truth is concerned. All of us have to produce theories of the world, all the time, just to be able to deal with it and carry on living. There is no yardstick by which these accounts can be judged true or false: they are all equally valid versions of truth arrived at by meaning-attributing human beings. In effect, ethnomethodology is telling conventional sociology that its descriptive, analytical and theoretical aims cannot be achieved – that sociology cannot be done. (As you can imagine, this has not made ethnomethodologists particularly popular with other kinds of sociologists.)

For ethnomethodology, the only thing we can describe with certainty is the one thing we all *do* have in common: the sense-making methods all humans, sociologists or not, have to use to arrive at our respective accounts, and this is what sociology should study. It is thus interested in the practice of making sense of the world, in how members accomplish social life. Though members are always the architects of social order in any social occasion, ethnomethodology believes it cannot tell the truth about *what* they have built by their efforts, only *how* they built it. This is why ethnomethodologists wish to change the focus and interest of the sociological enterprise. Hamstrung by their membership of the social world, they believe sociologists can never provide proven explanations of the causes of social phenomena. However, they can reveal the procedures and methods by which humans make sense of the settings in which they find themselves. Indeed, since sociological research is another example of precisely this activity, the research act itself can be used as data. Though sociologists can never arrive at anything other than a subjective explanation of social life, this does not mean they cannot describe *how* they arrived at this view. In short, instead of *verstehen* being the *instrument* sociology uses to understand and explain actors' meanings, it becomes the *topic* – the object of research – whether used by sociologists or non-sociologists.

Further Reading

Symbolic interactionism

Becker, Howard: *Outsiders: studies in the sociology of deviance*, Free Press, 1967.
Burns, Tom: *Erving Goffman*, Routledge, 1992.
Ditton, Jason: *The View from Goffman*, Routledge, 1980.
Downes, D. and Rock, Paul (eds): *Deviant Interpretations*, Martin Robertson, 1979.
Goffman, Erving: *Asylums*, Penguin, 1968.
Goffman, Erving: *Strategic Interaction*, Blackwell, 1969.
Goffman, Erving: *Stigma: notes on the management of spoiled identity*, Penguin, 1990a.

Goffman, Erving: *The Presentation of Self in Everyday Life*, Penguin, 1990b.

Goffman, Erving et al.: *The Goffman Reader*, Blackwell, 1997.

Manning, Philip: *Erving Goffman and Modern Sociology*, Polity, 1992.

Meltzer, B. N. et al.: *Symbolic Interactionism*, Routledge and Kegan Paul, 1975.

Plummer, Ken: *Modern Homosexualities: fragments of lesbian and gay experiences*, Routledge, 1992.

Rock, Paul: *The Making of Symbolic Interactionism*, Macmillan, 1979.

Rose, A. (ed.): *Human Behaviour and Social Processes*, Routledge and Kegan Paul, 1962.

Wootton, Anthony and Drew, Paul: *Erving Goffman: explaining the interaction order*, Polity, 1988.

Phenomenology and ethnomethodology

Atkinson, J. M.: *Discovering Suicide*, Macmillan, 1978.

Bauman, Zygmunt: *Hermeneutics and Social Science*, Hutchinson, 1978.

Benson, D. and Hughes, J. A.: *The Perspective of Ethnomethodology*, Longman, 1983.

Douglas, Jack: *Understanding Everyday Life*, Routledge and Kegan Paul, 1974.

Filmer, Paul et al.: *New Directions in Sociological Theory*, Collier-Macmillan, 1972.

Garfinkel, Harold: *Studies in Ethnomethodology*, Polity, 1984.

Roche, Maurice: *Phenomenology, Language and the Social Sciences*, Routledge and Kegan Paul, 1973.

Sharrock, W. W. and Anderson, R. J.: *The Ethnomethodologists*, Ellis Harwood, 1986.

Silverman, David: *Harvey Sacks: social science and conversation analysis*, Polity, 1998.

7 MICHEL FOUCAULT: DISCOURSE THEORY AND THE BODY-CENTREDNESS OF MODERNITY

Michel Foucault

© Bettman/CORBIS

Michel Foucault: born Poiters, France, 1926, died Paris, 1984

Major works

Madness and Civilisation (1965)
The Order of Things: An Archaeology of the Human Sciences (1966)
The Archaeology of Knowledge and the Discourse on Language (1969)
The Birth of the Clinic: An Archaeology of Medical Perception (1975)
Discipline and Punish: The Birth of the Prison (1979)
The History of Sexuality, vols 1–2 (1980–5)

Introduction

Michel Foucault is both a sociologist of the body and a post-structural theorist. His version of post-structuralism is usually called **discourse** theory (see Glossary: Discourse (2)). These elements of his work are closely linked since he uses post-structural theory to explain the way in which social and cultural influences on the body define its universal, natural features in different ways, depending on time and place. Of course, sociologists of the body do not deny that the bodies of males and females have the same organic constitution irrespective of the societies in which they live. However, they argue that these natural features mean different things in different cultural settings. According to many such sociologists, this is because people in different social worlds are taught to think differently about their bodies.

Foucault's sociology of the body concentrates on the way in which cultural definitions of normal and abnormal behaviour regulate people's ideas about their bodies and what they should and should not do with them. Furthermore, he believes we can make sense of the presence of these different social rules in different times and places by understanding the wider social and historical contexts in which different kinds of societies are located. He is particularly interested in how and why, in modern societies, the body needs to be managed and regulated in ways not necessary in pre-modernity.

The body in modernity

Foucault suggests that modern societies have two crucial reasons for the systematic regulation of the body:

- the population pressures produced by urbanization
- the needs of industrial capitalism.

The regulation of the individual body – e.g. rules governing sexuality – he calls **anatamo-politics**. The regulation of bodies en masse – e.g. health and safety rules or rules governing physical movement around cities – he calls **bio-politics**.

As a post-structuralist, Foucault is interested in the way in which different forms of knowledge – different versions of what is true and false, right and wrong – produce different ways of life. He uses the term *discourse* to refer to a knowledge-based way of thinking and acting. According to Foucault, the most significant aspect of a society becoming modern is not so much the fact it has a capitalist economy (Marx) or a new form of solidarity (Durkheim) or that it is the outcome and embodiment of rational action (Weber). It is the way in which new forms of knowledge – unknown in pre-modernity – emerge. For him, it is these new discourses that define modern life.

Discourse theory

We acquire discursive knowledge in the same way as we acquire language, and the chances of us resisting this knowledge are as remote as our chances of not learning a particular language as we grow up. This is not the same as *repressive* power (the exercise of power to stop us doing things), though. It is the exercise of power to *enable* us to be human (rather than remaining merely animals), and possess the knowledge we need to attach meaning to our experiences. Just as the child is only able to become properly human through learning some language or other, so we are only able to know truth and falsehood, right and wrong, as a result of the influence of discourses of some kind or other. However, this does not mean we can therefore claim to know things for certain. We are only able to know the truths provided for us by our discourses; we are clearly hamstrung and restricted by the particular discourses we encounter. Just as a child has no choice about the language(s) it has to learn as it grows, so we have no choice about the particular knowledge about the world we have to acquire. To put this another way, for Foucault, it is through the discourses that dominate a time in history and a place in the world that people acquire their mind-set, or world-view. This way of looking at things provided by discourse Foucault calls an **'epistème'**.

So, for Foucauldians, if you want to understand human behaviour in a particular place and time, find out the discourses that dominate there. And if you want to know why particular discourses came to power, be a sort of social archaeologist: trace the origins of a way of knowing by deconstructing it and examining the foundations on which its rise to power rested. We will look more closely at these ideas in the next chapter.

Discourses and modernity

Powerful discourses whose function is bio-political – the management and regulation of bodies en masse – come into being as part of the development of modernity. For example, planning and planners begin to organize the utilization of urban areas, while transport experts emerge to regulate the movement of bodies through space. Penology and penologists provide the knowledge base for the management and punishment of criminal bodies: prisons confine and control such bodies. Demographers devise instruments to gain knowledge of the characteristics and attributes of large populations; if you are reading this book, you probably already know something about that ubiquitous aspect of modern life – the social survey. Theories of education promulgated by educationalists inform the management and discipline of immature bodies in the schools in which they are confined. All of these are modern forms of knowledge deemed necessary to control and police the accumulation, concentration and congregation of bodies in modern environments. The exercise of such knowledge, argues Foucault, is the exercise of a certain kind of power – bio-politics. However, for him, the most important discourses in modernity are those which regulate both the social body and the individual body. According to Foucault, Western medicine provides us with the best example of a modern form of knowledge that exercises both considerable bio-power and anatamo-power.

Bio-medicine

To understand life in modernity, says Foucault, you only need to realize the huge extent to which we modern humans have become subject to the power of medical definitions of normality and deviance – that is, the extent to which we are so preoccupied with our bodily health. According to Foucault, the power of notions of health and illness in our lives is analogous to the power of notions of good and evil in the lives of pre-modern humans. Foucault characterizes the exercise of a discourse's power as a form of *surveillance* to ensure the conformity of a population to particular notions of truth and falsehood, good and bad. He concocted the idea of the *gaze* of a discourse and its enforcers to represent this. Thus he describes the shift from the dominance of religion in pre-modernity to the dominance of medicine in modernity as the emergence of the *Medical Gaze* or the *Clinical Gaze*.

There are a large number of discursive ways in which health and illness are understood by human beings. Why someone should fall ill when others remain well is the question many of these forms of knowledge address. Being bewitched (attacked by witchcraft); having affronted a deity; being punished for a misdeed in this or another life; being unable or reluctant to behave appropriately in relationships with others; being unable to cope with the stresses and difficulties of everyday living – all these kinds of explanation, and many others, link bodily illness to external causes. The body is the site of an illness of course, but its origins lie elsewhere, and therapies are prescribed accordingly.

In contrast, much Western bio-medicine merely treats the physical/bodily symptoms rather than the origins of illness; it concentrates on eradicating the disease present in the body rather than on a search for an external cause. This is what distinguishes it from so-called *holistic*, or whole-person therapies which typically understand health and illness in terms of a relationship between the social, the mental, the emotional and the physical – between the mind, the spirit and the body. External causes are recognized by bio-medicine, of course, but they are also usually assumed to be physical, such as viruses, bacteria, tobacco or alcohol. Preventive medicine is therefore also body-centred: eat properly, take exercise, avoid dangerous substances and so on. For most of the time, the kinds of non-physical sources of bodily ill-health presumed to be potential causes by other perspectives – misery, social isolation and loneliness, feelings of helplessness and low self-esteem – are relatively neglected.

How bio-medicine treats illness

The body-centredness of bio-medicine results in a diagnostic and therapeutic regime with which we are all familiar. It is usually the persistence of physical discomfort of some kind or other that leads us to visit a doctor's surgery. During the course of a (usually very short) consultation, the GP – whom we may or may not know – attempts to diagnose our condition by interpreting what is happening to our body. This is achieved in two main ways: first, we try to describe the physical sensations we are experiencing as best we can and second, if deemed necessary, the doctor will physically examine the relevant area of the body by sight, sound and/or touch. If a diagnosis is still difficult, or supporting evidence of the GP's opinion is needed, further tests on the body take place. This usually involves testing blood, urine, stools, saliva, or other bodily products. These and other kinds of highly technical testing can also take place in a hospital – a building and organization designed for the purpose of examining and treating diseased bodies. Hospitalized bodies are either out-patients or in-patients. As out-patients, we attend clinics, where bodies are examined by hospital medics. After examination, we are usually free to leave the building. Confined as an in-patient, the body becomes subject to the hospital regime. We eat, drink, sleep, dress, receive visitors, take medicines, are tested further and undergo surgery as we are told to. The body is under the strict control of the hospital staff; the needs of the organization take precedence over the personal whims and fancies of the person whose body is hospitalized. Indeed, one of the most common criticisms of the management and regulation of hospitalized sick bodies is the **depersonalization** involved. Unless this is specifically addressed, there is always a tendency for large organizations and buildings to demand the rational and efficient control of their populations and this is particularly true of hospitals. For individuals used to a considerable degree of choice in their everyday behaviour, the strict ordering, management, regulation and surveillance involved in hospital life can be difficult to adjust to. To be treated as 'the liver in bed 6'; or as 'a difficult patient' if personal autonomy is insisted upon; or to be given only the minimum information about the treatment one's body is undergoing; or to have to request to do the kinds of things taken for granted in the world outside the hospital; or to be forced to do things one would not normally choose to do can seriously erode feelings of autonomy and **agency** and create a powerful sense of dependency. To have so much attention focused on you as a body rather than you as a person with ideas, feelings and emotions can also lead to feelings of helplessness, isolation and powerlessness – many people's definition of alienation. As we saw in chapter 6, the symbolic interactionist Erving Goffman has provided a famous and telling account of this process, which he describes as 'the mortification of the self' (Goffman, 1968).

The medicalization of modern life

According to Foucault and his followers, the policing power of the medical gaze in modernity can also be seen in the widespread

medicalization of modern life. This term refers to the way in which universally experienced features and functions of human existence are, in modernity, appropriated and commandeered by medicine, defined in terms of its essential categories of health and illness and managed accordingly.

The medicalization of childbirth

Thus, many writers (e.g. Ann Oakley, 1980; 1984; 1993), have pointed to the medicalization of childbirth in modernity – the domineering way that medical discourse demands control over the biological reproduction of children in modern societies. Once conception is confirmed, unless a woman fights hard to resist, medicine routinely and systematically polices and monitors both her body and that of her unborn child throughout the pregnancy. The complaint is that such non-stop technological surveillance and control reduces the mother to merely a body – a reproductive machine – dehumanizing and depersonalizing her experience. In effect, the argument goes, the appropriation of pregnancy and childbirth by medicine defines this most natural of human events as an illness, thus stripping it of what should actually be its essence – a process filled with the wonder and fulfilment that comes from giving the gift of life to another person.

The medicalization of marriage and the family

In many ways, the management of marriage and family life in modernity could also be said to have become heavily medicalized (Cheal, 1991). In times of difficulty, it has become perfectly normal for married couples to turn to quasi-medical experts such as marriage guidance counsellors and sex therapists. Furthermore, family therapy, as the name suggests, is an approach to family problems, particularly popular in the USA, that treats them as 'illnesses', whose symptoms can be eradicated by expert intervention in just the same way as bio-medicine deals with organic disorder.

The medicalization of madness

Other commentators, including Foucault himself (Foucault, 1965; 1975), tell a similar tale about the medicalization of madness. Unhappiness, hopelessness, distress, fear, social estrangement and social marginalization are all inevitable aspects of the human condition and all human worlds deal with them in some way or other. But only in modernity is madness medicalized – defined as mental *illness* and therefore subject to medical intervention, regulation and control. As a society modernizes, psychiatry and psychiatrists emerge to define, police and manage this kind of illness with their ultimate power residing in their ability to confine and control mad bodies in mental hospitals and other places of surveillance.

The medicalization of death

Finally, just as modern humans are brought into the world under the control of medicine, so most of us are also ushered out of it under its supervision, a process known as the medicalization of death. In pre-modern societies, someone's death is seen as much as a com-munity matter – a rent in the social fabric that needs to be repaired – as it is the loss of an individual. A death is therefore handled by the community as a whole, as is shown in the protracted public funeral rites that typically take place. Not so in medicalized modernity. Most of us will either die in hospital or else under medical supervision at home. A death in hospital is in essence a *sequestered* death (Giddens, 1991), hidden away from the public world in which the dying person's life has been lived, deliberately organized so that it is left unobserved and unnoticed except by the hospital staff and close loved ones. For in a body-centred society dedicated to the triumph of the physical, death is an affront. The body – our principal source of identity and the object of so much of our attention while alive in modernity (a central part of modern existence that we go on to discuss in more detail below) – must die. No wonder death must be hidden away: how could we maintain our commitment to the body if its inevitable decay and demise were an ever-present part of the life of the living? No, ageing, frail and incontinent bodies are best kept out of sight during the 'death sequence', in 'old people's homes' and suchlike, and death itself best sequestered away, witnessed only by other sick and dying bodies.

Body-centredness in modernity

Foucault links the rise to power of bio-medicine in modernity to the needs of its characteristic form of production – capitalism. In order for industrial and commodity production to be effective bodies need to be reliably placed in the production process. However, this is not just a matter of the rational organization of bodies. They also need to be fit and healthy so that their productivity can be maximized. According to Foucault, it is therefore unsurprising that modern capitalist societies have the discursive promotion of bodily health as a strong and central cultural feature. Medical ideas about maintaining bodily health and avoiding illness by means of diet, exercise, the avoidance of bad/unhealthy habits such as smoking and drinking all emerge to regulate and discipline the population. In premodern worlds religious prescriptions focus on the soul, stressing the importance of living good, virtuous and sin-free lives in order to achieve salvation in an afterlife. In modernity, in contrast, medical prescriptions focus on the here and now, stressing the importance of 'looking after' oneself physically in order to gain maximum benefit from life on earth.

Body fetishism

Rather as an incoming tide gradually soaks and then covers in water more and more of a beach, so, as discourses become entrenched and gain in influence, they begin to direct more and more of a population's concerns. In a medicalized, body-centred society, people become increasingly obsessed with their bodies. Living a good or happy life becomes not so much about possessing spiritual virtues as physical ones. The moral obligation to be healthy develops beyond the strictly medical – avoiding illness and treating the symptoms of bodily disease when they occur – to advertising the fact as well. How the body appears to others takes on a new importance, with huge implications for consumption and, therefore, production. Body-centred products flood the market place, advertising them is everywhere and shopping for them can verge on the obsessive.

This narcissism does not just result in fatly stocked wardrobes and chests of drawers so that we can clothe our bodies fashionably and to suit every occasion. It also re-defines the function of the bathroom and the bedroom from places in which we clean and rest ourselves to ones in which we adorn and transform ourselves. As well as non-prescribed medicants which, of course, we have been taught to depend upon for our bodily health, the shelves and cupboards of these rooms groan with all manner of lotions, creams, perfumes, conditioners, powders, gels, waxes, deodorants, oils, mascaras, rouges, lipsticks, varnishes, glosses and depilatories. Body fetishism is rampant, fuelled by the beauty industry, the fashion industry, the youth industry, the diet industry and the fitness industry. Nothing matters more than how we look and the resulting obsession with slimming and dieting, working out, looking young and keeping fit reaches its zenith (or nadir) for those wealthy enough to buy the 'benefits' of cosmetic surgery. These days this can extend to women choosing to give birth by caesarean section, so as to minimize the impact on their bodies of being in labour. Among the very rich, there are even cases of surrogate mothers being hired to carry the child conceived by IVF, so that the biological mother's bodily appearance need not be affected by the ravages of pregnancy. Such a discourse is promoted by a panoply of medical and quasi-medical experts. These repositories of modern knowledge range from GPs, hospital consultants and dentists to dieticians, beauty therapists, fitness trainers, hairdressers, chiropodists and so on.

A Marxist would explain this phenomenon as market manipulation by profit-seeking pharmaceutical companies and their promotional allies. Feminists would point to the gendered nature of such body-centred consumption, though the rapidly increasing proportion of males preoccupied with their bodily appearance obvious today raises question marks about such an analysis. But the Foucauldian approach, while acknowledging the partial relevance of such accounts, prefers to see it as fundamentally the inevitable outcome of the penetration of body-centred discursive regulation into the very limits of contemporary human existence. It is traceable back to the rise of body-centred medicine which itself has its foundation in the needs of modernity.

A case study in Foucauldian analysis: female sexuality

In principle, physical sexual urges can be satisfied by all manner of bodily activities. But in all cultures, only some of these activities are considered legitimate; for Foucauldians, that is, all cultures derive their rules about sexuality from the power of some discourse or other. For example, members of societies governed by religious knowledge 'know' that certain forms of sexual activity are good (right) and others evil (wrong). Religious experts are on hand to enforce these rules of normality and deviance and these prescriptions are preached in the pulpit, the confessional or wherever. In secular cultures it is more common for ideas about what is 'natural' and 'unnatural' to provide the knowledge base from which designations of normal and deviant sex are derived. Typically, such discursive regulation is conspicuously gendered; it is usual for male and female bodies to be subject to very different prescriptions regarding sexual activity.

One of the most striking forms of regulation to which only the female body is subject is *Female Genital Mutilation* (FGM). This is a practice which is extraordinarily widespread; according to The World Health Organization (1997), it is estimated that some 130 million women in the world today have had their genitals altered by physical intervention. The mildest form of mutilation involves circumcision – the excision of the clitoris. The most extreme is infibulation – the sewing up of the labia. The consequences of such intervention, in terms of ease of sexual congress, bodily fluid retention and risks to health, are pretty obvious.

How should this sort of practice be understood? While feminists portray it is as a particularly visceral and vicious form of patriarchy, a Foucauldian reading seeks to explain it in a more *materialist* way, by linking it to both the realm of biology and reproduction and to the realm of property production, management and distribution – the economy.

Female sexuality and property transference in pre-modernity

By definition, pre-modern societies lack the institutions of modernity that we take for granted and upon which we depend for our physical, economic and emotional survival. Very often this means living without any form of government, local or central, to order our lives, agencies of law and order to protect us, or welfare agencies to assist us in times of need. It often means living without money or literacy. It also means surviving without the features of capitalism most of us depend upon – for example, without waged work to finance our lives or any kind of profit-dependent organization to sell us the goods and services we need. In such circumstances the basic necessities for existence – safety, security and physical nourishment – need to be acquired in other ways. This is why families – or, more accurately, groups of kin – play such a crucial role. The kin group is the basic unit of survival, providing most of the emotional support, physical protection and access to wealth upon which any individual depends. Because of this, how such groups are formed, reproduced and sustained is of crucial importance. As a result, the role of women and, in particular, their unique physical ability to conceive and give birth, becomes pivotal. Since close blood kin cannot have sex, in order for a kin group to survive and reproduce itself women from other groups need to be brought in. This is why marriage is so important: it allows a man to produce his heirs. Typically, property is owned collectively. Land, crops and animals – the basis of cultivating and pastoral economies – belong to families, not individuals. Economically, a kin group acts as a kind of corporation whose members own wealth in common. Retaining and reproducing this property is clearly crucial but so is its transference through time. 'Keeping it in the family', to use a modern phrase, is a much more serious necessity in pre-modernity. The group's survival (and, to repeat, any individual's survival therefore) depends upon the birth of new generations who will legitimately inherit, and act as the custodians of, its wealth, and who in turn will spawn another generation that will do the same.

A Foucauldian view of FGM argues that the practice needs to be understood in this context. If the point of marriage is so that the husband acquires children to reproduce his kin group and to whom he can transfer his property, rules governing female sexuality are inevitable. Without a woman's virginity guaranteed, a newly married husband could never be sure that the only claimants on his wealth will be his biological children. Equally, without ensuring her fidelity after marriage, the same concern would be present. Brutal and horrific though it is to us, FGM is the mechanism in millions of cases to guarantee a wife's virginity and fidelity, and it reveals the elemental link between physical and economic survival and a woman's body in tribal societies.

In pre-modern Europe where exactly the same link needed enforcing, this role of regulating female sexuality in order to facilitate property transference was undertaken by the Church. Religious ideas about sex and marriage can be seen as a discursive alternative to the physical method of FGM. According to religious teaching, sex outside marriage – fornication – was a sin and the dutiful wife was a woman whose body and reproductive capacities remained the exclusive property of her husband. To thwart this rule would bring eternal damnation. Furthermore, for a woman to be reluctant, or refuse, to live the virtuous life of a wife/mother could bring earthly retribution as well. As Bryan Turner (1995) puts it:

> Women were closely associated with witchcraft, because it was argued that they were particularly susceptible to the sexual advances of the devil . . . Women were seen to be irrational, emotional and lacking in self-restraint; they were especially vulnerable to satanic temptation . . . Between 1563 and 1727, somewhere between 70 and 90 per cent of witchcraft suspects throughout Europe were female . . . The attack on women as witches was primarily a critique of their sexuality. (pp. 88–9)

The medical regulation of female sexuality in modernity

With modernity, and secularization, bio-medicine and bio-medical accounts of bodily illnesses took on the role of regulating the female body, with psychiatry and psychiatrists in the van. Invoking its ever-present natural/unnatural dichotomy, women who resisted medical definitions of a healthy life were in danger of being classed as ill. In some places, having a child out of wedlock could lead to a diagnosis of mental imbalance and disturbance. (There are old women alive today who have been forced to live out their years in mental hospitals on precisely this initial justification.) The desire to explore your sexuality with a number of different male partners – being 'promiscuous' or 'loose' – could well lead you to being diagnosed with nymphomania, an illness of the time, like hysteria, from which only women could suffer. Indeed, at the end of the nineteenth century, medicine had been so influential in linking female sexuality with bodily health that the antidote for hysteria – abnormally neurotic behaviour – could well be a hysterectomy. (The Greek word for womb is hystera.) This treatment reveals much about bio-medical assumptions concerning the relationship between a woman's body and her personality at the time. Only by living a normal, healthy family life – a virgin before marriage, faithful yet productive afterwards – could a woman avoid suspicions of mental or physical illness.

In more recent times, medicine continued to exert its control over women. Although deviant sexuality on the part of men – homosexuality was being treated as an illness in Britain up until the 1960s – could also be seen as evidence of sickness as well as the commission of crime, it was on women's bodies that the Medical Gaze was more sternly directed. Not to want to be married was unnatural. Once married, so was not wanting to have children. Once a biological bond between a woman and her child had been created, medicine ruled that it must be a sign of psychological disturbance not to be able to subordinate all other interests to being a mother. After all, according to medicine, nature takes over once a child has been born; the mother's maternal instinct will guarantee her commitment, her parenting ability and, thereby, the safety and health of her child. To find motherhood difficult, exhausting or unrelentingly stressful was (and to some extent still is) also to invite medical intervention. Often, it is not until the birth of a child that the enormity of the responsibility of being a mother sinks in for a woman, especially in a world where mothers are often isolated from wider kin or other support networks. Asking for help, even if a sensible and practical move, can, in a medical culture, raise suspicions of 'not being able to cope' (mental instability) or, even more alarmingly, evidence of 'post-natal depression'. As with all powerful discourses, the inability to match up to its definitions of normality can bring with it not only the threat of outside intervention but can engender feelings of failure and worthlessness.

Self-surveillance

As Foucault explains, it is this combination of external enforcing and internal self-policing and self-surveillance that gives discourses their irresistible power. As we have seen from our examples, a discourse always has its experts to enforce normality and punish deviance. However, one of Foucault's key points is that it is because, as humans, we constantly assess what we should and should not do in relation to the cultural knowledge we have acquired – because *we police ourselves* – that the delivery of a discursively directed order is ensured. He compares the life of a human being in a discourse-directed world – and there *can* be no other kind – to the life of a prisoner in a panoptican. The panoptican was a prison designed by Jeremy Bentham in 1843. The prison warders were located in a circular tower surrounded by the cells that also formed a circle. The idea was to ensure that the prisoners could never escape surveillance – or, rather, that the prisoners could not guarantee that they were *not* being observed by the warders. This knowledge, Bentham believed, would lead the inmates to obey the prison rules at all times – that is, that they would police themselves and constantly monitor their behaviour – just in case. Though this prison was never built, Foucault used it as a metaphor for self-surveillance in everyday life – a phenomenon he termed **panopticism**. As Foucault describes self-surveillance: 'Just a gaze. An inspecting gaze which each individual under its weight will end by exteriorizing to the point that he is his own overseer, each individual thus exercising this surveillance over and against himself' (Foucault, 1980, p. 155).

However, according to Foucault, no discourse, however dominant, gets away without opposition from competing forms of knowledge forever. Except in very unusual circumstances, resistance to its definitions of truth and falsehood, right and wrong, always eventually emerges. This is particularly so in modern societies where alternative discursive depictions are liable to be publicized and promoted in ways generally extremely unlikely in pre-modern, traditional worlds. Living in modernity is about, among other things, the ventilation of competing ideas, often via electronic means of communication. One of the principal features of globalization is precisely this – the breaking-down of communicative walls between different world-views. Only by cutting off a world from outside influence can a modernized society deny alternative epistemes the oxygen they need to become established and exercise resistance. A good example of this process has been the twentieth-century emergence of feminist resistance to dominant ideas about the female body.

Discursive resistance: feminism and the female body

As we saw in chapter 5, feminism has waged its war against women's oppression and subordination on many fronts. The first wave concentrated on suffrage (votes for women) while the second, from the 1960s onwards, has focused on a range of other issues. For example, Marxist-feminism has attacked capitalism for its exploitation of women's work both in terms of domestic labour and in the world of paid employment. The extent of the inequalities experienced by women in both these arenas is still the subject of fierce debate and argument today. Much radical feminism has focused on the politics of family life, seeing gendered relations in the private, domestic sphere as the most appropriate battleground on which to confront and attack patriarchy. Dual-systems theorists wage their war in both these arenas, while anti-essentialists have opened up another front, fighting against the various sources of oppression experienced by non-white, non-middle class females.

However, another kind of battle, focusing on the female body, has been fought too. It began in a small, piecemeal way with the efforts of Marie Stopes in Britain, Margaret Sanger in the USA (1916; 1926; 1928) and others in the early years of the twentieth century. But from the 1960s onwards the female body became the site for a much more widespread campaign of resistance to, and confrontation with, dominant ideas concerning female sexuality and reproduction. From a Foucauldian point of view, the emergence of these forms of resistance demonstrate clearly the way the establishment of discursive dominance usually sows the seeds of opposition. The metaphor tells the story. From planting to flowering into full bloom often takes a long time but, once established and firmly rooted and with proper nourishment, strong growth often follows.

In the early years, opposition to medicine-inspired ideas about a woman's 'natural' sexual and reproductive destiny was limited. In Britain, Marie Stopes urged women to resist such notions by reclaiming their sexuality and reproductive abilities for themselves. Only by making their own decisions about these aspects of their bodies could they wrest the management and regulation of these away from men and medicine. Thus, a woman should see sex as not merely a matter of lying back and thinking of England – something done to her body by a man – but as a collaborative act in the pursuit of mutual personal fulfilment. Stopes not only encouraged women to use contraception (1920; new edition, 2000), but wrote the first sex manual for women (1916; new edition, 1996), describing the erotic benefits of different positions in intercourse. For many modern women of the time this was the first real depiction of their anatomical potential they had ever encountered. Naturally, such heresy met with heavy and concerted opposition.

It was not until the second wave of feminism in the 1960s that this battle over the female body was rejoined. The marches and protests of the time with bra-burning at their heart bore testimony to the importance of bodily liberation for these feminists. Soon, however, it became more than mere symbolism. At the end of the sixties women were provided with the technological keys to unlock the discursive chains binding their bodies and by none other than medicine itself. Although its opponents mounted a fierce rearguard action, eventually the Pill became available on the NHS, and for both married *and* unmarried women. In retrospect, this was as liberating a law for modern women as the victory over suffrage had been in the 1920s. But more was to come. Though again fiercely resisted, an Act legalizing abortion was eventually passed, in 1967, so that termination no longer needed to be a furtive affair in the proverbial back-street.

At the same time too, radical feminists such as Andrea Dworkin (see chapter 5), though hugely vilified for it, were making links between the symbolic violence against women's bodies represented in gender advertising, men's magazines and other visual pornography and actual bodily violence and sexual assaults by men against women. Though such a focus brought gendered violence into public view for the first time (the 'Reclaim the Night' campaign of the 1970s gained widespread support from men too), many commentators saw the further claim by such radical feminists – that penetrative sex is also a form of symbolic violence by men against women – a claim too far.

Body language

One of the best ways in which we can get a sense of the balance of power between competing discourses at a particular juncture is by reflecting on the language used to describe things. The shift from the universally pejorative way homosexuality used to be described – homosexuals were routinely derided as poofs, nancy-boys, queers, arse-bandits, bum-boys and so on even up to the 1980s – to the neutral and even positive use of the word 'gay' and the new use of the word 'queer' is a case in point. The shift in the balance of discursive power between competing definitions of the female body in recent years is also revealed by language. For example, in matters of sex women have traditionally been subject to linguistic castigation in a way men have not. A sexually unresponsive woman could be frigid whereas there was no such thing as a frigid man. Men could not suffer from hysteria or nymphomania, nor could they be harlots or whores. More recently, sexually active women could be sluts, tarts, slags, or slappers but men could not. These days, however, things have changed. Not only are these terms used in a less pejorative, more jokily affectionate way, but they can be used to describe men too. This demonstrates a new set of circumstances for women; an alteration to the discursive rules governing sexual expression.

This example demonstrates that language can tell us a great deal about cultural content, which is hardly surprising, since knowing the meanings of words is the only way we are able to discover what our world is like. It is only by learning a language that we are able to go beyond mere sensory experience and acquire the knowledge we need to be able to function as human beings. But post-structuralists like Foucault go further than this. For them, our language does not just describe a world – it actually *creates* that world. It is to these ideas that we now turn.

Further Reading

Danaher, Geoff, Schirato, Tony and Webb, Jen: *Understanding Foucault*, Sage, 2000.

Jones, Colin and Porter, Roy: *Reassessing Foucault: power, medicine and the body*, Routledge, 1994.

McHoul, Alec and Grace, Wendy: *A Foucault Primer: discourse, power and the subject*, Routledge, 2002.

McNay, Lois: *Foucault: a critical introduction*, Polity, 1994.

Oakley, Ann: *Women Confined*, Martin Robertson, 1980.

Oakley, Ann: *The Captured Womb: a history of the medical care of pregnant women*, Blackwell, 1984.

Oakley, Ann: *Essays on Women, Medicine and Health*, Edinburgh University Press, 1993.

Poster, Mark: *Foucault, Marxism and History*, Polity, 1984.

Rabinow, Paul (ed.): *The Foucault Reader*, Penguin, 1991.

Sanger, Margaret: *What Every Girl Should Know*, M. N. Naisel, 1916.

Sanger, Margaret: *Happiness in Marriage*, Brentano's, 1926.

Sanger, Margaret: *Motherhood in Bondage*, Brentano's, 1928.

Scott, Sue and Morgan, David (eds): *Body Matters: essays on the sociology of the body*, Falmer, 1993.

Shilling, Chris: *The Body and Social Theory*, Sage, 1993.

Smart, Barry: *Foucault*, Routledge, 1988.

Stopes, Marie: *Married Love*, Orion, 1996. (This refers to the work she published in 1916.)

Stopes, Marie: *Birth Control and Other Writings*, ed. Lesley A. Hall, Thoemmes Press, 2000.

Turner, Bryan: *Regulating Bodies: essays in medical sociology*, Routledge, 1992.

Turner, Bryan: *The Body and Society: explorations in social theory*, Sage, 1996.

8 LANGUAGE AND SOCIAL LIFE: STRUCTURALISM, POST-STRUCTURALISM AND RELATIVISM

Introduction

Language plays a pivotal role in action theory: from this point of view it is by far the most sophisticated means by which we are able to communicate our meanings to one another and thereby build what we call social order. The focus on the creative use of language by human beings reaches its extreme with ethnomethodology; here the nature of human language itself becomes the topic for sociological investigation. Thus, the technicalities of *how* it is used by humans to reveal the contents of each other's minds is the concern of the best-known ethnomethodological research device – conversational analysis. The argument is that since conversation represents the principal symbolic means by which members construct order in social situations, how this is done must be understood by any sociology concerned with members' methods.

For action theorists then, language and the ability to use it reflects the distinguishing feature of human life; it demonstrates our possession of consciousness and our ability to interpret, and attach meaning to, the world around us. There is a twist in the tail however. Paradoxically, an interest in language is also at the heart of a school of sociological theorizing whose dedicated aim is to kill off and bury such action-theory assumptions about human beings and human social life. The aim of *structuralism* and *post-structuralism* is to bring about the '*death of the subject*' (though sometimes this enterprise is given a less gory description, when the declared aim is to '*de-centre*' the subject). It aims to point to the reasons why we should discard action theory's conception of the actor/agent/member/subject as the source of meaning and the architect of a consciously created social reality. This is also true, either implicitly or explicitly, of other forms of structural theory, like functionalism and Althusserian Marxism. However, the objections from these viewpoints are rooted in their representation of societies as social structures, or systems made up of social institutions. The objections from structuralism and post-structuralism originate elsewhere. In effect, they steal the clothes from action theory and then try to strangle it with its own principal garment. These traditions agree that language is of vital importance for human social life, but not for the reasons action theory claims it is. The irony is that language – the very instrument which their intended victim uses to point to the triumph of the human subject's mind and consciousness in social life – is the same instrument that structuralists and post-structuralists use to try to murder and bury such claims.

Language and social life

A useful starting-point from which to understand structuralism and post-structuralism is the famous stricture of philosopher **Ludwig Wittgenstein** (1889–1951) against the possibility of a *private* language. As Doyal and Harris say, following Wittgenstein: 'If words did not already mean what they do mean, then they could not be used to express what you mean to say' (1986, p. 84). Furthermore, since thought depends on languages that pre-exist us – you cannot have an idea or a concept unless you learn what to call it – thoughts themselves are social in origin. Thus, according to Wittgenstein (1973), 'you learn the concept "pain" when you learn the language'. Similarly, in answer to a question about how he knew a colour was red, Wittgenstein (1973) responded: 'It would be an answer to say I have learnt English.' As Doyal and Harris put it: 'You must learn from others the language you employ to describe even your most intimate and private feelings; thus even the way you describe yourself to yourself can only happen by using words publicly available, and learnt, by you' (Doyal and Harris, 1986, p. 82).

Of course, post-structuralists recognize that we experience reality as soon as our senses – our ability to see, hear, touch, smell and taste – begin to work. But they are arguing that we cannot know what these experiences *mean* until words are learnt. Furthermore, since we do not have any choice over the meaning of words, we cannot have any choice over the knowledge of the world that they provide us with either.

Clearly, then, we must make a distinction, as the linguist Saussure does, between *speech* – what particular individuals say to each other – and *language*, the public and social system of signs, symbols and referents which speakers have to use to think and speak. A system of language exists independently of its learners and users, and they are obliged to use the meanings referred to by its constituent symbols both to think for themselves and to exchange thoughts with others.

If all this is so, then the importance of individual thought and consciousness, so central to action sociology, is minimal: *language* determines these thoughts and it is language we must explain. Roger Trigg puts this argument as follows:

> The nature of language and culture, viewed as systems, cannot be discovered at the level of the subject . . . this kind of structuralism offers a threat to any idea that man is the centre of the universe. The very categories of human thought are given to us . . . we can no longer be understood as subjects thinking about an independently existing world and devising language to describe it. We are not the source of language or of culture. Being human involves living in a world which has already been determined. (Trigg, 1985, pp. 190–1)

For structuralists and post-structuralists, then, language occupies the same status as institutional structures do for Marxists and functionalists. Just as, for these theories, institutional structures exercise constraint by compelling certain kinds of belief and behaviour, so, for structuralism and post-structuralism, ways of thinking and talking which we are obliged to use exercise similar compulsion over us. In effect, our way of knowing about the world is provided for us in the languages which pre-exist us and which we learn.

The reason for using the term 'structuralism' to refer to ideas about language and its role in social life is clear; as with functionalism and Althusserian Marxism, the individual actor, agent, or subject, is irrelevant. The origin of social life lies in structural influences beyond the actor; but here it is a system of *language*, rather than a social system of functioning *institutions*, that we must understand and explain. Thus, not only does social life depend upon language, but language defines social reality for us. Since language creates the world as it is understood by actors, two obvious problems arise here. First, where does language come from? And second, does this mean that speakers of different languages inhabit different worlds?

In the work of two Frenchmen, **Claude Lévi-Strauss** (1908–1990), an anthropologist and leading structuralist, and Michel Foucault (1926–1984), the most famous post-structuralist, we have examples of two different kinds of answers to these questions. Though Lévi-Strauss died some time after Foucault, Lévi-Strauss's answers nonetheless came first and, as the name suggests, the *post*-structuralist (*after*-structuralism) answers of Foucault build upon this position, providing a different account.

Lévi-Strauss and structuralism

Like his fellow Frenchman and predecessor, Emile Durkheim, Lévi-Strauss argues that the structure of social life is an independent entity which constrains the behaviour and beliefs of actors. Where Lévi-Strauss departs from Durkheim is in his definition of these structural constraints. For him, the defining features of human existence are:

- language, which humans encounter upon entering life, and
- the fact that the underlying structure of all language is the same.

According to Lévi-Strauss, language originates in the unconscious human mind. Since all human minds work in the same way, whatever differences languages may appear to exhibit, they are in fact organized on the same principles. Furthermore, culture is also the creation of these same unconscious thought processes; thus, the structural features of social organization inevitably mirror those of language. In effect, according to Lévi-Strauss, human thought structures the world of language and of behaviour (social organization) in the same way.

Lévi-Strauss is thus interested in the form, not the content, of language and culture. Culture, like language, is a system of signs and symbols whose organization reflects the manner of human thought. Trigg's view of Lévi-Strauss is that:

> He interprets myths and symbols in this way, saying that 'the world of symbolism is infinitely varied in content but always limited in its laws' . . . he analyses kinship systems in a similar way, viewing them as languages . . . He is concerned . . . to uncover the systems, whether of kinship or language . . . which are built by the mind, as he puts it, 'at the level of unconscious thought'. (Trigg, 1985, pp. 190–1)

There is nothing in social life that is the innovative creation of the conscious or imaginative mind then; human beings are not the authors of their life-stories, for these are written for them, in language and in culture. Nothing could be further from the world of Weber, Goffman, Schutz and Garfinkel.

Foucault and post-structuralism

Though agreeing about the linguistic authorship of human life-stories, Foucault goes beyond the kinds of ideas produced by Lévi-Strauss in two ways. First, he rejects the idea that there are universal features underpinning all languages. Second, he is principally interested in the exercise of *power* involved in the establishment and use of a language.

Foucault follows the structuralist line in placing language at the centre of the picture. But the 'languages' in which he is interested are not the kind that are normally referred to by the term – like English, French and Spanish. He is concerned to show how specific ways of thinking and talking about aspects of the world are forms of *knowledge* which work like languages and which we learn in the same way as we learn ordinary languages. As we saw in the previous chapter, he calls such 'languages' – systems of connected ideas which give us our knowledge of the world – *discourses*, which is why his post-structuralism is sometimes called *discourse theory*.

Discourse theory

As we saw earlier, according to Foucault, acquiring a discourse is the only human way of *knowing* about reality there is; the only reason we can only think/talk at all is by using a discourse of one kind or another. Furthermore, since we are compelled to know by means of discourses, they exercise *power* over us. Who we are – what we think, what we know, and what we talk about – is produced by the various discourses we encounter and use. Thus, the 'subject' – the creative, freely choosing and interpreting agent at the centre of action theory (and at the heart of philosophies like existentialism) does not exist. People's subjectivity and identity – what they think, know and talk about – is created by the discourses in which they are implicated. The post-structuralist jargon used to describe this is that the individual is *constituted* by discourses. So discourses – ways of thinking, knowing and talking – provide us with the only ways we can 'be' anybody at all. They provide us with our thoughts and our knowledge and, there-fore, can be said to direct, or be behind, any actions we choose to take. This link between thought, language, knowledge and action Foucault summarizes by the phrase *'discursive practices'* – meaning that social life consists of activities promoted by discourses.

For Foucault, the study of history involves working out how and why different discourses came to be established when they did, because this will achieve the historian's goal – to discover why people thought, said and did what they did. According to Foucault, this is ultimately a question of power, too. The question here is: 'By what means and for what reasons did *this* form of discourse come to be established and to prevail at *this* time in history?' That is, Foucault sees the historian's task as unearthing the foundations of different discourses. The use of the archaeological metaphor is not accidental. Foucault himself describes his aim as the digging out of evidence about past discourses in an archaeological fashion; his project is literally to discover what lies underneath the emergence of various discourses.

To summarize then, Foucault's argument is that identity is constituted by discourse. People are who they are – they think what they think, know what they know, say what they say and do what they do – because of their implication in a configuration of different, and sometimes competing, discourses. The underlying reasons for the existence of these discourses can be unearthed by the historian/ archaeologist; discovering these is, in essence, discovering the basis of a particular kind of knowledge and a particular kind of power. For above all, according to Foucault, the study of discourse is essentially the study of power. For Foucault then, power is exercised in two ways. First, it is exercised in order that a discourse will come into being. Second, it is exercised *by* a discourse, since it constitutes identity – it determines what people think and know, and therefore how they act. So, for Foucault, discursive practices are at the root of social life; the exercise of power through discourse is everywhere.

Deconstructing discourses: the examples of medicine and madness

A brief look at Foucault's own historical work shows the sorts of factors he regards as significant in providing the foundations for the establishment of particular discourses. As we discussed in the previous chapter, Foucault has become famous for his accounts of the history of the body in terms of the various discourses that have defined it. He argues that the emergence of particular ways of knowing and talking about any area of social life depends on the prior existence of specific organizational and institutional arrangements.

Post-structuralists use the term *deconstruction* to describe a method of unearthing the origins of a way of thinking and knowing. For example, he argues that it was only the appearance of the clinic that made medical discourse possible. As we saw earlier, because we now live in a world where the presence of medical concepts and their use in various areas of social life is taken for granted, it is a little difficult for us to appreciate just how pervasive such a discourse has become. For us, notions of 'health' and 'ill-health' are not just applied to bodies, but to societies (as in the ideas of Durkheim), desires, sexual orientations, appetites, pastimes, interests, families, marriages, economies, and so forth. This list shows how contagious (another use of medical discourse!) the use of such concepts has become. It therefore draws attention to the constitution of thinking and consciousness that Foucault argues a discourse can achieve. It is evidence of the power of both the discourse and the practitioners who enforce such a way of knowing about the world.

The reasons behind the emergence of the idea of madness as illness is another good example of Foucault's deconstruction of the past. The interpretation of 'mad' as 'without reason' is a feature of a discourse facilitated by the emergence of Enlightenment views about the virtue of reason and rationality, and the possibility of progress via science – that is, by the creation of ideas of modernity. Yet madness was not deemed to be 'illness' until rather later when, in effect, it then became another condition to be consumed by medical discourse. In Medieval Europe the eradication of leprosy left the buildings used to confine lepers empty. This provided the circumstances for the possibility of the exclusion from ordinary society of other categories of persons – particularly the 'insane'. The creation of asylums made possible the discipline of psychiatry, with the result that mental 'illness', the mental hospital, psychiatry and psychiatrists all grew up alongside one another. The exercise of the power to incarcerate people now defined as 'sick' is deemed to be 'therapy' and the provision of 'medical treatment'. However, the net effect, i.e. the social control of people exhibiting behaviour disturbing to others, is the same as it ever was, except that now *medical* discourse provides the justification for control, via hospitalization.

This is typical Foucault. As we have seen throughout the book so far, the task for theorists engaged in the project of modernity is to generate knowledge which can then be used to enable societal progress and make possible individual freedom and liberation. For Foucault, however, forms of knowledge are used to regulate, control and discipline. Thus he turns the modernist definition of knowledge on its head, saying that since we can only know reality through discourse, this knowledge must control who we are. We do not use knowledge to create better worlds; social change simply means the emergence of new discourses, which in turn define and control subjects in new ways. These 'new' ways of knowing are not 'better' or 'worse' than what has gone before – they are simply different, reflecting different forms of power. Defining madness as the possession of sacred knowledge, as representing lack of reason, or as evidence of a diseased mind, is not a matter of 'falsehoods' being replaced by 'truth'. It is simply a shift in power relations – the replacement of one way of defining reality by another. Foucault's thinking is thus a good example of *relativism*.

Relativism

A relativist believes there is no such thing as 'objective' truth; there are only competing ways of looking at things and competing ways of knowing about things. As Pascal put it: 'What is truth on one side of the Pyrenees can be falsehood on the other.' 'Reality' thus has no meaning apart from what is *believed* to be real by some groups of believers. Because of the way we embrace modernism, take science and scientific knowledge for granted, and regard them as 'superior' to other forms of knowledge, it is perhaps hard for us to grasp this. However, the relativist would argue that even scientific knowledge and practice – scientific discourse, as Foucault would call them – cannot be said to be objectively superior to other forms of knowledge which are believed to be true in other times and places. Thus, says the relativist, believing in the notion that the world is as it is because God made it that way, that witchcraft causes misfortune, that the conjunction of the planets can cure warts, or whatever, is not a belief in falsehoods except from the point of view of another definition of truth (in this case scientific). Even though we live in a world where scientific discourse prevails this does not mean that it is therefore superior to other claims for truth. For relativists, it is the other way round; scientific knowledge is not powerful because it is true; it is true because it is powerful. Thus the question is not 'What is true?' but 'How did *this* version of what is true come to dominate in *these* social and historical circumstances?' It is a question, in fact, for the sociology, politics and history of knowledge. The earliest and most famous relativist account of scientific knowledge is that of **Thomas Kuhn** (1922–).

Relativism and the social construction of scientific knowledge

In 1962, Kuhn, a historian of science, published a work called *The Structure of Scientific Revolutions* which has had a profound impact on the way science and scientific knowledge has since been understood. In effect, Kuhn argues against the claim that science collects knowledge in a purely objective way, dealing only with facts and excluding judgements. His argument is that the production of scientific truth is always influenced by fashion and trend, by politics and the exercise of power, and by choices about what should be known about and what should not, just like any other form of human production. Of course, the attraction of science for the project of modernity has been its claim to be unlike other forms of knowledge, to deal *only* with facts, to provide demonstrable proof and to enable certain knowledge. Consequently, Kuhn's argument represents a major assault on the foundations upon which much modernist theorizing has been built.

He claims that an examination of the history of the natural sciences shows how a process of value-based selection always has to occur – that scientists not only have to choose which phenomena to research but they also have to choose a theoretical approach in order to carry out this research. Furthermore, argues Kuhn, these choices are always made in social contexts; there are always social and political influences affecting how scientists do their work. He describes this by arguing that any scientific knowledge is produced from within a particular tradition, or *paradigm*, which determines what research is done and how it is carried out. Scientists belong to one of these traditions or another; scientific work always takes place from within one paradigm or another.

The history of a science is the history of the rise and fall of paradigms. For some periods of time only one paradigm prevails, and any ideas which threaten it are despatched away from the centre of the stage. In such times, scientific work takes the form referred to by Kuhn as 'normal science'; nearly all scientists work within the dominant paradigm, and different ways of looking at the world are treated with scorn. In this way, dominant paradigms exercise power and sustain dominance as 'dogma'.

The rise and fall of paradigms: the case of medicine

Medicine provides a good contemporary example of such a state of affairs. Despite the wide range of therapies available – homeopathy, hypnotherapy, acupuncture, faith-healing, hydrotherapy and many others, the practice of Western medicine is dominated by one version of medical truth. The medical establishment (represented in Britain by the British Medical Association, the BMA), funding bodies, research institutes and teaching hospitals, all practise and thereby reproduce one form of therapy. There is one dominant way of looking at illness (as organic in origin and treatable by physical intervention – by drugs or surgery for example). So, when you turn up at your doctor's surgery, you are not asked to make a choice from the array of alternative therapies in existence. You are obliged to have a consultation with a doctor trained in one particular way, to the exclusion of others. In Kuhn's terms, there is a dominant medical paradigm.

Things are changing in medicine, however. Whereas faith-healers and hypnotherapists, for example, used to be called 'quacks', they are now called 'alternative' or 'complementary' practitioners. Today, a British general practitioner (GP) is more likely to offer homeopathy or acupuncture or psychotherapy as part of NHS treatment – a state of affairs that would have been unthinkable thirty years ago. The former 'fringe' medicines are slowly becoming more respectable; their version of what makes people ill, and how they should be treated, is gaining more and more legitimacy. In fact, we could be seeing the beginning of the demise of orthodox medicine as a dominant paradigm, and the emergence of a world where alternative versions of medical truth compete with each other on equal terms – for patients and funding and for legitimacy and authority. Kuhn describes how the fall from grace of a dominant paradigm in any science produces a time of ferment and uncertainty in the science – a time, as he describes it, of revolution.

As in all revolutions, old certainties are abandoned, competing versions of truth and virtue multiply and confusion reigns. Peace and certainty can only break out again when a victor emerges from the conflict among those who would be king. However, this can only happen when the power of one of these pretenders becomes so great that its competitors are defeated. From its newly acquired position of dominance, the victorious paradigm can then begin to dictate the practice of the science, and 'knowledge' and 'progress' can race ahead once more. In effect, the emergence of a new dominant paradigm means the production of a new version of truth and certainty. According to Trigg: 'Scientists once believed in a substance called phlogiston and now they do not. They once believed the atom could not be split, whereas now they continue to search for sub-atomic particles' (Trigg, 1985, p. 13).

Kuhn uses this famous drawing, which can be seen as either a duck or a rabbit, to illustrate how the world is seen differently after the destruction of an old dominant paradigm, and the emergence of a new one. Kuhn (1962) says: 'What were ducks in the scientific world before the revolution are rabbits afterwards' (p. 110).

Why do scientists change their paradigms? Since the emergence of a prevailing paradigm is the result of social influences – through the practice of the politics of persuasion – we should expect such influences to be behind the decision of individual scientists to abandon previously held beliefs in favour of new ones. Kuhn says scientists choose a new paradigm: 'for all sorts of reasons and usually several at once . . . Some of these reasons . . . depend upon idiosyncrasies of autobiography and personality. Even the nationality or the prior reputation of the innovator and his teachers can sometimes play a significant role' (Kuhn, 1962, p. 151).

So science, instead of being the steady, value-free accumulator of more and more evidence about reality, is in fact just what communities of believing scientists are led to do at a certain time in history, in a particular set of social circumstances. The dominance of one paradigm and the knowledge its practitioners purvey is not, therefore, caused by any monopoly over truth it may have. It is because of its monopoly over *power* and, as a result, its means to control socially what *counts* as truth. The production of scientific knowledge is thus underpinned by choices, preferences and judgements not freely chosen by scientists, but orchestrated and reinforced by the political activity of a scientific establishment. This is why relativists say that scientific knowledge is not powerful because it is true; it is true because it is powerful. This is made explicit by the relativist philosopher of science, **Paul Feyerabend** (1924–94).

According to Trigg, Feyerabend contends:

that there is no more ultimate way of referring to reality than through the particular tradition we belong to. Instead of reality controlling our beliefs, at least to some extent, it seems as if the beliefs of a tradition determine what is to count as real. Within any one of them, we can gain the illusion that knowledge can be and has been attained. Yet once we see that many conflicting traditions have the same conceit, we realize, it is alleged, that judgements of truth only have relative validity. They hold for our colleagues in the tradition to which we are attached, but not for those outside. (Trigg, 1985, p. 116)

The sociology of science – the investigation of the social and political origins of particular paradigmatic 'certainties' or 'truths' – therefore becomes highly important. Trigg puts it like this: 'Societies or traditions determine what we count as knowledge . . . what we believe or claim to know is merely the product of social forces of which we may be utterly ignorant' (Trigg, 1985, p. 16).

This can happen at both the structural and the interpretive level. At the level of structure, the institutional and ideological means by which scientific communities attempt to exercise political and social control over the production of knowledge in their name should be explored. At the level of action and interpretation, the construction of scientific knowledge as an outcome of meaningful interaction and negotiation in laboratory settings should be the topic. This is why, for the relativist:

'Reality' has no meaning apart from what is believed real by some group. The very concept of an objective world, independent of all points of view, has disappeared. Ontology has thus become dependent on epistemology. What there is is seen as the product of our strategies for finding things out. If our epistemology changes, as when we move from one worldview to another, so do our beliefs about what is real. (Trigg, 1985, p. 22)

This sort of argument is the very antithesis of the claims about knowledge made by proponents of the 'project of modernity'. As we have seen, for modernists the application of reason, exemplified by science, enables humans to discover *the* truth about the nature of reality, to understand the causes of social life in the way natural science has revealed the workings of nature. Such knowledge allows us the chance of progress, social development and individual liberation and freedom. The more we discover, the better we can construct our world; the more we know, the greater our opportunities for human emancipation.

In chapter 4, we looked at the views of Max Weber, for whom the construction of modern, rational society represented the imprisonment and destruction of the human spirit. Relativists too, though for different reasons, also cast profound doubt on the optimistic assumptions underpinning the idea of modernity. Since from this viewpoint 'truth' is relative and a product of the historical and social world in which we are implicated, knowledge itself has to be understood as socially constructed. For relativists, there is no way of acquiring any certainty about reality. Truth and knowledge are culturally and historically specific; whatever we 'know' is constructed for us – it is the product of the time in history and the location of the world in which we find ourselves. Whatever structural sociology we use – whether we define the process whereby we acquire truths as a product of interconnecting discourses, as socialization into prevailing ideas, as ideological indoctrination, or whatever – the relativist cannot escape the fact that what we are and what we know is a social creation. Indeed, from this point of view, locked as we inevitably are in the discourses/traditions of time and place, the fact that we are constituted by such phenomena means we have no way of standing back and making objective judgements anyway. For even the criteria by which we judge truth or falsehood are themselves social constructions, provided for us by our social world. As Feyerabend puts it: 'Each tradition, each form of life, has its own standards of judging human behaviour . . . a citizen will use the standards to which he belongs: Hopi standards, if he is a Hopi: fundamentalist Protestant standards, if he is a fundamentalist' (Feyerabend, 1981, p. 27). If this sort of relativist claim is correct, then for the project of modernity it is catastrophic. The argument is that although our 'socialness' makes ordered life possible, it nonetheless denies us the chance of ever knowing 'reality' except from our own point of view. The construction of sociological theories does not beckon the dawning of truth and liberty then, for these prescriptions are themselves social products and cannot be said to be right or wrong – just different.

The implications of this sort of relativist argument have led some commentators to argue that we should abandon any hope of acquiring truth or knowledge about an objective reality, and accept that all sociological accounts – even *all* humanly constructed accounts of reality – have equal validity. No single, over-arching theory can point the way to a modern utopia; we have gone beyond the time when we should believe that such a *meta-narrative*, or grand account of all history and all social life, like functionalism, Marxism or feminism can have any credibility. We must therefore accept we are in a *postmodern* world, where grand theoretical designs are obsolete, and where it is inevitable that multiple claims to truth compete with each other for our support. The fact that some of these theories, like Foucault's, claim that we have no choice about what we do think, whereas others disagree, does not change the truth about the pluralistic character of knowledge. For postmodernists, in fact, this is the *only* truth. Their argument is that we must accept that modernist concepts like reason and progress provide us with no purchase at all on the way we live, or the way we will live in the future. We will now examine these postmodernist ideas, and the alternative approaches of some of the theorists who criticize them, in our final two chapters.

Further Reading

Fuller, Steve: *Thomas Kuhn: a philosophical history for our times*, University of Chicago Press, 2000.

Gellner, Ernest: *Relativism and the Social Sciences*, Cambridge University Press, 1986.

Hollis, Martin: *The Philosophy of Social Science*, Cambridge University Press, 1994.

Hollis, Martin and Lukes, Steven: *Rationality and Relativism*, Blackwell, 1985.

Kuhn, Thomas: *The Structure of Scientific Revolutions*, 2nd edn, University of Chicago Press, 1970.

Margolis, Joseph: *The Truth about Relativism*, Blackwell, 1991.

Norris, Christopher: *Against Relativism: philosophy of science, deconstruction and critical theory*, Blackwell, 1997.

Trigg, Roger: *Understanding Social Science*, Blackwell, 1985.

9 POST-MODERNITY AND POSTMODERNISM

Introduction

First, we must make a distinction between **post-modernity** and **postmodernism**. Post-modernity refers to the view that the institutions and ways of living characteristic of modernity have been replaced by new institutional features to such a profound extent that it is no longer plausible to see the twenty-first century as a continuation of modernity. That is, modernity has ended and we now live in a new era, of post-modernity, and we need new ways of making sense of this transformed world. As Bauman puts it: 'a theory of post-modernity . . . cannot be a modified theory of modernity . . . it needs its own vocabulary' (1992, p. 188). In contrast, postmodernism, though obviously intimately connected to post-modernity, is a term that refers to new ways of thinking about *thought* – to new ways of understanding *ideas*, *beliefs* and *knowledge* – rather than to new ways of living and organizing social affairs.

From modernity to post-modernity?

It is clear that in recent times, the preoccupations of the classic theorists of modernity have been found wanting when it comes to making sociological sense of significant elements of social existence today. For obvious reasons, Durkheim, Marx and Weber say nothing about issues that are of crucial importance for us living now, such as threats to the environment, the dangers posed by the proliferation of nuclear weapons, and the risks and uncertainties associated with scientific and technological advances. It is less obvious why they should have neglected the need to look at gender and race issues, or issues surrounding war and nationalism, but these, too, are major concerns for our times which require us to go beyond traditional theorizing to properly address. It is to produce conceptual frameworks that allow us to understand the world as it is today that has driven the work of some of sociology's major living theorists, such as **Anthony Giddens** (1938–), **Jürgen Habermas** (1929–), **Ulrich Beck** (1944–) and **Manuel Castells** (1942–). We will look at some of the ideas of Habermas, Giddens and Beck in the next chapter.

But such writers, though sensitive to the new concerns that need to be addressed by sociology today, are most certainly not postmodernists. They believe that the contemporary world is still best interrogated by building on the intellectual and theoretical tools that have helped us understand modernity and modernism. It is this, still modernist, approach that postmodernists disagree with, arguing that radical new ways of being sociological are needed to make sense of what is, for them, a new Great Transformation.

Social life in the twenty-first century

In chapter 1, we briefly summarized the transformations to life ushered in by the emergence of modernity. These included the rise of capitalism, of mass production techniques, of large urban conglomerations, of the nation-state, of Western global dominance and of the secularization of knowledge. The question here is: what have been the dramatic alterations to these characteristic elements of modern life that have led some to talk of contemporary life as a time of post-modernity? For many commentators, one of the key features of life today is known as globalization. There is much debate about the meaning and precise significance of this concept and we do not have the space here to even begin to do justice to the different viewpoints involved. It is therefore important to remember that what follows below is merely an outline sketch of some of the features of our lives today referred to by the term.

Dimensions of globalization

Global capitalism

Capitalism has dramatically altered since its establishment as the economic dynamic behind modernity. It has long since left its moorings in the harbours of individual countries and today is rampant on the high seas of the world. No longer confined to the West, the relentless pursuit of profit has penetrated into the furthest reaches of the world. It has become a global phenomenon, far out of reach of national regulation. The significant players in contemporary capitalism are the multinational, or, more accurately, *transnational* corporations. Owing no allegiance to particular nations, transnationals operate *in* countries, but not *for* countries. Profitability determines the location of manufacturing. If wage costs can be kept down by locating production in countries without trade unions and therefore without established wage-bargaining procedures – using so-called 'sweat-shop' labour – then this is considered good business. Research and development may still have to be located in the educated West but the manufacturing of the developed product usually takes place where returns can be maximized. This profit-driven tendency to relocate production away from the West has seen a corresponding expansion of the service industries in Europe and the USA and the rise of fears about long-term mass unemployment in these countries.

The nation-state in the twenty-first century

The emergence of these features of global capitalism has in turn threatened the power of the nation-state. Even if corporate decisions seem against their national interests there seems little that governments can do to restrict the rampaging dominance of transnational capitalism. Indeed, it could be argued that the only time transnational corporations consult national governments is when it makes good business sense – when there is something in it for them. For example, getting production (and therefore jobs and thereby reducing unemployment) located in the West is often a matter of governments having to offer considerable financial incentives to transnationals for them to be prepared to do so.

Population growth and urbanization in the twenty-first century

Along with the decline in power of the nation-state, two other original features of modernity have been reversed. Today, rapid population growth and urbanization is taking place in the Third World whereas cities are in decline in the First World. Furthermore, there has been a real shift in global power relations; recent years have seen a considerable expansion of wealth and power in Asia at the expense of Europe.

The globalization of markets and marketing

Markets have become global too. Go into any supermarket and look at the place of origin of the products on sale there, or go into a clothes store such as Gap, French Connection, or Cult Clothing and look at the labels which tell us where the garments were made. The global nature of manufacturing production and distribution will become all too apparent. The marketing of these products is another global activity. Advertising and promotion knows no national boundaries and exactly the same techniques of image-construction and branding designed to entice and seduce can be found in all parts of the world, West, East, North and South. However, unlike the production process in early modernity, the mass production of a standardized good is a thing of the past. Mass production has been replaced by a much more flexible system enabling both a wider range and faster turnover of goods, and mass marketing has been replaced by promotion tailored to local circumstances, a process known as 'niche marketing'.

The network society

The Information Revolution – the way in which instant electronic communication has obliterated traditional notions of time and space – has been another principal impetus behind globalization. It has transformed the management of capitalism, particularly finance capitalism: dealing in investments of various kinds is now a global activity and mainly conducted electronically. Mass media communication is another global phenomenon, of course. Because of TV, video and film, few parts of the world are unaffected by the images and narratives pumped out on a 24/7 basis by the media. This means our knowledge of the world is no longer limited by time and space. We now routinely peer into the worlds of others whose existence we would never have known about unless we had physically visited them. This communication revolution has been, for the Spanish social theorist, Manuel Castells, *the* defining transformation to our existence; indeed, he labels our contemporary global world the 'network society' (Castells, 1996).

These changes involved in globalization are recognized by all kinds of contemporary theorists. What is distinctive about the analysis of the supporters of the idea of post-modernity are the conclusions and inferences they draw from them and the emphases they place in their account.

Identity in post-modernity

Our world is being remade. Mass production, the mass consumer, the big city, big-brother state, the sprawling housing estate, and the nation-state are in decline: flexibility, diversity, differentiation, and mobility, communication, decentralization and internationalization are in the ascendant. In the process, our own identities, our sense of self, our own subjectivities are being transformed. We are in transition to a new era. (Hall et al., 1988, pp. 24–9)

As the penultimate sentence in this quote indicates, it is the relationship between institutional changes and *identity* that has been the focus of much sociological attention in recent years. This is particularly true of postmodernist analyses. One of the principal elements in a typical postmodernist account concerns the way postmodern humans live their lives and see themselves. In modernity the centrality of work in people's lives found expression both in their sense of themselves – 'I am what I do' – and in the work-based social groupings to which they belonged. For example, as we noted in chapter 1, two of the distinctive features of modernity are class membership based on occupational rewards and the existence of workplace organizations, such as Trade Unions, set up to engage in collective bargaining with employers/managers.

For many post-modernists, one of the central features of *post-modernity* is the way work and production have given way to **consumption**, both as the lynchpin of social cohesion and as the source of individual identity. One of the leading supporters of the idea of post-modernity is **Zygmunt Bauman** (1935–) and this is how David Lyon describes Bauman's view of this profound shift in our lives:

Bauman rightly argues that for the first part of its history, modern capitalism placed work (or at least paid employment) in a central position. Work held a pivotal role, linking the individual motivation of the worker, the means whereby a network of social relationships and friendships was developed, and the way that the whole system was kept running efficiently. But work as paid employment has undergone some radical changes over the past quarter-century, and the idea of a secure lifelong job, trade or profession has increasingly become history. Employment has become casualised, part-time, uncertain and insecure (and this affects both women and men), and the multiple career, retraining and early retirement (or layoff) seems more like the norm. This is hardly a basis for personal motivation, let alone the fostering of stable communities and liveable localities. (Lyon, 2000, p. 227)

For Bauman, since we can no longer slot into pre-existing identities based on occupation and class, we have to be more creative in the way we construct ourselves. For him, this is where the purchase of consumer goods comes in. According to Bauman, what is post-modern about these circumstances is the way consumption has become the central feature of our existence as we have turned to focusing on possessions as the main means of expressing who we are. Lyon summarizes this view as follows:

> The consumer system needs credit-card-happy shoppers, and there is also a sense in which consumers feel themselves bound to shop. They are pressurised both by the constant need to keep up with others and to demonstrate their style, up-to-dateness and social fit; and also by merchandising companies who both define the good life – above all through relentless advertising – and go to great lengths to channel the choices of consumers . . . Both symbolic rivalry and social management together form, not a mode of pressure felt by oppression, but a system of (what Pierre Bourdieu (1984) calls) seduction. (Lyon, 2000, p. 227)

According to Bauman, this preoccupation with consumption produces a new form of stratification. For those with the means to join in, consumption fetishism offers a choice of lifestyle unimaginable in modernity. But for those whose lack of means disenfranchises them from living in consumer society – who Bauman calls 'flawed consumers' – their inability to acquire possessions makes their outsider status only too visible. However, even for those happily on holiday, inside the shopping mall or tuned in to the shopping channels, post-modern life brings new uncertainties and insecurities. This is how Lyon characterizes Bauman's take on this aspect of post-modern existence:

> Any apparent 'order' is local, transient and emergent, rather like a river whirlpool that maintains its pattern but is constantly renewed. Rather than use 'society', the term 'sociality' should be adopted to express the processual, the play of randomness and pattern, and the notion of structure as an emergent accomplishment. Human agency . . . is foregrounded, such that choices made in the agent's life add up to self-constitution or self-assembly. The corresponding item to be dropped is any notion of 'progress'. Mobility and change there may well be, but not in any clear direction. Time is thus unbound, in that ties with the past are weakened, leaving less space for the future to be colonised. (Lyon, 2000, p. 228)

This leads us neatly to the other element of postmodernist thinking – the rejection of modernist notions of progress through truth. That is, we turn our attention away from the nature of post-modern*ity* to the ideas of postmodern*ism*.

From modernism to postmodernism?

Postmodern thinking applies not only to social organizations, but also to all other realms of human activity and production, like art, architecture, and literature, for example. The focus is on pluralism and on competing accounts of the nature of virtue, style, truth and falsehood. It is also on the impermanence and instability of such definitions – the transience of certainties and the chronically brief life of truths. Postmodernism thus represents a reaction to the Enlightenment-sponsored modem search for *the* truth, ultimate meaning, and the nature of reality. Instead, the superficial and ephemeral nature of contemporary human life is emphasized, where, because of the persistently impermanent character of claims to truth, it is fashion, trend and image that have come to matter more than substance and meaning. In particular, the cultural dominance of the mass media is emphasized, where reality and identity are constructed for us by advertising, popular music and television soap operas. So although the mass media shrinks our world, because of its ability to transcend time and space, this gives us no more meaningful a purchase on 'reality' – it simply multiplies the number, frequency and impermanence of the accounts of reality we consume. What we 'see' via the media inevitably constitutes a major source of our knowledge in a postmodern world – but what we see and know, and therefore are, is merely for here and now, and only until another story comes along.

We can draw an analogy between this postmodernist account of the acquisition of notions of knowledge and the social construction of taste and fashion. It does not take much thought to realize the pivotal role of media manipulation in the establishment of (deliberately transitory) notions of what is fashionable and what is not in the minds of consumers. Take clothing, for example. The exercise of power in advertising is designed to produce in the consumer a belief in the attractiveness of, and (sometimes) therefore the desire to possess, an item of clothing. As power is exercised to sell new styles, so the idea is that the consumers change their minds about what is attractive. (A look at old photos of yourself in clothes you believed then to be the bee's knees but which today you would not be seen dead in tells you all you need to know about this process.)

According to postmodernism, this is how the social construction of knowledge works too. Just as consumers of clothes are subject to the power of advertising and promotion, so the consumers of, for example, moral positions are subject to the power of *their* promotion. There is no objective or inherent beauty in one item of clothing that elevates it over another. One *appears* more beautiful than the other as a result of the power exercised on its behalf to define it as more beautiful. For postmodernism, the same is true of moral positions. There is no moral judgement that is objectively right and another wrong. One appears right and the other appears wrong because more power is being exercised to promote one rather than the other.

Modernism versus postmodernism

This debate about the nature of knowledge between modernists and postmodernists is reflected in their respective views on the nature of freedom. For modernist thinkers we can only become free if we live as they tell us we should, whereas for postmodernists we will only be free when nobody feels able to tell us how to live.

Modernists believe that only their analysis of existence – their meta-narrative – is the correct one. It is therefore perfectly understandable – indeed, inevitable – that such custodians of the Truth should see it as their principal obligation to preach their message to the unconverted. They become, in effect, Truth merchants – the purveyors of the one and only answer. The missionaries we normally encounter in our every-day lives are religious ones – for example, Mormon elders (though in my experience they are always very young men) who stop us in the street to talk to us about their faith. What they are doing is trying to sell us what they know to be true.

But all promoters of modernist meta-narratives are secular mission-aries, really. For example, Marx used the word *praxis* to describe the importance of not just knowing the truth – understanding the human world – but of taking political action to re-organize it according to these insights. Thus, in good modernist Truth merchant fashion, he demanded that the 'Workers of the world unite! You have nothing to lose but your chains!' Feminists have been among the twentieth-century heirs to this unification of theory and practice: from the suffragette movement onwards, feminist theorists have preached the importance of women taking action on behalf of feminist analysis. This is the meaning of the term 'consciousness-raising' after all. Whether their goal is anti-racism, anti-sexism, anti-homophobia or whatever, activists always represent the political wing of a modernist theoretical analysis.

Such political action in support of the Truth can take place on a grander scale too. These words are being written six weeks after the 11 September 2001 attacks on the USA by Islamic fundamentalists. The resulting war against the Taliban in Afghanistan has in the meantime been self-consciously portrayed by the protagonists – particularly in the rhetoric of President George Bush and Prime Minister Tony Blair – as a 'crusade' on behalf of freedom, liberty and democracy. That is, they see it as justified in moral terms as well as retaliatory and strategic ones. But their enemies see their fight in exactly the same terms: a *jihad* is a holy war, fought against infidel unbelievers, and also on behalf of freedom and liberty. How can this be? How can two sides in a bloody war be fighting for the same thing?

For postmodernism, of course, it is because notions of freedom and liberty are *relative* – someone who is a terrorist from one standpoint will almost certainly be a freedom fighter from another. It is this fact – that they see human concepts such as right and wrong, truth and falsehood or good and bad as inevitably relative to the way the world is looked at – that has led postmodernists to reject modernist thinking.

From this point of view, missionary work by Truth merchants is actually no more than cultural imperialism – the imposition of one cultural version of truth on others. Like most imperialism, it is carried out in the name of liberation, of course, but, again like most imperialism, it is in fact no more than the (often vulgar) exercise of power. It is the use of power to degrade and, ultimately to destroy, other, equally legitimate, ways of thinking and living simply because these others are powerless to protect themselves and resist. According to postmodernism, only when we come to accept that there can be no objectively 'True' human knowledge, just as there can be no 'True' human language, will we be free. And this will be a freedom from the dogmatism, bigotry and intolerance that always characterizes the behaviour of those who believe they have a monopoly over Truth. For postmodernism, humankind does need liberating – not *by* 'the Truth' but *from* the whole idea of 'the Truth'. Real liberty means being given the freedom to be different – to be tolerated even though we are 'the Other'. This kind of liberty means being free to be who we have to be, as our knowledge permits, without being distrusted or despised or hated or punished for it, just as those different from us can be who they have to be, also free to live as their knowledge directs. Postmodernism insists that the only real freedom possible for culturally constructed human beings is the freedom that comes from abandoning the Enlightenment-sponsored modernist fallacy that humans can use reason to know things as they really are. Such a view implies that using reason somehow gives us the means to be able to step outside our culture and its influence and know right and wrong, truth and falsehood for certain. For postmodernism, however, since we can never escape culture, we can never know anything for certain. Humans can only ever know via language and discourse and languages and discourses can never be true or false or right or wrong.

10 CRITICAL RESPONSES TO POST-MODERNITY AND POSTMODERNISM

Introduction

Many different kinds of objections have been made to the post-modernist account of human existence. Here we will examine four of the most important ones, reflected in the ideas of the philosopher **Ernest Gellner**, the German social and political theorists **Jürgen Habermas** and **Ulrich Beck** and one of Britain's leading social theorists and public intellectuals, **Anthony Giddens**. Formerly Professor of Sociology at the University of Cambridge, Giddens is at the time of writing Director of the London School of Economics.

Ernest Gellner and scientific truth

The first critique comes from those who reject the postmodernist claim that humans can never know things for certain because they can never step outside the culture that has made them. According to this criticism, postmodernists are probably right to claim that humans will never be able to know right and wrong, good and bad, except from a cultural point of view. However, they are quite wrong to also argue that humans can never know facts – what phenomena exist and what do not – for certain, uninfluenced by culture. The one way they can do this is by being scientific. This position insists that we must distinguish between **moral**, or **cultural relativism**, and **cognitive relativism**, and one of its most forceful proponents has been the philosopher **Ernest Gellner** (1925–95).

Gellner accepts that scientific knowledge can never tell us how to live or how to organize ourselves. That is, we cannot expect science to provide us with moral guidelines: these are always going to be cultural constructions. But this is not the same thing as saying that science cannot tell us the truth about the facts of our existence. According to Gellner, because of the unique method it employs – relying exclusively on empirical evidence in an attempt to falsify hypotheses – science is the one form of knowledge production that produces the same results wherever it is employed. Even if the argument of Kuhn is accepted, and it is conceded that the origins of areas of scientific interest are culturally influenced, this is not the same thing as saying that the scientific testing of these culturally generated hypotheses is also inevitably infected with culture. No matter what culture a scientist lives in, no matter what time and place in the world an experiment is performed in, so long as it is performed in the same way, it will always produce the same results. This is because, during testing procedures at least, science has no place for human opinion or hopes or fears or desires or dreams – only the facts. These facts are often frightening, depressing and dispiriting. Science often reveals the world to be a cold, ugly and inhospitable place and scientists, like all humans, may well wish things were otherwise – that their loved ones did not have to feel pain, or fall ill, or die, for example. But things are as they are, whether we like it or not, and the reason science can tell us these truths is because it is the one form of human investigation that concerns itself solely with the facts and nothing but the facts. As Gellner puts it: 'Truth is not beauty; nor virtue, nor utility, nor the advancement of any political cause' (Gellner, 1979, p. 144). Science 'desecularizes, disestablishes, disenchants everything substantive: no privileged facts, occasions, individuals, institutions or associations. In other words, no miracles, no saviours, no sacred churches or sacramental communities' (Gellner, 1992, p. 81). It is because science is wholly unconcerned with what we might wish our world to be like that we can rely on it to tell us the truth about it.

In any case, insists Gellner, the proof of the pudding is in the eating. Wherever scientific knowledge has been applied, it has totally transformed human existence. After all, it is only because of the application of scientific knowledge that the incredible transformation from pre-modernity to modernity has been possible. Furthermore, he argues, if this was not the case, and science did not tell us the factual truth, why is it that undeveloped, unmodernized societies are so desperate to use science to transform and become modern themselves?

No, according to Gellner, cognitive relativism is a nonsense; morals may well be relative, but facts most definitely are not.

Gellner's attack on relativism concerns the human ability to know the factual truth. But others go further, arguing that it is also possible to establish moral judgements that can apply in different cultural settings as well; that is, they reject moral relativism too. Such thinkers do not deny that humans are culturally constituted – that our ideas of right and wrong, good and bad are cultural constructions. But they insist that even though this is true, there is no need to draw the postmodernist conclusion about the incommensurability of cultural values, since humans nevertheless possess the ability to reach agreements with others, even others from very different cultural traditions, about the way we should behave. This position argues that just because we come from radically different cultural backgrounds does not mean that we cannot have an open and honest dialogue about our differences and, so long as there is a genuine desire to do so, thereby establish a cross-cultural consensus about correct values and morals.

To claim this must mean that such thinkers believe that there is a culture-free way of assessing right and wrong – that in the assessment of morality, there is the equivalent of the role of the scientific experiment in the assessment of facts. One of the most influential thinkers in this tradition is the German social and political theorist **Jürgen Habermas** (1929–). For Habermas, just as science is able to use the laboratory experiment to know the truth about facts, so we can use language and communication to construct a truth about values. According to Habermas, the unique human ability to use language to communicate can give us moral knowledge in the same way as the laboratory can give us factual knowledge.

Jürgen Habermas and communicative rationality

Habermas is very much the modern heir to the ideals of the Enlightenment. He is a fierce advocate of the virtues and continued relevance of modernist thinking for our times, rejecting the postmodernist assault on the possibility of humans achieving progress through Truth. For Habermas, we can – and must – keep faith with the Enlightenment belief in the power of human rationality to enable us to know things for certain, because in our basic human ability to speak to each other

Jürgen Habermas

© Anne Selders

we possess the rational means to iron out culturally founded differences. For him, we are not hamstrung by culture, as the postmodernists argue. No matter how divergent our cultural background, no matter how radically different our life-experiences, humans always have one thing in common – our unique ability to use language to communicate. Habermas insists that so long as we are earnest in our desire to do so, it is this ability to communicate through language that will always enable us to reach out to each other, across cultural divides, and forge a cross-cultural moral community.

Habermas has been influenced by a wide range of theories and his approach represents an imaginative fusion of previously disparate ideas. In particular, he makes strategic use of important Marxian, Weberian and action theory concepts as major constituents in his perspective.

Habermas and Marx

From Marx he uses the equivalent of the base/superstructure distinction: thus he divides social existence into two realms – the *social system* and the *life-world*. The social system is the world where things are made and where structural phenomena exercise influence, while the life-world is the realm of action and meanings.

Habermas and Weber

From Weber, he sees modernity as crucially about the rise of rationalization as the underpinning of action. Like Weber, Habermas distinguishes between two types of rational action – *instrumental rationality*, action oriented to the achievement of efficiency in human life, and *value-oriented rationality* – the use of reason to distinguish between right and wrong. As we saw in chapter 4, Weber saw instrumental rationality gaining a tighter and tighter grip on human behaviour in modernity and was profoundly pessimistic about the chances of this stranglehold ever being broken. For Weber, the modern preoccupation with efficiency, calculation and predictability means the increasing neglect of spiritual matters, a process he termed **disenchantment**. He saw the future for modern life in extremely bleak terms. He predicted a future characterized by an overwhelming obsession with how to get things done in the most efficient ways possible with little or no thought given to values – to notions of good and bad, right and wrong. That is, he foresaw a world with concern about what should be the essence of being a human – a concern with how we *should* live, with how we *should* behave, with what kinds of people we *should* be – becoming increasingly irrelevant. For Weber, then, modernity is not just the triumph of rationality, but of instrumental rationality. It is not the fault of rationality as such. We could use reason to think about how we should live as well as using it to calculate how to be efficient, but we hardly ever do, and we will do so less and less. This is why the prospect for humankind is such a depressing, soulless and disenchanted one.

Habermas does not agree. He accepts that the use of reason since the Enlightenment is as Weber describes – that human rationality has principally been harnessed to the search for instruments of effectiveness. But, unlike Weber, he sees the potential for using reason for more noble ends – to enable us to do good and be good – as enormous. All that is required is a new belief in the power of value-oriented rationality. The problem, says Habermas, is that we have allowed instrumental rationality to be our yardstick in areas of life where it is inappropriate. He is certainly perfectly happy for the pursuit of efficiency to dominate in those realms of human activity where it is appropriate – that is, in the social system. Where we have gone wrong, he says, is that we have allowed instrumental rationality to be our yardstick in matters of value as well; as he puts it, we have made the mistake of allowing the life-world to be *colonized* by instrumental rationality. For Habermas, a new future beckons if we use our capacity for reason to guide us in the search for right and wrong as well as, where appropriate, to enable us to be efficient in organization and production. But how are we to do this? How can we create a better world, where the pursuit of efficiency applies only where it should and where members of different cultures talk to each other about matters of good and bad? To answer these questions, Habermas turns to those schools of thought that are concerned with language, interaction and communication – action theories. One of the action theories that makes an appearance in this element of Habermas's work is ethnomethodology.

Habermas and ethnomethodology

As we discussed in chapter 6, ethnomethodology is concerned to lay bare what it believes lies at the heart of human social life and which it believes other perspectives ignore – the work humans put in to make the occasions in which they are involved ordered ones. To repeat what we said earlier, for ethnomethodology, the main reason human social life works is that all of us assume it has an order to it. In fact, social occasions only work because we use our sense-making abilities to make them work but we do not realize this. We think there is already meaning and order in our world and we interact with each other sharing this assumption. Since we assume life is ordered, we approach our encounters with others not expecting to have to start from scratch each time, and expecting that others will corroborate our interpretations. And of course, because they are assuming exactly the same thing, social occasions work. All of us are open and honest with each other because we are all after the same thing – to be reassured things are as they seem. For example, according to Garfinkel, this is why conversation works. When we talk to others we assume – and we are nearly always right – that they want the same thing out of the encounter as we do: that it will make sense. And this is why it nearly always does – we make sense of it together. For ethnomethodology, this is humankind's greatest gift – the ability to create order together. In order for human social life to work it has to be collaborative enterprise; we have to want the same things when we communicate with each other otherwise we will make no sense to each other.

Habermas and communicative action

For Habermas, what we therefore have to do in order to establish a moral bridgehead with members of other cultures is to do what we, as humans, do all the time, in every social occasion in which we are implicated. We must talk to each other in order to find common ground and establish a consensus with these others over meaning. It is because we are capable of being rational and reasonable in these matters in order to co-exist at all with others in our everyday social encounters that we can employ exactly the same techniques to reach across cultural divides too. The point is that nobody enters into a conversation with another without assuming an agreement can be reached about meaning. For example, a customer does not communicate with a shopkeeper except in the belief that the shopkeeper wishes to serve him. Likewise, the shopkeeper speaks to the customer in the belief that he or she wishes to make a purchase. That is, they share a view of their encounter that informs the way they communicate with each other. Each of them reasons that the other will behave reasonably in order to achieve a reasonable outcome.

According to Habermas, much less mundane encounters can operate in the same way. Take political arguments, for example. So long as the parties to a communicative exchange have an equal opportunity to state their views, so long as they treat each other as equals and honestly seek agreement, this is always possible. It is only impossible if the exchange is one-sided or the desire to reach agreement is fraudulent. Obviously, humans can talk at each other until they are blue in the face and never agree if reaching agreement is not what they want. If a powerful person wants to use a communicative encounter to humiliate and subjugate a weaker one then of course this can be done. If one person is determined not to listen to other points of view and not be prepared to shift position then of course communication will get nowhere. We are all familiar with communicative encounters where this is precisely what is being aimed at. But if the parties to an exchange genuinely do want to agree and where everyone has the same chance to state their views, an agreed outcome is always achievable.

That is, so long as an encounter is approached rationally – with reason – differences can be overcome. Of course we can be pig-headed and unreasonable if we want to be. But, by the same token, we can also be reasonable and rational instead, if we choose to. Rational communication is unique to human beings and Habermas argues that it is precisely this ability that gives us the chance of living in a world that is not just physically shared but morally shared too.

Anthony Giddens: analysing late modernity

Anthony Giddens attacks postmodernism on other grounds. First, as we saw earlier, he rejects the term post-modernity since it implies we no longer live in modernity – that human existence has left modernity behind. He thinks this is a serious misrepresentation. The point about contemporary life for Giddens is that modernity has altered and is characterized by new circumstances, new forces and new turbulence and uncertainty, but not that it no longer exists. As a result, for him, the sociology of modernity still provides us with the right conceptual tools with which to make sense of social existence today.

Anthony Giddens

Second, he rejects the postmodernist portrayal of the human actor as wholly in the thrall of discursive influences and incapable of independent, creative action. For Giddens, the subject is most certainly not dead. But neither is he or she in any sense the ethnomethodological member, building social order in the total absence of any structural features or constraints. Giddens gives us an account of contemporary existence – *late modernity*, as he terms it – at both the level of structure and at the level of action. Furthermore, for him, these realms, the macro and the micro, are inextricably linked. As he argues in his purely theoretical work on *structuration* (1984), no actor makes choices except in specific structural circumstances and no structural features can come into being except as a result of the consequences of intentional action. In fact, it can be reasonably argued that Giddens's account of life in late modernity is structuration theory in practice.

Structuration theory

Giddens's theory refers to the 'duality of structure'. Not only do structures constrain and determine certain forms of behaviour, but they also *enable* behaviour; they provide opportunities, as well as limitations. Furthermore, the structural circumstances within which human action, or 'agency' as Giddens calls it, takes place are thereby reproduced, or redefined, by this action. That is, while an action inevitably takes place within a structural context, this context in turn may be regenerated, or transformed, by the action. There is thus a *dialectical* relation between structure and action. This is how Giddens summarizes this notion of 'duality of structure': 'Every act which contributes to the reproduction of a structure is also an act of construction, a novel enterprise, and as such may initiate change by altering that structure at the same time as it reproduces it' (Giddens, 1976, p. 128).

Kevin Bonnett offers the following comment on this depiction by Giddens:

> This leads to a very different idea of structure to the common models in sociology. We often think of structures as like physical, immovable steel frames. Instead of this, Giddens distinguishes structure and system. He uses 'system' to refer to the lasting social arrangements and institutions that generally get reproduced over time; they are not immune to change, but they give a lasting context for action. This usage of 'system' is very close to what many sociologists have called 'structure'. In contrast, Giddens uses the concept 'structure' in a very particular

way to refer to the moving body of rules and resources that agents use for action. Because these 'structures' are fluid and not institutionalised, they can be continually modified as they are used in action. For example, we all use the English language in a way that is constantly changed and renewed as we use it, but we can pick up changes and still make sense of one another. The formal rules of 'correct' English lag far behind this practical usage. (Bonnett, 2002, unpublished manuscript)

Using structuration theory: the case of the 2001 foot-and-mouth epidemic

The origins and consequences of the foot-and-mouth epidemic in Britain in 2001 demonstrate the dialectical relationship between structure and action embodied in structuration theory clearly. Although at the time of writing no prosecution has taken place, one allegation is that the epidemic began because of the actions of a pig-farmer in Cumbria. This farmer knew that local restaurants and schools where he lived were in the habit (one which is quite normal for catering establishments of course), of disposing of their slops, or unconsumed food, as waste. Seeing an opportunity to feed his pigs cheaply, the farmer arranged with some of these outlets to let him have this waste. His argument was that since they were going to get rid of their surplus food anyway, they might as well let him feed his herd with it. They agreed.

So, what we have here is a farmer taking account of his structural circumstances and choosing to take advantage of the opportunities they offered for the benefit of his business. The farmer did not intend to start the foot-and-mouth epidemic, of course, but because, unknown to him, the waste food became contaminated, this is what happened. As a result, the agricultural and tourist industries in rural Britain were thrown into turmoil, the government was forced to radically rethink its farming support policy and British farming will never be the same again. That is, the structure of agricultural production has been irrevocably altered and individual farmers will now have to operate in wholly transformed circumstances. For example, they are much more likely to choose to act as 'custodians of the countryside', playing a conservation and land management role, rather than concentrating exclusively on food production. They will still have to be agents, making choices, of course, but not in the world in which they lived before.

The same is true of the rest of us, the consumers of food. Food is likely to become more expensive (the reduction in subsidies for farming will see to that) and we will have to decide how we react to these changed circumstances. Do we choose different foodstuffs from before to save money? Now, especially after the BSE (the so-called 'Mad Cow' disease) scare of recent years, we have a greater sense of the risks involved in food consumption, do we choose to change our diets? For example, do we choose to eat organic foods? Making choices always has structural implications. For example, choosing to 'go organic' is bound to have serious economic repercussions for both organic and non-organic producers, and, as is already happening, may encourage farmers to jump on the organic bandwagon.

These transformations would probably never have happened (or at least not in the way they did) without the pig-farmer's actions, and from now on, when deciding how to live our lives, we will all have to accommodate the new circumstances he set in train. That is, the action he chose to take made sense to the pig-farmer in the circumstances in which he found himself but the unintended consequences are that now other people's choices have to be made in a new, completely different, set of structural features. Structuration theory emphasizes that choices *always* have to be made in structural circumstances and that the act of choosing *always* has implications for the nature of these circumstances.

This example not only shows how structuration analysis works, but also highlights the centrality in our lives of what for Giddens is one of the defining features of modernity today – *risk*. According to him, the notion of risk 'unlocks some of the most basic characteristics of the world in which we now live' (Giddens, 1999, p. 21).

Risk

Giddens distinguishes between two types of risk – *external* risk and *manufactured* risk. External risk 'is risk experienced as coming from the outside, from the fixities of tradition or nature', whereas manufactured risk is 'risk created by the very impact of our developing knowledge upon the world' (Giddens, 1999, p. 26). In essence, as Giddens explains, it is the difference between worrying about what nature can do to us – in the form of floods and famine, for example – and worrying about what we have done to nature, for example, the emergence of threats to the environment such as global warming. He argues that it is the emergence of manufactured risk that is one of the hallmarks of late modernity. However, Giddens does not see risk in contemporary life as merely a matter of the potential for global catastrophes such as nuclear accidents or nuclear wars, important though this is to his analysis. He also characterizes our personal lives as suffused with risk too.

In traditional worlds, whether based on agricultural or industrial production, to a large extent people did not have to work out how to live and who to be in the way we have to now. This is what living 'traditionally' means – being able to know that things in the future will be substantially the same as they were in the past. Living in late modernity, says Giddens, means that we cannot depend on continuity and stability in this way and, as a result, we have to accommodate change and uncertainty by creating and recreating our lives on a lifetime basis – an activity he calls **reflexivity**. We will look at this characterization of late modern personal existence in more detail shortly.

Ulrich Beck: a risk society

The centrality of the notion of risk in Giddens's account of contemporary existence echoes many of the ideas of the German sociologist **Ulrich Beck** (1944–).

Ulrich Beck

© Armin Pongs

As with the other thinkers in this chapter, Beck rejects post-modernism. He acknowleges the very new circumstances in which our lives are lived today, but prefers to call this emerging world a 'new modernity', not one of post-modernity. Like Giddens, Beck analyses contemporary life at both the structural and the action levels, and lays much of the blame for the increase in manufactured risk and the failure to manage it properly at both these levels on science. As he puts it: 'Science has become the protector of a global contamination of people and nature. In that respect, it is no exaggeration to say that in the way they deal with risks in many areas, the sciences have squandered until further notice their historic reputation for rationality' (Beck, 1992, p. 70).

One of Beck's key points concerns the way our relationship to science and scientists has changed in recent years. In the past, not only did we take for granted the fact that science could be relied on to tell us the truth, but that scientists were the experts we could depend upon to guide us in circumstances of uncertainty. It was a case of 'Trust us, we're scientists,' as much as 'Trust me, I'm a doctor.' As Giddens puts it:

> In Western society, for some two centuries, science functioned as a sort of tradition. Scientific knowledge was supposed to overcome tradition, but actually in a way became one in its own right. It was something that most people respected, but was external to their activities. Lay people 'took' opinions from the experts. (Giddens, 1999, p. 31)

Of course, there were failures and mini-disasters during this time, but these could always be explained away as the result of individual inefficiency or negligence, thus allowing us to retain our faith in science and scientists. For it is one thing to blame an individual practitioner, but quite another to blame the profession itself. That is, we could retain our trust in science and derive a sense of security from its benevolent presence in advancing our lives so long as there were sufficient malpractising or inept individuals around to blame mistakes on.

Beck argues that this no longer describes our relationship with science and scientists. According to him, the consensus so characteristic of modernity – that the use of science and technology leads inexorably to a golden future in which we humans can harness the power of nature for our own purposes – began to break down in the 1970s. It is no coincidence that this happened at a time when new social movements and protest groups such as Greenpeace and Friends of the Earth began to employ their own scientists to critique those establishment scientists working in government or business. As Beck (1992) puts it, science began to turn in on itself, undermining the very foundations on which the reliance on science rests – that the expert knows best. Now the 'experts' not only fought among themselves, but began to be seen to fight among themselves. And the more it became apparent that these hugely important sources of our sense of security were divided about matters of facts and truth, the more risk management had to become a matter of personal responsibility. As a result, in everyday life, our uncertainties began to multiply and our sense of risk began to increase. As Giddens portrays this new world:

> We cannot simply 'accept' the findings which scientists produce, if only because scientists so frequently disagree with one another, particularly in situations of manufactured risk. And everyone now recognises the essentially mobile character of science. Whenever someone decides what to eat, what to have for breakfast, whether to drink decaffeinated or ordinary coffee, that person takes a decision in the context of conflicting and changing scientific and technological information. (Giddens, 1999, p. 31)

Beck characterizes this process as *reflexive modernization* and stresses that it operates at both a structural and a personal level. To quote Giddens again:

> Whichever way you look at it, we are caught up in risk management. With the spread of manufactured risk, governments can't pretend such management isn't their business. And they need to collaborate, since very few new-style risks have anything to do with the borders of nations ... But neither, as ordinary individuals, can we ignore these new risks – or wait for definitive scientific evidence to arrive, As consumers, each of us has to decide whether to try to avoid genetically modified products or not. These risks, and the dilemmas surrounding them, have entered deeply into our everyday lives. (Giddens, 1999, p. 34)

Risk management thus involves both institutional and individual reflexivity. But Beck and Giddens see the presence of risk in our personal lives as so pervasive that it is not just a matter of second-guessing scientific knowledge. It is about managing uncertainty in *all* areas of our everyday existence. Thus, as Beck puts it: 'newly formed social relationships and social networks now have to be individually chosen; social ties, too, are becoming *reflexive*, so that they have to be established, maintained, and constantly renewed by individuals' (Beck, 1992, p. 97).

For Beck and Giddens, then, twenty-first-century life is not only much more uncertain and risky in terms of the management of inexorable change and the unknowability of the future at the macro level. It is also much more uncertain and suffused with risk for us as individuals in our personal lives as well and this means it is necessary to understand late modern life at the micro level too. And this is not just a matter of understanding risk and uncertainty as both an objective fact and a matter of perception – the difference between *objective* and *subjective* risk – important though this distinction is. It is that our identities – who we are – are no longer established and sustained for us by institutional certainties. This is how a culture of risk and uncertainty born of, and reproduced by, constant and rapid change impacts on individual lives. We saw earlier that Giddens developed his structuration approach to be able to deal with the dialectical relationship between structure and agency in social life, and it is the use of this theoretical framework to analyse risk and uncertainty in what he calls late modernity that we now turn.

Giddens: reflexivity in late modernity

At the level of structure, Giddens insists that any satisfactory commentary on the way things are now in modern society has to highlight the incredible changes we are undergoing. As we have just seen, they include the emergence of new dangers and risks – for example, those posed by nuclear weapons and threats to the environment. We saw earlier that these also include rapid globalization, which impacts not only at a global level but also at the local – the level of everyday experience – just as much. The technological transformation in methods of human communication, with its obliteration of traditional categories of time and space, is also hugely significant.

Because of this structural focus, Giddens is contemptuous of the postmodernist preoccupation with meaning – of the fact that its central argument sees reality as discursively created and exclusively a function of the powerful forms of cultural knowledge that define it. For Giddens, it is absurd to conceive of human existence as solely a matter of discursive definition, or only about meanings. For him, there is nothing more real than, for example, the threat of nuclear war, or the dangers posed to the world by hardly managed and barely manageable environmental change, or global relations of wealth and inequality.

But this structural analysis is insufficient by itself, for Giddens has tied himself to the mast of the theoretical indivisibility of structure and action. His account of the nature of individual experience in late modernity is the other, equally important half of his narrative. His point is that the enormous structural changes in the world he identifies have had huge consequences for the way we live our lives and think of ourselves. Because we exist in such different circumstances from any other humans who have ever lived, we have had to find new ways of living and coping. In effect, not only do modern humans today have to be interpreting, creative agents as never before but this agency will have inevitable consequences for the structure of our world.

Identity in late modernity: the emergence of the reflexive self

As was mentioned above, according to Giddens, in both pre-modern and modern traditional settings people acquired both a sense of social order, and of their having a settled, defined place in it, from the presence of established institutional pegs on which to hang their selves – their identities. Giddens calls this existential condition **ontological security**. Marriage, family life, working life and community life had a sense of permanence and stability. There were established – traditional – ways of living to be used as a life-script and as a result it was a relatively easy matter for us to know ourselves and know our futures. Not so now. According to Giddens, one of the crucial consequences of rapid structural and institutional change is its impact on the everyday business of living – the business of knowing yourself and knowing what to do. Giddens gives the following example:

> Two or three generations ago, when people got married, they knew what it was they were doing. Marriage, largely fixed by tradition and custom, was akin to a state of nature – as of course remains true in many countries. Where traditional ways of doing things are dissolving, however, when people marry or form relationships, there is an important sense in which they don't know what they are doing, because the institutions of marriage and the family have changed so much. Here individuals are striking out afresh, like pioneers. It is inevitable in such situations, whether they know it or not, that they start thinking more and more in terms of risk. They have to confront personal futures that are much more open than in the past, with all the opportunities and hazards this brings. (Giddens, 1999, pp. 27–8)

For Giddens, living in modern societies today means we have to make and re-make our selves in order to cope with the changes buffeting us from all around. Since new circumstances constantly arise and have to be made sense of, we have to manage and attach meaning to a world that is inherently *un*stable. We cannot turn to old ways of living since they have become redundant in this new 'runaway world' (Giddens, 1999). Our only course of action is to constantly monitor our circumstances and shape our selves accordingly. This means routinely adapting to our sense of what is going on; sculpting a self, an identity, to suit today but not necessarily tomorrow. This is the process Giddens describes as *reflexivity*. Thus, living in late modernity is a (lifelong) *reflexive project*: making sense of how things are and how we should live has to be undertaken over and over and over again as the conditions under which we live alter and alter and alter again. We can expect nothing else so long as we live in a world famously described by Giddens as follows:

> A runaway engine of enormous power which, collectively as human beings, we can drive to some extent but which also threatens to rush out of our control and which could rend itself asunder. The juggernaut crushes those who resist it, and while it sometimes seems to have a steady path, there are times when it veers erratically in directions we cannot foresee. The ride is by no means unpleasant or unrewarding; it can often be exhilarating and charged with hopeful anticipation. But, so long as the institutions of modernity endure, we shall never be able to control completely either the path or the pace of the journey. In turn, we shall never be able to feel entirely secure, because the terrain across which it runs is fraught with risks of high consequence. (Giddens, 1990, p. 139)

At the level of the agent or actor then, the emergence of late modern life has meant the dissolution of the institutional forms of identity characteristic of more traditional settings, with the result that a sense of self can only come from within. Late modern life is about writing and re-writing an emotional and mental script for oneself: reflexivity is the name Giddens gives to this search for ontological security in the absence of external, culturally defined signposts.

Managing personal uncertainty – the rise of therapy

According to Giddens, it is this aspect of the reflexive project that explains the dramatic rise in significance of professionals to help you do it. If living life has become a matter of making your own decisions about who you are, the explosion in recent years of various forms of counselling and therapy as aids in this task comes as no surprise. Giddens has been criticized for wrongly assuming that recourse to therapy is a late modern phenomenon, when it is in reality only a late modern phenomenon among those (like him) in possession of the cultural and economic resources to use it. But there seems no doubt that, at least for some, living in late modernity has involved an increasing use of professional guides in the business of trying to map out the directions to take on your personal odyssey.

The reflexive body

This emphasis on self-reflexivity in late modernity also leads Giddens to offer a very different account of contemporary body-centredness from Foucault. Because, theoretically, Giddens insists that we recognize agency as a principal constituent of human existence, he rejects the Foucauldian view that the kinds of body obsession and body fetishism characteristic of contemporary life that we reviewed in chapter 7 are discursively constructed phenomena. Giddens argues that in fact they are symptomatic of reflexivity.

Interactionists like Goffman have traditionally pointed to the creative use of the body in social interaction. For him, as we saw in chapter 5, effective impression management relies heavily on the self-conscious use of the body. Our ability to manipulate our appearance, demeanour, expression and so on is routinely pressed into service in social encounters so that they can proceed in ways with which we feel comfortable. We use our body in a theatrical way, as part of a public performance. In some of these little dramas we are being 'true to ourselves' whereas sometimes we are not.

Giddens, however, is saying something rather different. For him, life in late modernity means we can no longer let our job, or where we come from, or where we live, or who our family is speak for our selves. We have to find other ways of both being our selves and representing these selves to others. For this reason (and here he provides a similar analysis to Bauman), the rampant consumerism that is such a major feature of contemporary life becomes understandable. If possessing things is the way we reveal the self, it is the material elements of consumer culture that become our expressions of identity. As Bauman puts it: 'The roads to self-identity, to a place in society, to a life in a form recognizable as that of meaningful living, all require daily visits to the market place' (Bauman, 1992, p. 26).

This is why the body becomes so important. It becomes one of the plates on which a reflexively chosen identity is etched: our physical appearance becomes emblematic of who we are. This is how Elizabeth Jagger summarizes this element in Giddens's account:

> By providing a series of 'expert knowledges', for instance in relation to lifestyle, health, fashion and beauty, consumer culture is understood ... to have contributed to an increasingly reflexive understanding of the self, an awareness that identity is chosen and constructed ... As Giddens (1991) has pointed out, the self in 'late modernity' has become a reflexive project; it is created (and re-created) through a plurality of consumer choices and lifestyle decisions. In his view, individuals can now draw on a wide repertoire of symbolic goods with which to fashion and display their own identities. (Jagger, 2000, pp. 51–2)

In effect, as Giddens (1991, p. 31) himself puts it, in late modernity the body becomes 'a visible carrier of self-identity and is increasingly integrated into the lifestyle decisions which an individual makes'.

Giddens and theorizing modernity: conclusion

For Giddens then, postmodernism is a social theory that gets things wrong on three counts:

- it neglects the institutional realities of living in the twenty-first century
- it wrongly sees the human individual as powerless in the face of discursive influences, and
- it cannot make any useful contribution to the business of making our world a safer and better place because it denies that we can ever have the capacity to know how things really are.

As such, according to Giddens, postmodernism is wholly inadequate as a sociological theory. For him, just as it was for the classic sociological theorists, sociology and its theories are nothing if they cannot help in influencing for the better the human condition.

Further Reading

Postmodernity

Bauman, Zygmunt: *Intimations of Postmodernity*, Routledge, 1992.
Harvey, David: *The Condition of Postmodernity*, Blackwell, 1989.

Lyotard, Jean-François: *The Post-Modern Condition*, Manchester University Press, 1984.

Postmodernism

Berman, Marshall: *All That Is Solid Melts Into Air: the experience of modernity*, Verso, 1983.
Cahoone, L. (ed.): *From Modernism to Postmodernism: an anthology*, Blackwell, 1996.
Callinicos, Alex: *Against Postmodernism: a Marxist critique*, Polity, 1989.
Dews, Peter: *Logics of Disintegration*, Verso, 1987.
Gellner, Ernest: *Postmodernism, Reason and Religion*, Routledge, 1992.
Lash, Scott: *Sociology of Postmodernism*, Routledge, 1990.
Sarup, Madan: *An Introductory Guide to Post-structuralism and Postmodernism*, 2nd edn, Harvester-Wheatsheaf, 1993.

Habermas

None of the many works by Habermas is listed here. Though I have included some texts throughout the Further Reading sections in this book that are difficult to follow, this is particularly so in the case of Habermas's own writing. In my view, the commentaries on his work are more appropriate to recommend in a text designed to be an introduction to social theory.

Ashenden, Samantha and Owen, David: *Foucault contra Habermas*, Sage, 1999.
Held, David: *Introduction to Critical Theory*, Hutchinson, 1980.
McCarthy, Thomas: *The Critical Theory of Jürgen Habermas*, Polity, 1984.
Outhwaite, William: *Habermas: a critical introduction*, Polity, 1994.
Outhwaite, William: *The Habermas Reader*, Cambridge, Polity, 1996.
Scambler, Graham: *Habermas, Critical Theory and Health*, Routledge, 2001.
White, Stephen K.: *The Cambridge Companion to Habermas*, Cambridge University Press, 1995.

Beck

Beck, Ulrich: *Risk Society: Towards a New Modernity*, Sage 1992.
Beck, Ulrich, Giddens, Anthony and Lash, Scott: *Reflexive Modernization*, Polity, 1994.

Giddens

(This list includes only Giddens's relatively recent works)
Bryant, C. G. A. and Jary, David (eds): *Giddens' Theory of Structuration*, London, Routledge, 1991.
Cohen, I.: *Structuration Theory*, Basingstoke, Macmillan, 1989.
Giddens, Anthony: *The Constitution of Society: outline of the theory of structuration*, Polity, 1984.
Giddens, Anthony: *The Consequences of Modernity*, Polity, 1990.

Giddens, Anthony: *Modernity and Self-Identity: self and society in the late modern age*, Stanford, Stanford University Press, 1991.

Giddens, Anthony: *Runaway World: how globalisation is reshaping our lives*, Profile Books, 1999.

Giddens, Anthony: *The Transformation of Intimacy: sexuality, love and eroticism in modern societies*, Polity, 2001.

Giddens, Anthony and Pierson, Christopher: *Conversations with Anthony Giddens: making sense of modernity*, Polity, 1998.

Held, David and Thompson, John: *Social Theory of Modern Societies: Anthony Giddens and his critics*, Cambridge University Press, 1989.

O'Brien, Martin, Penna, Sue and Hay, Colin: *Theorising Modernity: reflexivity, environment and identity in Giddens' social theory*, Longman, 1998.

POSTSCRIPT

So, now we are at the end of this book, where does this litany of debate and dispute in theorizing in sociology leave us? At least we are now in a position to ask appropriate questions. For example, as human beings, are we creative agents, writing our own life-stories? Or are we constituted subjects, whose destinies are dictated by biographical forces outside our control? If so, how should we make sense of such forces? Are they normative, material, cultural, discursive or what? Or is human life best understood from both structural and action viewpoints – as a time when, though we can try to be who we want to be, we nevertheless have to do so in structural circumstances not of our choosing?

Furthermore, how should we acquire knowledge of social life? Should we embrace science, reject it, or see the construction of scientific knowledge as itself a process requiring sociological understanding? Can the knowledge we acquire be judged true or false, or is human understanding inevitably relative – a product of a time and place? If so, should we dispense with the search for 'truth' altogether? If we choose to do that, how can we confront and attempt to manage the tremendous changes that characterize our times? The answers to these kinds of questions may be elusive, but the obligation to look for them is not just a price we have to pay for being human. It is also a privilege no other living thing can enjoy.

BIBLIOGRAPHY

Abbott, Pamela and Wallace, Claire: *An Introduction to Sociology: feminist perspectives*, London, Routledge, 1990.

Anderson, Perry: *Considerations on Western Marxism*, London, New Left Books, 1976.

Anderson, R.: 'Listening to conversation', in Meighan R., Shelton I. and Marks T. (eds), *Perspectives on Society*, Sunbury-on-Thames, Nelson, 1979.

Ariès, P.: *Centuries of Childhood*, Harmondsworth, Penguin, 1973.

Ashenden, Samantha and Owen, David: *Foucault contra Habermas*, London, Sage, 1999.

Atkinson, J. M.: *Discovering Suicide*, Basingstoke, Macmillan, 1978.

Badham, R.: *Theories of Industrial Society*, London, Croom Helm, 1986.

Baert, Patrick: *Social Theory in the Twentieth Century*, Cambridge, Polity, 1998.

Barrett, Michèle: *Women's Oppression Today: problems in Marxist feminist analysis*, London, Verso, 1988.

Bauman, Zygmunt: *Hermeneutics and Social Science*, London, Hutchinson, 1978.

Bauman, Zygmunt: *Intimations of Postmodernity*, London, Routledge, 1992.

Bauman, Zygmunt and May, Tim: *Thinking Sociologically*, 2nd edn, Oxford, Blackwell, 2001.

Beck, Ulrich: *Risk Society: towards a new modernity*, London, Sage, 1992.

Beck, Ulrich, Giddens, Anthony and Lash, Scott: *Reflexive Modernization*, Cambridge, Polity, 1994.

Becker, Howard: *Outsiders: studies in the sociology of deviance*, New York, Free Press, 1967.

Benson, D. and Hughes, J. A.: *The Perspective of Ethnomethodology*, Harlow, Longman, 1983.

Berman, Marshall: *All That Is Solid Melts Into Air: the experience of modernity*, London, Verso, 1983.

Bernstein, R. J.: *The Restructuring of Social and Political Theory*, Oxford, Blackwell, 1976.

Beynon, H.: *Working for Ford*, Harmondsworth, Penguin, 1973.

Bilton, Tony et al.: *Introductory Sociology*, 1st edn, Basingstoke, Macmillan, 1981.

Bilton, Tony et al.: *Introductory Sociology*, 3rd edn, Basingstoke, Macmillan, 1996.

Bilton, Tony et al.: *Introductory Sociology*, 4th edn, chapters 17, 18, 19, Basingstoke, Palgrave, 2002.

Bloor, D.: 'A sociological theory of objectivity', in Brown S. C. (ed.), *Objectivity and Cultural Divergence*, Cambridge, Cambridge University Press, 1984.

Bocock, Robert and Thompson, Kenneth (eds): *Social and Cultural Forms of Modernity*, Cambridge, Polity, 1992.

Bottomore, T. (ed.): *Interpretations of Marx*, Oxford, Blackwell, 1988.

Bottomore, T. and Rubel, M.: *Karl Marx: Selected Writings*, Harmondsworth, Penguin, 1963.

Bouchier, David: *The Feminist Challenge*, Basingstoke, Macmillan, 1983.

Bowles, S. and Gintis, H.: *Schooling in Capitalist America*, London, Routledge and Kegan Paul, 1976.

Brownmiller, Susan: *Against Our Will*, Harmondsworth, Penguin, 1976.

Bryant, C. G. A. and Jary, David (eds): *Giddens' Theory of Structuration*, London, Routledge, 1991.

Burns, Tom: *Erving Goffman*, London, Routledge, 1992.

Butler, Judith: *Gender Trouble*, London, Routledge, 1990.

Butler, Judith and Scott, Joan Wallace (eds): *Feminists Theorise the Political*, London, Routledge, 1992.

Cahoone, L. (ed.): *From Modernism to Postmodernism: an anthology*, Oxford, Blackwell, 1996.

Calhoun, Craig et al.: *Classical Sociological Theory*, Blackwell's Readers in Sociology, Oxford, Blackwell, 2002a.

Calhoun, Craig et al.: *Contemporary Sociological Theory*, Blackwell's Readers in Sociology, Oxford, Blackwell, 2002b.

Callinicos, Alex: *Is There a Future for Marxism?* Basingstoke, Macmillan, 1982.

Callinicos, Alex: *Against Postmodernism: a Marxist critique*, Cambridge, Polity, 1989.

Castells, Manuel: *The Rise of the Network Society*, Oxford, Blackwell, 1996.

Cheal, D.: *Family and the State of Theory*, Hemel Hempstead, Harvester Wheatsheaf, 1991.

Cohen, I.: *Structuration Theory*, Basingstoke, Macmillan, 1989.

Collins, Patricia Hill: *Black Feminist Thought: knowledge, consciousness, and the politics of empowerment*, London, Unwin Hyman, 1990.

Craib, Ian: *Modern Social Theory*, 2nd edn, Hemel Hempstead, Harvester-Wheatsheaf, 1992.

Craib, Ian: *Classical Social Theory*, Oxford, Oxford University Press, 1997.

Cuff, E. C., Francis, D. W., Sharrock, W. W.: *Perspectives in Sociology*, 4th edn, London, Routledge, 1998.

Danaher, Geoff, Schirato, Tony and Webb, Jen: *Understanding Foucault*, London, Sage, 2000.

Davis, Angela, Y.: *Women, Race, and Class*, New York, Random House, 1981.

Delphy, Christine: *Close to Home: a materialist analysis of women's oppression*, London, Hutchinson, 1984.

Dews, Peter: *Logics of Disintegration*, London, Verso, 1987.

Ditton, Jason: *The View from Goffman*, London, Routledge, 1980.

Dodd, Nigel: *Social Theory and Modernity*, Cambridge, Polity, 1999.

Douglas, Jack: *Understanding Everyday Life*, London, Routledge and Kegan Paul, 1974.

Downes, D. and Rock, Paul (eds): *Deviant Interpretations*, Oxford, Martin Robertson, 1979.

Doyal, L. and Harris, R.: *Empiricism, Explanation and Rationality*, London: Routledge and Kegan Paul, 1986.

Durkheim, Emile: *Suicide*, ed. George Simpson, London, Routledge and Kegan Paul, 1970.

Durkheim, Emile: *Sociology and Philosophy*, New York, Free Press, 1974.

Durkheim, Emile: *The Elementary Forms of Religious Life*, London, Allen and Unwin, 1976.

Durkheim, Emile: *The Rules of Sociological Method*, ed. Steven Lukes, trans. W. D. Halls, Basingstoke, Macmillan, 1982.

Dworkin, Andrea: *Pornography: men possessing women*, Women's Press, 1981.

Eisenstein, Zillah, R.: 'Developing a theory of Capitalist Patriarchy and Socialist Feminism', in Eisenstein, Zillah, R. (ed.), *Capitalist Patriarchy*, New York, Monthly Review Press, 1979.

Elster, Jon: *Making Sense of Marx*, Cambridge, Cambridge University Press, 1985.

Elster, Jon: *An Introduction to Karl Marx*, Cambridge, Cambridge University Press, 1986a.

Elster, Jon: *Karl Marx: a reader*, Cambridge, Cambridge University Press, 1986b.

Farganis, James (ed.): *Readings in Social Theory: the classic tradition to post-modernism*, 3rd edn, New York, McGraw-Hill, 2000.

Fenton, Steve: *Durkheim and Modern Sociology*, Cambridge, Cambridge University Press, 1984.

Feyerabend, P.: Philosophical Papers, vol. II, *Problems of Empiricism*, Cambridge, Cambridge University Press, 1981.

Fidelman, Ashe: *Contemporary Social and Political Theory: an introduction*, Milton Keynes, Open University Press, 1998.

Filmer, Paul et al.: *New Directions in Sociological Theory*, London, Collier-Macmillan, 1972.

Firestone, Shulamith: *The Dialectic of Sex*, London, Cape, 1971.

Foucault, Michel: *Madness and Civilisation*, New York, Vintage, 1965.

Foucault, Michel: *The Birth of the Clinic: An Archaeology of Medical Perception*, New York, Vintage, 1975.

Foucault, Michel: *Power/Knowledge: selected interviews and other writings, 1972–1977*, ed. Colin Gordon, New York, Prentice-Hall, 1980.

Freedman, Jane: *Feminism*, Milton Keynes, Open University Press, 2001.

Friedan, Betty: *The Feminine Mystique*, New York, Dell, 1974.

Fuller, Steve: *Thomas Kuhn: a philosophical history for our times*, Chicago, University of Chicago Press, 2000.

Garfinkel, Harold: *Studies in Ethnomethodology*, Polity, 1984.

Gellner, Ernest: *Spectacles and Predicaments: essays in social theory*, Cambridge, Cambridge University Press, 1979.

Gellner, Ernest: *Relativism and the Social Sciences*, Cambridge, Cambridge University Press, 1986.

Gellner, Ernest: *Postmodernism, Reason and Religion*, London, Routledge, 1992.

Giddens, Anthony (ed.): *The Sociology of Suicide*, London, Frank Cass, 1971a.

Giddens, Anthony: *Capitalism and Modern Social Theory: an analysis of the writings of Marx, Durkheim and Max Weber*, Cambridge, Cambridge University Press, 1971b.

Giddens, Anthony: *Emile Durkheim: selected writings*, Cambridge, Cambridge University Press, 1972a.

Giddens, Anthony: *Politics and Sociology in the Work of Max Weber*, London, Macmillan, 1972b.

Giddens, Anthony, *New Rules of Sociological Method*, London, Hutchinson, 1976.

Giddens, Anthony: *The Constitution of Society: outline of the theory of structuration*, Cambridge, Polity, 1984.

Giddens, Anthony: *Social Theory and Modern Sociology*, Cambridge, Polity, 1987.

Giddens, Anthony: *The Consequences of Modernity*, Cambridge, Polity, 1990.

Giddens, Anthony: *Modernity and Self-Identity: self and society in the late modern age*, Stanford, Stanford University Press, 1991.

Giddens, Anthony: *Runaway World: how globalisation is reshaping our lives*, London, Profile Books, 1999.

Giddens, Anthony: *The Transformation of Intimacy: sexuality, love and eroticism in modern societies*, Cambridge, Polity, 2001.

Giddens, Anthony and Pierson, Christopher: *Conversations with Anthony Giddens: making sense of modernity*, Cambridge, Polity, 1998.

Goffman, Erving: *Strategic Interaction*, Oxford, Blackwell, 1969.

Goffman, Erving: *Stigma: notes on the management of spoiled identity*, Harmondsworth, Penguin, 1990a.

Goffman, Erving: *The Presentation of Self in Everyday Life*, Harmondsworth, Penguin, 1990b.

Goffman, Erving: *Asylums*, Harmondsworth, Penguin, 1968.

Goffman, Erving et al.: *The Goffman Reader*, Oxford, Blackwell, 1997.

Hall, Stuart et al.: 'New Times', *Marxism Today*, October 1988.

Hall, Stuart, Held, David and McGrew, Tony (eds): *Modernity and its Futures*, Cambridge, Polity, 1992.

Hartmann, Heidi: 'Capitalism, patriarchy and job segregation by sex', in Eisenstein, Zillah, R. (ed.), *Capitalist Patriarchy*, New York, Monthly Review Press, 1979.

Hartmann, Heidi: 'The Unhappy Marriage of Marxism and Feminism: Towards a More Progressive Union', in Sargant, Lydia (ed.), *Women and Revolution*, London, Pluto Press, 1981.

Harvey, David: *The Condition of Postmodernity*, Oxford, Blackwell, 1989.

Held, David: *Introduction to Critical Theory*, London, Hutchinson, 1980.

Held, David and Thompson, John: *Social Theory of Modern Societies: Anthony Giddens and his critics*, Cambridge, Cambridge University Press, 1989.

Hollis, Martin: *The Philosophy of Social Science*, Cambridge, Cambridge University Press, 1994.

Hollis, Martin and Lukes, Steven: *Rationality and Relativism*, Oxford, Blackwell, 1985.

hooks, bell: *Ain't I a Woman? Black women and feminism*, New York, South End Press, 1981.

hooks, bell: *Yearning: race, gender, and cultural politics*, New York, South End Press, 1990.

Jackson, Stevi (ed.): *Women's Studies: a reader*, Hemel Hempstead, Harvester, 1993.

Jaggar, Alison, M.: *Feminist Politics and Human Nature*, Hemel Hempstead, Harvester, 1983.

Jagger, Elizabeth: in Hancock, Philip, et al., *The Body, Culture and Society*, Milton Keynes, Open University Press, 2000.

James, Joy and Sharpley-Whiting, T. Denean (eds): *The Black Feminist Reader*, Oxford, Blackwell, 2000.

Jones, Colin and Porter, Roy: *Reassessing Foucault: power, medicine and the body*, London, Routledge, 1994.

Kelly, Liz: *Surviving Sexual Violence*, Cambridge, Polity, 1988.

Kolakowski, L.: *Main Currents of Marxism*, vols 1–3, Oxford, Oxford University Press, 1978.

Kuhn, Thomas: *The Structure of Scientific Revolutions*, 1st edn, Chicago, University of Chicago Press, 1962.

Kuhn, Thomas: *The Structure of Scientific Revolutions*, 2nd edn, Chicago, University of Chicago Press, 1970.

Kumar, Krishan: *Prophecy and Progress: the sociology of industrial and post-industrial life*, Harmondsworth, Penguin, 1978.

Lash, Scott: *Sociology of Postmodernism*, London, Routledge, 1990.

Lee, David and Newby, Howard: *The Problem of Sociology*, London, Hutchinson, 1983.

Lemert, Charles (ed.): *Social Theory: the multicultural and classic readings*, New York, Westview Press, 1993.

Lemert, Edwin: *Human Deviance, Social Problems and Social Control*, Englewood Cliffs, Prentice Hall, 1967.

Lovell, Terry (ed.): *British Feminist Thought: a reader*, Oxford, Blackwell, 1990.

Lukes, Steven: *Emile Durkheim: his life and work*, Harmondsworth, Penguin, 1973.

Lyon, David: 'Post-modernity', in Browning Gary, Halci, Abigail and Webster, Frank, *Understanding Contemporary Society*, London, Sage, 2000.

Lyotard, Jean-François: *The Post-Modern Condition*, Manchester, Manchester University Press, 1984.

McCarthy, Thomas: *The Critical Theory of Jürgen Habermas*, Cambridge, Polity, 1984.

McHoul, Alec and Grace, Wendy: *A Foucault Primer: discourse, power and the subject*, London, Routledge, 2002.

McLellan, David: *Karl Marx: his life and thought*, Basingstoke, Macmillan, 1973.

McLellan, David: *The Thought of Karl Marx*, 2nd edn, Basingstoke, Macmillan, 1980.

McLellan, David: *Karl Marx: the first 100 years*, London, Fontana, 1983.

McLellan, David: *Marxism: essential writings*, Oxford, Oxford University Press, 1988.

McLellan, David: *Marxism after Marx: an introduction*, 3rd edn, Basingstoke, Macmillan, 1998.

McLellan, David: *Selected Writings of Karl Marx*, 2nd edn, Oxford, Oxford University Press, 2000.

McNay Lois: *Foucault: a critical introduction*, Cambridge, Polity, 1994.

Malinowski, B.: *Argonauts of the Western Pacific*, London, Routledge and Kegan Paul, 1922.

Mann, Michael: *The Sources of Social Power*, vol. 2, Cambridge, Cambridge University Press, 1993.

Manning, Philip: *Erving Goffman and Modern Sociology*, Cambridge, Polity, 1992.

Margolis, Joseph: *The Truth about Relativism*, Oxford, Blackwell, 1991.

Marshall, Barbara, L.: *Engendering Modernity*, Cambridge, Polity, 1994.

Marx, K.: *The 18th Brumiaire of Louis Napoleon*, Moscow, Progress Publishers, 1954.

Marx, K. and Engels, F.: *The German Ideology*, New York, International Publishers, 1963.

Marx, K. and Engels, F.: *Collected Works*, London, Lawrence and Wishart, 1976.

Matthews, Betty (ed.): *Marx: 100 Years On*, London, Lawrence and Wishart, 1983.

May, Tim: *Situating Social Theory*, Milton Keynes, Open University Press, 1996.

Maynard, M.: *Sociological Theory*, Harlow, Longman, 1989.

Meltzer, B. N. et al.: *Symbolic Interactionism*, London, Routledge and Kegan Paul, 1975.

Millett, Kate: *Sexual Politics*, London, Virago, 1977.

Mitchell, Juliet: *Psychoanalysis and Feminism*, Harmondsworth, Penguin, 1975.

Mitchell, Juliet and Oakley, Ann: *What is Feminism?* Oxford, Blackwell, 1986.

Nicholson, Linda, J. (ed.): *Feminism/Postmodernism*, London, Routledge, 1990.

Norris, Christopher: *Against Relativism: philosophy of science, deconstruction and critical theory*, Oxford, Blackwell, 1997.

Oakley, Anne: *Sex, Gender and Society*, London, Maurice Temple Smith, 1972.

Oakley, Ann: *Women Confined*, Oxford, Martin Robertson, 1980.

Oakley, Ann: *The Captured Womb: a history of the medical care of pregnant women*, Oxford, Blackwell, 1984.

Oakley, Ann: *Essays on Women, Medicine and Health*, Edinburgh, Edinburgh University Press, 1993.

Oakley, Ann and Mitchell, Juliet: *Who's afraid of feminism? Seeing through the backlash*, Harmondsworth, Penguin, 1997.

O'Brien, Martin, Penna, Sue and Hay, Colin: *Theorising Modernity: reflexivity, environment and identity in Giddens' social theory*, Harlow, Longman, 1998.

Outhwaite, William: *Habermas: a critical introduction*, Cambridge, Polity, 1994.

Outhwaite, William: *The Habermas Reader*, Cambridge, Polity, 1996.

Parkin, Frank: *Max Weber*, London, Tavistock, 1982.

Parsons, T.: *Societies: evolutionary and comparative perspective*, Englewood Cliffs, Prentice-Hall, 1966.

Parsons, T.: *The System of Modern Societies*, Prentice-Hall, 1971.

Pearce, Frank: *The Radical Durkheim*, London, Unwin Hyman, 1989.

Plummer, Ken: *Modern Homosexualities: fragments of lesbian and gay experiences*, London, Routledge, 1992.

Polanyi, Karl: *The Great Transformation*, New York, Octagon Books, 1973.

Poster, Mark: *Foucault, Marxism and History*, Cambridge, Polity, 1984.

Rabinow, Paul (ed.): *The Foucault Reader*, Harmondsworth, Penguin, 1991.

Rich, Adrienne: 'Compulsory heterosexuality and lesbian existence', in *Signs*, 5(4), 1980, 631–60.

Richards, Janet Radcliffe: *The Skeptical Feminist*, London, Routledge, 1980.

Ritzer, George: *Sociological Theory*, 5th edn, New York, McGraw-Hill, 2000.

Ritzer, George (ed.): *The Blackwell Companion to Major Social Theorists*, Oxford, Blackwell, 2002.

Roche, Maurice: *Phenomenology, Language and the Social Sciences*, London, Routledge and Kegan Paul, 1973.

Rock, Paul: *The Making of Symbolic Interactionism*, Basingstoke, Macmillan, 1979.

Rogers, Mary, F. (ed.): *Contemporary Feminist Theory: a text/reader*, New York, McGraw-Hill, 1998.

Rose, A. (ed.): *Human Behaviour and Social Processes*, Routledge and Kegan Paul, 1962.

Sanger, Margaret: *What Every Girl Should Know*, New York, M. N. Naisel, 1916.

Sanger, Margaret: *Happiness in Marriage*, New York, Brentano's, 1926.

Sanger, Margaret: *Motherhood in Bondage*, New York, Brentano's, 1928.

Sarup, Madan: *An Introductory Guide to Post-structuralism and Postmodernism*, 2nd edn, Hemel Hempstead, Harvester-Wheatsheaf, 1993.

Scambler, Graham: *Habermas, Critical Theory and Health*, London, Routledge, 2001.

Schutz, A.: Collected Papers, vol. 1, *The Problem of Social Reality*, Dordrecht, The Netherlands, Kluwer Academic Publishers, 1962.

Scott, Sue and Morgan, David (eds): *Body Matters: essays on the sociology of the body*, London, Falmer, 1993.

Seidmore, Steven: *Contested Knowledge: social theory in the postmodern era*, Oxford, Blackwell, 1998.

Sharrock, W. W.: 'The problem of order', in Worsley, P. (ed.), *Introducing Sociology*, Harmondsworth, Penguin, 1977.

Sharrock, W. W. and Anderson, R. J.: *The Ethnomethodologists*, Chichester, Ellis Harwood, 1986.

Shilling, Chris: *The Body and Social Theory*, London, Sage, 1993.

Silverman, David: *Harvey Sacks: social science and conversation analysis*, Cambridge, Polity, 1998.

Skidmore, W.: *Theoretical Thinking in Sociology*, Cambridge, Cambridge University Press, 1975.

Smart, Barry: *Foucault*, London, Routledge, 1988.

Stanko, Elizabeth: *Intimate Intrusions: women's experience of male violence*, London, Routledge, 1985.

Stopes, Marie: *Married Love*, Sussex, Orion Fiction, 1996. (This refers to the work she published in 1916.)

Stopes, Marie: *Birth Control and Other Writings*, ed. Lesley A. Hall, Bristol, Thoemmes Press, 2000.

Taylor, Steve: *Durkheim and the Sociology of Suicide*, Basingstoke, Macmillan, 1982.

Thomas, W. I.: in Janowitz, M. (ed.) *Organisation and Social Personality: Selected Papers*, Chicago, University of Chicago Press, 1966.

Thompson, Denise: *Radical Feminism Today*, London, Sage, 2001.

Thompson, Kenneth: *Emile Durkheim*, London, Routledge, 1982.

Tong, Rosemarie Putnam: *Feminist Thought: a more comprehensive introduction*, New York, Westview Press, 1998.

Trigg, Roger: *Understanding Social Science*, Oxford, Blackwell, 1985.

Turner, Bryan: *For Weber: essays on the sociology of fate*, London, Routledge and Kegan Paul, 1981.

Turner, Bryan: *Regulating Bodies: essays in medical sociology*, London, Routledge, 1992.

Turner, Bryan: *Medical Power and Social Knowledge*, 2nd edn, London, Sage, 1995.

Turner, Bryan: *The Body and Society: explorations in social theory*, London, Sage, 1996.

Turner, Bryan (ed.): *The Blackwell Companion to Social Theory*, 2nd edn, Oxford, Blackwell, 2000.

Uberoi, J. Singh: *The Politics of the Kula Ring*, Manchester, Manchester University Press, 1962.

Veblen, Thorstein, *The Theory of the Leisure Class*, New York, Prometheus Books, 1998.

Walby, Sylvia: *Theorising Patriarchy*, Oxford, Blackwell, 1990.

Wallis, R.: in Mann, M. (ed.) *The Macmillan Student Encyclopaedia of Sociology*, Basingstoke, Macmillan, 1983.

Weber, M.: *The Methodology of the Social Sciences*, New York, Free Press, 1949.

Weber, M.: *Economy and Society* (eds Guenther Roth and Claus Wittich), New York, Bedminster Press, 1968.

Weber, M.: *The Protestant Ethic and the Spirit of Capitalism*, London, Allen and Unwin, 1977.

Whimster, Sam and Lash, Scott (eds): *Max Weber, Rationality and Modernity*, London, Allen and Unwin, 1987.

White, Stephen, K.: *The Cambridge Companion to Habermas*, Cambridge, Cambridge University Press, 1995.

Winch, P.: *The Idea of a Social Science*, London, Routledge and Kegan Paul, 1970.

Wittgenstein, L.: *Philosophical Investigations*, Oxford, Basil Blackwell, 1973.

Wootton, Anthony and Drew, Paul: *Erving Goffman: explaining the interaction order*, Cambridge, Polity, 1988.

World Health Organization: *Female Genital Mutilation*, WHO, 1997.

Worsley, Peter: *Marx and Marxism*, London, Tavistock, 1982.

GLOSSARY

action

In interpretive sociology, the term that stresses the consciously intended nature of human social behaviour.

action theory/ interpretive theory

Approaches to human social behaviour that explain it as the product of the choices and intentions of actors, such as Weber's social action theory, symbolic interactionism, phenomenology and ethnomethodology. Social life is seen as the creation or accomplishment of conscious human beings whose mental abilities to interpret or attach meaning to reality enable them to make sense of each other and thereby interact in ordered ways.

agency

The term favoured by Giddens and his followers to refer to purposive, intentional action. Probably used more often than action today.

alienation

A crucial concept in Marxist thinking, just as anomie is in Durkheimian thought. It summarizes the nature of existence for a member of an exploited class. Forced to work for someone else in order to live, such a worker not only has little or no control over how this work is carried out but does not own what it produces either. Such workers are alienated from both work itself and its product.

anatamo-politics

A Foucauldian term which refers to the exercise of power in order to encourage people to think about and manage their bodies in particular ways.

anomie

Durkheim's term for egoistic, self-centred, anti-social behaviour, which, for him, is always the result of inappropriate or inadequate socialization.

belief system

A set of interrelated ideas which together form a coherent view of the world.

bio-medicine

The approach to health and illness which treats these as matters essentially to do with the body and its constituent organs.

bio-politics

A Foucauldian term which refers to the exercise of power in order to promote particular forms of physical behaviour in a population of bodies.

bourgeoisie

The Marxist term for the owners of productive wealth in capitalism: employers, shareholders and investors.

capitalism

The hiring of workers to produce goods and services for sale in order to make a profit for their employers.

class consciousness

According to Marx, only the overthrow of false consciousness will make the dominated, exploited class aware of their true, collective circumstances. Only then will they become conscious of their class identity and the need to take action as a class if they are to become free.

cognitive relativism

The view that all factual knowledge, such as that produced by science, is a cultural construction and therefore can never be held to be objectively correct.

collective conscience

A crucial pre-condition for social solidarity, Durkheim's term for the sharing of beliefs, judgements and world-views and, as a result, the fostering of a sense of a shared identity among a population of different individuals. According to Durkheim, the principal function of religion is the vital one of generating and fostering a collective conscience.

compulsory heterosexuality

The term employed by Adrienne Rich to describe the cultural privileging of male-female sexual relations over all others and the resulting conviction that the only normal and natural source of sexual fulfilment is derived from penile-vaginal penetrative sex.

consumption

The activity of purchasing goods for personal use, as in shopping.

depersonalization/ mortification of the self	According to Goffman, these are the principal consequences of institutionalization. The terms refer to the way the enforcement of organizational rules reduces the capacity of humans to choose who to be and to decide for themselves how to behave.
discourse (1)	The particular words chosen in order to express meaning.
discourse (2)	A depiction of reality and a set of prescriptions for behaviour based on a particular form of knowledge, as in medical discourse, religious discourse.
disenchantment/ dehumanization	According to Weber, the huge drawback of the dominance of rationalization in modernity. For him, the obsession with efficiency and calculability which typifies modern existence results in the absence of any real interest in the finer things in life – spiritual, emotional and aesthetic considerations in particular.
division of labour	Durkheim's term for the extent to which members of a society play different roles and live different lives. The more traditional a society, the simpler the division of labour; the more modern it is, the more complex the division of labour.
economism/ economic determinism	Usually used pejoratively (as a criticism), these terms refer to an analysis that sees economic activity as the only area of human life that needs to be understood in order to make sense of human behaviour.
empiricism	The exclusive reliance on the human senses, particularly observation, to demonstrate the existence of things.
the Enlightenment	The name given to the moment in history around the middle of the eighteenth century when it was realized that because human beings, uniquely among living things, have the mental ability to reason for themselves and thereby act rationally, they need no longer rely on religion-inspired accounts of reality, which typically explain it as the creation of non-human, higher beings, such as gods or spirits. This emphasis on the potential of human reason encouraged the establishment of scientific reasoning and practice as the embodiment of rationality and marginalized religious thinking and practice, a process known as secularization.

epistème	Foucault's term for the world-view promoted by a particular discourse.
false consciousness	Marx's term for the inability of an exploited, oppressed class to appreciate the reality of its circumstances and to realize that it needs to act to free itself from these. For Marxists, false consciousness is explained by the presence of powerful ideologies – false depictions of the world – which make up such a large part of the superstructure of a class society.
forces of production	The Marxist term for the tools and techniques used in productive or economic activity: for example, a hoe, a tractor, an assembly line, a computer or a robot.
functionalism	A theoretical approach to human societies which emphasizes their integrated, interdependent, structured features. Functionalists often portray the workings of social systems as analogous to those of organic systems.
globalization	The name used to describe the ways in which the boundaries between different societies have been eroded. Those who claim that globalization is a central feature of contemporary life point to the transformations of world existence wrought by such features as the power of transnational corporations, electronic communication and global trading in both finance and manufacturing.
historical or dialectical materialism	The terms used to describe Marx's theory of history, in which he sees all human societies passing through the same epochs or times (though not at the same speed), and in which each is defined by different economic or productive systems.
ideal type	A Weberian concept, this refers to the deliberate portrayal of an aspect of human existence in as stark and one-sided a way as possible. The point is to omit the complexity you are perfectly well aware exists in favour of making your selected emphasis as clear as could be.
ideology	Sometimes used as a synonym for a belief system (a set of interrelated ideas) but more sensibly used to refer to a set of beliefs which deny the believer an understanding of the true nature of reality. For example, Marxists and some feminists point to the

ways in which ideologies are false depictions of reality which obscure, or at least justify and legitimate, class- and gender-based inequalities.

indexicality

The term used by ethnomethodologists to refer to the context-bound, or contingent, nature of human action. That is, the decision to act in a certain way can only make sense in the social context in which the action takes place. It therefore follows that any action can only be understood properly by appreciating this social context.

individualism

An approach that explains human behaviour as the product of an individual's unique characteristics, such as psychological makeup and personality traits.

infrastructure/ economic base

For Marxists, the foundation or base on which any social system is built. In Marxist thought, the basis of any society is its particular form of economic or productive activity.

institutionalization

Goffman's term for the process whereby the establishments in which people live demand complete conformity from their inmates to rules of behaviour deemed necessary for organizational efficiency.

instrumental rationality/ instrumental reason

For Weber the principal preoccupation in modernity, these terms refer to the application of the uniquely human ability to think and work out what to do solely in order to calculate the most efficient way of achieving something. That is, the pursuit of technical efficiency – for example, how to do things as cheaply as possible – prevails over all other considerations, such as working out whether something is good or bad, whether it is the right thing to do.

materialism

An approach that explains people's behaviour as the product of the physical facts of their lives.

mechanical solidarity

The type of solidarity found in pre-modern, traditional societies where social order is automatically, or mechanically, achieved because the inhabitants live similar lives and share similar beliefs.

medicalization

The exercise of medical power in order to regulate behaviour in realms of existence that have little or nothing to do with the body. This often means treating morality – concerns about right and wrong – as matters of health and illness, as in the medicalization of the family or the medicalization of sexuality.

mode of production	The Marxist term for a type of economy or way of producing goods and wealth. Apart from communistic economic activity, each mode – slavery, feudalism and capitalism – is based upon one dominant class exploiting the labour of a subordinate one in order to produce wealth. This wealth then becomes the private property of the dominant class.
modernism	The belief that humans, by the use of reason, can discover certain, objective truth about the nature and meaning of things and events and use this knowledge to improve the conditions of human existence.
modernity	The name given to the Enlightenment-inspired changes which began in the nineteenth century and which matured during the twentieth; its central features included industrial capitalism, scientific activity, huge population growth, urbanization and the secularization of knowledge.
moral/cultural relativism	The view that all values and value-judgements are inevitably cultural constructions and therefore can never be held to be objectively correct and of universal validity.
naturalism	An approach that explains human behaviour as a product of natural forces such as genetic makeup, evolution and the satisfaction of animal-like needs.
ontological security	The term Giddens uses to refer to the sense of safety and security, the equanimity that comes from the conviction that your world is morally and socially ordered and your place in it secure.
organic solidarity	The type of solidarity found in modern societies. Here people live very different lives from each other but because they are dependent on each other's different activities in order to survive, organic solidarity emerges. It is the solidarity that grows from the interdependence of different individuals.
panopticism	Foucault's term for the ways in which individuals regulate their own behaviour in case they are being observed. The panoptican was designed to be a prison in which the inmates knew they could never escape the surveillance of their guards.
patriarchy	The exercise of power in all its forms by men over women.

positivism	The approach which argues that an account of reality can be accepted as true only if it can be proved to be.
postmodernism	The view that contemporary existence is characterized by a loss of faith in the possibility, so central to Enlightenment ideals, that people can ever acquire objective truth or certain knowledge. Postmodernism holds that all human knowledge is inevitably a cultural creation. Since human beings can never stand outside the cultural influences that have made them who they are, human knowledge will always be a product of time and place.
post-modernity	The view that it is no longer accurate to say that we continue to live in modernity. According to postmodernists, the world has been so transformed in recent years that we have gone beyond modernity and now live in post-modern times. As a consequence, we need to develop new ways of making sense of this transformed existence.
project of modernity	Activities based on the belief that the acquisition of certain knowledge by the use of reason will enable humans to achieve continuing progress for themselves and their societies.
proletariat	The Marxist term for the class in capitalism that sells its labour power to employers in return for the wages its members need in order to survive.
rationalization	For Weber, the hallmark of modernity – the process whereby modern humans become so preoccupied with calculating how to do things efficiently.
reductionism/ reductive thinking	These terms refer (pejoratively) to any analysis, such as one guilty of economic determinism, which ignores the possibility that many causal factors may be at work in favour of the view that only one matters.
reflexivity	The routine monitoring of yourself and your behaviour in order to decide who to be and how to live.
reification	The mistake of treating a concept as though it is a real thing. For example, to talk of the ideas or beliefs of a society, when in fact only human beings can have ideas and beliefs, is to reify the concept.

relations of production	The Marxist term for the ways in which individuals interact with each other in economic activity. Different economic systems or modes of production are characterized by different relations of production: for example, between the master and the serf in feudalism; between the employer and the wage-earner in capitalism.
secularization	The process whereby religious beliefs and practices lose social significance and influence.
social solidarity	Durkheim's term for the presence of social order in a society whose structure is solid and well-organized.
social structure	The characterization of human societies as a set of interrelated and interlocking features that make up an organized whole.
social system	A description of the ways in which the different elements in a social structure work and change together over time, such as in the analogy between the workings of a living organism and the workings of a society often drawn by functionalism.
stereotyping	Associated with labelling theory, this term summarizes the decision to attribute a complete identity to someone on the basis of their possession of one characteristic alone, as in 'All black men are . . .' or 'All women are . . .'.
superstructure	According to Marxists, all the elements in a social system that are not to do with its economy – the superstructure of non-economic activities, institutions, ideas and beliefs – are built upon and emerge from the economic base.
value rationality	A Weberian term, this involves the application of reason in order to decide what is right, or good, and what is bad, or wrong; that is, deciding what should be done.

INDEX

Note: Page references in italics indicate illustrations.

Index compiled by Meg Davies
(Registered Indexer, Society of Indexers)